STE

STERLING

Its Use and Misuse
A Plea for Moderation

Douglas Jay

Oxford   New York

OXFORD UNIVERSITY PRESS

1986

To H.G.J. and M.L.J., with love and gratitude

Oxford University Press, Walton Street, Oxford OX2 6DP
Oxford New York Toronto
Delhi Bombay Calcutta Madras Karachi
Kuala Lumpur Singapore Hong Kong Tokyo
Nairobi Dar es Salaam Cape Town
Melbourne Auckland
and associated companies in
Beirut Berlin Ibadan Nicosia

Oxford is a trade mark of Oxford University Press

First published 1985 by Sidgwick & Jackson Ltd.
First issued, with Douglas Jay's Foreword to the paperback edition, as
an Oxford University Press paperback 1986

British Library Cataloguing in Publication Data
Jay, Douglas
Sterling: its use and misuse: a plea for moderation.
1. Money—Great Britain—History
I. Title
332.4'941   HG939.5
ISBN 0–19–285159–4

Library of Congress Cataloguing in Publication Data
Jay, Douglas, 1907–
Sterling: its use and misuse.
(Oxford paperbacks)
Bibliography: p.   Includes index.
1. Monetary policy—Great Britain—History.
2. Pound, British—History.   3. Inflation (Finance)—
Great Britain—History.   4. Great Britain—Economic
policy—1945–   .   I. Title.
HG935.J39   1986   332.4'941   86–681
ISBN 0–19–285159–4 (pbk.)

Printed in Great Britain by
The Guernsey Press Co. Ltd.
Guernsey, Channel Islands

Contents

Part IV: Money, Demand, and Employment

Foreword

A record of the use and misuse of one currency in the past may help, I believe, towards better management of it in the future. This book sets out the reasons for believing that the heavy unemployment in the United Kingdom and the rest of the Western world today, with all its human evils, is not due to natural causes, or inevitable, or beyond human wisdom to overcome. It is the result of mistakes of economic and monetary policy, and notably the failure to control monetary flows in the modern economy. Those who are primarily concerned with the present day rather than history can, if they wish, omit the earlier chapters of this book, and start with Part IV: Money, Demand, and Employment, which seeks to explain why the UK and other Western countries have lost control of their economies in the 1970s and 1980s and how they can be steered back on course. Others may agree that a clearer knowledge of past mistakes may ease the job of avoiding them from now on.

In the Appendix an attempt is made to set out a continuous measure of the purchasing power of the pound sterling from the thirteenth century to the 1980s. For the years from 1264 to 1954 this is based on Sir Henry Phelps Brown and Miss Sheila Hopkins' monumental *A Perspective of Wages and Prices*, and I am extremely grateful to Sir Henry for allowing me to reproduce these statistics, as well as for advice on their implications and for his valuable comments generally on the rest of this book. For the years 1955 to 1983, I am indebted to the long-term Index of Prices of Consumer Goods and Services compiled by the Central Statistical Office, and for assistance from that Office and the Oxford University Institute of Economics and Statistics in converting the CSO index on to a basis comparable with the Phelps Brown index.

My warm thanks are also due to Miss Margaret Reid and to Mr
Bryan Gould for advice on the manuscript; to the Library of All
Souls College, the Bodleian Library and the Library of the Oxford
University Institute of Economics and Statistics for their various
and valuable services; and especially to my wife for unflagging help
and support. The opinions expressed are naturally my own.

Minster Lovell   *Douglas Jay*
July 1984

Foreword to Paperback Edition

Events in the UK since the first edition of this book was published in
March 1985 have fully borne out the warning on p. 227 that 'no
convincing reason has yet been advanced why, unless active steps
are taken to increase demand, the economy should not stagnate at a
high level of unemployment for a very long time'. Unemployment
in 1985 remained very high, due to the squeezing of demand by the
Government through Budgetary cuts and excessively high interest
rates. The rise in unemployment lasted longer than in 1929–33, and
manufacturing output in late 1985 was still lower than in 1979. Only
in October 1985 was the 'M.3.' fetish formally abandoned. The loss
of national income due to unused resources has been running at over
£30 billions a year; and until the recovery policies described in the
later chapters of this book are adopted, all this damage must be
expected to continue.

Two charts have been added in this edition (p. 280 & p. 281)
recording the changes since 1800 in (Chart A) the sterling price
index, and (Chart B) UK industrial output per capita. A measure of
real GDP per capita would give much the same results as Chart B
(see National Income, Expenditure and Output of UK 1855–1965.
C. H. Feinstein 1972 p. T.42). These charts show that (before the
coming of cost-inflation) real output has tended to rise fastest when
money values were falling.

I would like to express my renewed gratitude to the Oxford
University Institute of Economics and Statistics, and in particular to
Mrs Gillian McNamara, for valuable help in preparing these charts.

Minster Lovell   *Douglas Jay*
November 1985

Author's Note

To assist those who like to know in advance the purport of an argument before plunging into detail, the following is a brief outline of the main theme of this book.

For any economy to run smoothly, money must act as both a measure of value and a medium of exchange. Naturally in early times, money's function as a measure of value seemed the most essential. But as the modern economy and the bank money system developed, money's function as a medium of exchange gradually became more important. This change has been only slowly understood, and many of our avoidable economic mistakes spring from disregard of it. In the case of the pound sterling the attempt to force on the British economy John Locke's fixed sterling price of gold – in the name of stabilizing the value of money – brought much distress and economic loss after both the Napoleonic Wars and the 1914–18 war.

A modern economy can only function properly and use all its resources if the total flow of money demand and total flow of producers' money costs are kept in reasonable balance. But there is no automatic force which brings these two into balance; and the nineteenth-century 'trade cycle' was largely a see-saw in which one or the other got the upper hand.

The Great Depression of 1929 was essentially a collapse of money demand which, for whatever reason, became more acutely deficient than ever previously, and might have brought the whole world near to a total economic stop if the UK and US governments had not been induced to alter the gold value of their currencies.

After this experience it began to be realized that unless conscious steps are taken to bring the two monetary flows of costs and demand into balance, there is little hope of reasonable progress in the real economy: i.e. in production, employment, and living standards. During the 1939–45 war in the UK and the USA the war economies were governed by the principle of using every scrap of physical and human capacity, and treating the pound and the dollar as means to this end. Everyone was astonished at the gigantic productive effort this achieved, and unemployment fell below 1 percent.

In the years 1945–70 a conscious and continuing effort was made in the UK and USA and many other economies to keep the demand and cost flows in balance and to use the currency for this purpose rather than primarily as a measure of value. As a result the world enjoyed the most rapid advance in output, employment, trade, and living standards which it has ever known. Real standards rose rapidly while money values were gradually falling. The intelligently managed free society was vindicated as against the Marxist cassandras and other fundamentalists.

In the late 1960s, not just in the UK but in most developed economies, and *before* the 'oil shock' of 1973–4, something went wrong. Prices and pay rates began to rise at an accelerating pace; and governments, taking fright, adopted restrictive and deflationary policies which stopped or reversed the real progress made in the preceding twenty-five years.

What really emerged in the late sixties, not at first generally understood, was what I have called the central dilemma, caused by a sudden acceleration in the rise of money pay rates in general. The ratio of the flow of money demand to money costs largely determines the rate of employment and output. But the ratio of money demand to the volume of goods and services available similarly determines prices. No basic difficulty emerges if – as broadly from 1945 to 1960 – cost rates (i.e. mainly money pay rates) do not rise faster than output can rise. But if pay rates do rise faster than output, then the following dilemma is unavoidable. If demand is raised as fast as costs, prices must rise (because demand will be rising faster than output). But if demand does not rise as fast as costs, unemployment must rise (because money demand will not cover the pay of all those able to work). In short, if pay rates rise faster than output, you must have either a rising price level, unemployment, or both.

This central dilemma, being at root an arithmetical truism, does not affect only the pound and the UK. In the USA, for instance, where potential productive capacity is so huge, it can be avoided for a time by a rising flow of physical output. But at some stage it would emerge. In the UK in 1975–6 it became acute, but was rightly met by the then government with an attempt to restrain the excess rise in costs. This attempt succeeded in actually reducing unemployment in 1978–9 and slowing the rise in prices at the same time.

Confusion on the whole issue, however, has been made worse by the revival of certain ancient fallacies in a form now popularly known as 'monetarism'. Moderate monetarists quite legitimately point out that an expansion of the stock of money is one factor that may affect the price level. This is a fair, but not an original, point.

Monetarism, however, as expounded by extremists, is cluttered with fallacies. The worst is the confusion between a demand-inflation and a cost inflation. Extreme monetarism rests on the assumption that the industrial countries in recent times have all been suffering from a demand inflation. This may well be true of certain South American and other economies. But most of the OECD (Organisation for Economic Co-operation and Development) countries in the 1970s (including the UK) have actually been suffering from a cost inflation, as is proved, apart from other evidence, by the fact that profits were falling in the relevant period. In demand inflations profits rise. Wrong diagnoses lead to wrong prescriptions.

The second most prevalent fallacy (encountered in every depression since 1800) is the belief that unemployment is caused by technical progress. But if this is so, why did unemployment suddenly rise, for instance in the UK, after May 1979? And why has the USA achieved a massive increase in employment in 1982–3–4? All modern economic history shows that unemployment in developed countries is a monetary phenomenon, a failure to keep money demand and costs in balance. President Reagan, since 1980 by means of huge budget spending, has generated a major rise in production and employment and has thus effectively, though unintentionally, proved wrong both the crude monetarists and the believers in technological unemployment.

Meanwhile in the UK the post-1979 government, by adopting the opposite policies, and by treating a cost inflation as a demand inflation, has in effect simultaneously cut down demand and let costs go on rising. This has produced exactly the effect which the critics of these policies predicted: a heavy fall in national output apart from oil, and unemployment of over 3 million; with all the damage resulting from this to the UK's future economic capacity.

The basic choice before the developed countries in the contemporary world is therefore this. If we control neither money demand nor money costs, the two will be constantly out of balance, and periods of high unemployment or rapidly rising prices will be usual, with both on occasions prevailing at the same time. Real economic growth will be slow, and standards lower than they need be; and the cause of this will be mismanagement of the monetary machine. If we try to control demand and not costs, or costs and not demand, the result will not be far different. All this applies generally; but the dilemma is particularly acute in the case of the UK and the pound because of other mistakes of economic policy made since the 1950s. With present policies, we are heading for a daunting crisis when our oil earnings run down in the 1990s.

Yet it is perfectly possible, though not easy, to combine full employment with only moderately rising price levels, if we can control reasonably effectively the flows of both demand and costs. My plea is therefore for moderation. Neither 'free collective bargaining', the 'money supply', nor 'public borrowing' should be treated as holy grails. The central objective should be to control *centrally* both money demand and cost levels; or in effect to extend the principle of law and order, rather than the rule of force, to wider areas of society.

This means developing a workable incomes policy, affecting prices and investment incomes as well as pay. Nobody denies that the practical difficulties of operating such a policy are great; but experience here and elsewhere shows that they are not insuperable. Any attempt in human affairs to substitute more civilized methods than force for resolving conflicts is apt to be troublesome, complicated, and laborious. It will always be opposed by those who think they will suffer from it. But the prize of success in this instance is very great. The alternative in the case of the UK is the needless but continuing enfeeblement of the economic vitality and so the strategic and political strength of a potentially great country. It is worth trying.

I would rather see finance less proud and industry more content.

Winston Churchill

Cecily, you will read your *Political Economy* in my absence. The chapter on the Fall of the Rupee you may omit. It is somewhat too exciting for a young girl.

Oscar Wilde

1

Means, not End

Money is a good servant, but a bad master. It is an essential means, without which the whole process of production, exchange and consumption, and so the satisfaction of human wants, cannot be advanced beyond a primitive level. If there were no money, the obstacle to the exchange of most people's skills would be insurmountable. The dentist who wanted food would have to find a farmer whose teeth needed attention. But the nearest farmer might want cigarettes instead, and the cigarette manufacturer might want no food and have nothing wrong with his teeth. But if they can all offer their services or goods for the same thing – money – then, given a system of law and order, the whole complex of myriad exchanges becomes possible. This indeed is just as true of a planned or socialist economy as of a mixed or wholly *laissez-faire* system, at least if the consumer is free to buy what he or she wishes. Barter – the direct exchange of goods for goods – though occasionally worthwhile, remains a clumsy substitute. Money made it easier for earlier societies to escape from slavery or serfdom.

But money, though essential, is only a means, not an end. You cannot eat it, drink it, wear it, or live in it. Its value almost wholly depends on what you can exchange it for: in other words, its value is its purchasing power. And it is the first basic contention of this book that many, perhaps most, of the major mistakes made in economic policy nowadays spring from the error of treating money as an end rather than a means.

The primary nature of money is as a 'unit of account', something in which value, price, or debt is expressed. If you wish to express or compare values, prices, or debts, you can only do so in numbers. And if you use numbers, they must be numbers of something. In a sense the name does not matter. But just as you can only measure or compare lengths in numbers of, say, inches or yards, you can only compare economic values in numbers of some unit of account. Here, however, a confusion may break in. It is strictly true that a yard is three times as long as a foot. And it is equally true that the price of something can be twice or three times that of something else. But it is not strictly true that one want or need, though it may be greater or less than another, can be three times greater – any more than one person's loves or hates, hopes or fears, can be three times as great as another's. Wants and needs cannot be truly measured in numbers, though the use of money and prices sometimes makes it seem that they can. The existence of a common price for some commodity does mean that each consumer can estimate the sacrifice he must make to acquire it. It does not mean that the want satisfied by that commodity is the same in intensity for all consumers, still less that it is twice as great as some other want even for one consumer. Nevertheless for practical purposes of measurement, calculation, and comparison, economic values must be expressed in numbers of some money of account.

Traditionally, and on the whole justifiably, money has been recognized as having three functions or uses: as a medium of exchange, as a standard or measure of value, and as a store of value. Its use as a medium of exchange, something which enables the whole economic process to develop, has already been described. It is primarily this use which makes a given thing 'money'. If people generally will accept something as payment for their produce or services, then it is money, even if it is a shell, a stone, a piece of paper, cattle or sheep.[1] Historically this is how it usually starts. But the same function, that of making economic activity possible, becomes even more crucial as both money itself and the modern economy, industrial and international, develop into the immensely complex and sophisticated mechanism we know today. As the potential benefits to mankind of economic activity grow, so does the harm done by mismanagement of money and the failure to supply an adequate volume of it.

Secondly, money functions, by reason of its nature as a unit of account, as a measure or standard of value. Because this enables calculations and contracts to be made, and debts to be incurred and discharged, a whole new range of economic advance is opened up.

Whereas money as a means of exchange is an object, even if only a paper one, money as a measure of value is, strictly, an abstraction. The actual value of the money unit at any one time ultimately depends, for the individual, on the satisfaction of those of his or her wants which that unit is able to buy, and the efforts and sacrifice he or she has to make in order to earn it.[2] But a basic practical difficulty in the management of money very soon raises its head. How do you ensure that the money unit in question retains substantially the same value for at least most people in different places and periods of time? If you do not, the public may hesitate to use it as a medium of exchange, and it will lose its essential usefulness.

Thirdly, money has to act as a store of value. Those who have earned it, or acquired it somehow, will want to keep some of it; often from their earlier years until old age. And they will want to be reasonably sure that it preserves its value over time; in effect that it will buy the same sort of things that it used to buy.

The three functions of money are thus closely interdependent. People use it as a medium of exchange because it provides them with a measure of value and enables them to judge whether a given transaction is worth their while. Conversely money tends to preserve its value because people know that it can be used as a means of payment – to buy goods or discharge debts – and also as a store of value. And it is in turn trusted as a store of value because of its ability to perform these other functions and because people believe that its value is likely to be preserved. From this very interdependence, however, it also follows that once the belief in one of money's virtues is undermined, doubts may spread about the others, and the whole house of cards totter towards collapse. Hence the talk which persists throughout the history of money about 'confidence', or lack of it, in the currency and its controllers.

Unhappily also, the very interdependence between the uses of money involves a conflict between them. The major conflict, which only fully revealed itself historically as the nature of money evolved in the vastly greater complexity of the nineteenth and twentieth centuries, is between money's functions as a measure of value and as a medium of exchange. Fundamentally, the dilemma is this. In certain circumstances it may be true that you can only preserve the value (purchasing power) of money by restricting or even curtailing the quantity of it available. But if you do so, you may also curtail the whole process of production and exchange, and so deprive the community of the 'real' supply of goods and services which alone give their money any value. In the Middle Ages, and indeed up to the nineteenth century, the mismanagement of money tended more usually to take the form of rapacious governments preferring the usefulness of money as a means of payment (by themselves) to its function as a stable measure of value. Hence traditional economic thought, feeding on history, has long been inclined, and is still inclined even now, to regard this mismanagement – excessive expansion of the quantity of money for short-term purposes – as the only, or at least much the most important, misuse of the money system.

Yet in the modern world the opposite mistake – the impulse to preserve the value of money even at the cost of bringing real economic life almost to a stop – has become equally if not more prevalent. Just because of abuses in earlier periods, and in ill-managed economies even in the twentieth century, the intellectual pendulum has swung back too far, as it often does; and in the 1980s the belief that money values are paramount is in danger of becoming a fetish which actually blocks the production of wealth. It is the second basic contention of this book that, though all the functions of money remain vital, in the present age money's function as a medium of exchange ought to be treated as more important than its other functions as a measure or store of value.

Notes

[1] China and India used cowrie shells for many centuries, and the Latin *pecunia*, money, is derived from *pecus*, cattle. The English 'salary' is derived from the Latin '*sal*' for salt, in which Roman soldiers were paid.
[2] A discussion of the nature of value in the full sense is, of course, outside the scope of this book.

Coins and Paper

The human race only stumbled very gradually, by trial and error, on the mechanism of money. Money proper developed in three stages, and eventually took three main forms: coins, notes, and bank deposits. It probably started with people using, for the three purposes described in Chapter 1, small units of precious metals, usually bronze, silver, or gold. These metals were valuable in themselves as ornaments; were easily kept and transferred; did not wear out through use; and lasted more or less indefinitely. But for practical purposes it was necessary to be sure that the given unit of metal really had the weight which it claimed. So from an early stage people brought their metal to be stamped with its weight and/or fineness by some authority which was generally trusted. At some point in the story the state stepped in and took on the job, first of designating the standard, and later of actually stamping the piece of metal. With the second of these functions the coin proper was born, and its production became in most cases the sole prerogative of the state. Herodotus may or may not be right in saying that the first genuine coins were struck by the kings of Lydia in the sixth or seventh centuries BC; but certainly by this period coined money had come into existence in the Mediterranean world. Much earlier than this, even, some states, without actually issuing coins of their own, had defined what weight and fineness of metal was to be the standard.

Understandably, from these early times onward the key question among sceptically minded persons was whether the weight and fineness of the metal were genuine. Since the issuer of the coins could, by exaggerating their value, obtain in exchange more than they were really worth, suspicion of 'debasement' and fraud became common. These suspicions arose only too naturally with the development of coinage itself; and they were often justified. Inevitably, therefore, concern with the value of the money unit became deep-rooted, and persisted into more recent times when the whole problem had grown far more complex.

The second and third types of money, notes and bank deposits, only came into their own in the modern world. Essentially both these devices are IOUs or promises to pay, but of two different forms. Very early in the history of economic life it must have been found convenient for A to say to B: 'I haven't got the money today, but if you will sell me the goods now, I will pay you at such and such a date.' Whereupon B replied that he would do this if A would sign a piece of paper promising to pay on time. Before long B would discover that, if A's word generally was trusted, his promise to pay could be passed on by B to C in return for something that B required before the relevant date arrived. So, in so far as the authors of the promises were generally trusted, promises to pay converted themselves gradually into 'money'; in other words something which most people were willing to accept in payment for goods and services or discharge of a debt.

At this point the state again saw its chance and found that it had the power to declare by legislation that such and such paper promises to pay (whether issued by itself or a bank or anyone else) were 'legal tender': that is, they could be used legally to pay labour or buy goods or discharge a debt. These promises to pay became what has been called 'fiat' money – almost worthless in themselves, but given a value in virtue of the constitutional and legislative power of the state to ratify in the courts their use as money. Just as Jehovah said, 'Let there be light', so the king or parliament said, 'Let this be a pound.' And as long as society accepted this legislative fiat, and as long as it was believed that it would be accepted, the new 'fiat' money – notes – circulated just as readily as the old. It had already become apparent, of course, that this principle applied also to coins. A copper coin declared to be legal tender was normally just as good as a silver coin (and much more profitable to the state as issuing authority), whatever relation the value of the actual copper bore to the value stamped on the face of the coin.

But this gradual monetary revolution created momentous consequences, at first not fully understood. First there was evidently little physical limit to the numbers of paper money units which the king or parliament could declare to be legal tender. How many, then, should he or they issue? Secondly, the discovery of 'promise to pay' money in fact made possible a huge expansion of trade, production, and employment. It therefore raised more than one far-reaching question. Had the state discovered a magic device for creating wealth? What would happen if this power was used without limit? And if some limit was necessary, what should it be? These questions were to provoke prolonged controversy among governments, bankers, economists, and others notably from the eighteenth and nineteenth centuries onwards.

Such controversies were made even more acute by the emergence in these centuries of the third main form of money (and second type of 'promise to pay' money): bank credit or bank deposits. The most fascinating aspect, perhaps, of the history of banking is the way in which bankers themselves for several generations tended to conceal what they were really doing;[1] then for another long period indignantly denied it, and only in the twentieth century were cajoled by economists and other interfering busybodies into generally admitting and justifying it. Yet in fact they were performing all the time the perfectly honourable and necessary function of creating money, without which modern industry, trade, and employment could never have developed as they have.

Money lenders had always existed, and banks had operated profitably in the later Middle Ages in Venice, Florence, Genoa, Amsterdam, and elsewhere. They received 'money', mainly coin, into safe custody and gave the owners IOUs in return. In England (and it was just 'England' at this stage), in London's Lombard Street in particular, goldsmiths had been lenders before the seventeenth century.[2] But they normally lent their own money, not that of others collected for the purpose. The turning point came in Amsterdam in the early seventeenth century as an indirect result of the influx of silver from Spanish America, and later in the same century in London. So much silver of varying quality had reached Amsterdam by 1609 that the merchants of that city decided to set up a bank, owned by the city, called the Bank of Amsterdam, which would receive deposits of silver, test it by weight, credit the true amount to the depositor, and give him a paper certificate to that effect. The depositor had the right to draw the silver if he wanted it, but otherwise the bank would keep it. Meanwhile the depositor's paper claim was found to be valuable money which he could transfer to someone else if he wished to do so.

But then the bank made another discovery. There was no point in leaving all the silver lying idle in the vaults if people mostly did not ask for it but instead used their claims on it for buying and selling. So why not lend some of this silver at interest, or create further paper claims on it and lend these to other people? This meant creating claims on more silver than remained in the bank, and had this been generally known at the time it would probably have been considered somewhat alarming: so the bank kept quiet. If, of course, the depositor and the borrower had each asked for their share of the same silver on the same day – or rather if they all did – the bank would not have been able to honour its promises and pay them. But the bank authorities found that this did not happen in practice. On any given day or week only some of the claimants asked for 'cash'. So the problem for the bank became purely quantitative. If you know from experience that your depositors and borrowers would never ask for more than, say, 50 per cent of your silver on the same day, then you could create claims for nearly twice as many monetary units as the worth of the silver you held. And you would thereby have created trustworthy money – as long as only a very few people understood what you were really doing.

Whether or not the Bank of Amsterdam first originated these practices, it certainly made them respectable and successful; and as such they became the basis of the banking system, and in large part the money system, of the modern world. If customers and critics in the seventeenth century had fully understood what was happening, they would probably have called it a fraud. But it was not really a fraud so much as a confidence trick, and one which, paradoxically and unintentionally, was a public service because modern industry and trade needed it. It was also an immediate success.

Throughout the eighteenth and nineteenth centuries the complexity of the banking system developed enormously; but the central principle of 'credit creation' remained the same, and orthodox bankers continued to conceal and deny, or at least obfuscate, what they were doing. They had some excuse if they looked at the problem from the point of view of their own individual bank rather than the whole system. Their most plausible argument was this. Banking, they said, was really just like the proverbial cloakroom ticket system. Bankers could only lend on what somebody else had deposited with them; and they really issued only as many tickets as they had packages. But the fallacy was this. If legal tender money such as coins or notes is handed to the bank, then money is simply transferred from one place to another, and no new money is created. The bank's assets are increased by the new cash and its liabilities (which in total must equal its assets) by the deposit which the customer acquires in exchange – a debt of the bank to the depositor. But if no cash is deposited, and the bank makes an 'advance' or grants an overdraft, new money is certainly created. What really happens in this case is that the customer exchanges his debt to the bank, the overdraft, for the bank's debt to him, the deposit. But since his debt would not be accepted by other people as money, and since the bank's debt *is* accepted in this way if the bank is well known, new money is created by the exchange. The recipient of the overdraft can use this new deposit created by the overdraft to buy goods or make a payment into another bank. Thus since the eighteenth century money has been created on an ever-increasing scale, not merely by central banks set up by governments, but also by ordinary commercial banks in so far as their promises to pay have been generally trusted. This central truth was only accepted generally by British bankers and public opinion as a whole, as well as by economists, after the publication in 1931 of the *Report on Finance and Industry* by the Macmillan Committee, which included both bankers and economists (J.M. Keynes among them). In a crucial passage the Macmillan Report said this:

> 'It is not unnatural to think of the deposits of a bank as being created by the public through the deposit of cash representing either savings or amounts which are not for the time being required to meet expenditure. But the bulk of the deposits arise out of the action of the banks themselves; for by granting loans, allowing money to be drawn on overdraft, or purchasing securities, a bank creates a credit in its books which is the equivalent of a deposit.'[3]

And (the Macmillan Report might have added) if the banks did not create money, where on earth had it all come from?[4]

The power of commercial banks to create money is not, however, unlimited. It is limited first by the willingness of the public to accept as money its promises to pay, and secondly by the wish of its customers to borrow. The latter wish is naturally constrained by, among other things, the rate of interest which the bank charges. Thirdly it is limited by the size of the reserve of 'cash' (normally notes and coins) which the bank believes it must keep to satisfy holders of its debts who want to change them into cash. The original Bank of Amsterdam had to keep *some* silver in its vaults because some people sometimes asked for it. In advanced countries in modern times a ratio of cash to total deposits of something like 8–10 per cent has been found safe and become normal. But it still remains true that if at any time prudence or the law allows the accepted reserve ratio to be lowered, then the power of the whole banking system to create money is automatically increased.

Naturally from the seventeenth century onwards it began to be felt, even if confusedly, among governments and learned men, and less learned men, that some control ought to be exercised over the operation of the banks. Might not these new-fangled banks, people asked, be monkeying about with the currency? Partly for this reason, and partly no doubt because English monarchs of the late seventeenth century tended to want a lot of money, the Bank of England was founded in 1694 to imitate and rival the Bank of Amsterdam. The functions of the new bank were to receive deposits, to issue notes, and above all to lend money to the government. And in time it became established that deposits held by other banks at the Bank of England could be counted as part of the other banks' cash reserve. This meant in turn that if the Bank of England chose to increase its loans, for instance by buying government securities, the other banks' cash could be proportionately expanded, and with it the power of the banking system as a whole to create money.

As this system spread in time to one country after another, the various implications became apparent, and various questions began to be asked. A mechanism had certainly, if accidentally, been devised which could permit over generations a vast expansion of commerce and trade. But should it be controlled by governments? Should they not exercise the same control over it which they had claimed for centuries over the unit of account and the coinage? What would happen if they did not? And more pointedly, what quantity if any of new money should they allow to be created? Did the banks' operations perhaps also affect the value of money? And finally, since the power of money creation was highly profitable, and since the creator earned interest by lending money which he had created at negligible cost to himself, should not the profit on creating credit accrue, like that of coinage, to the public as a whole and not to the banks? The latter question became curiously muted, compared with the others, though I do not believe we have yet heard the last of it. It will be easier, however, to answer these questions in the later chapters of this book if we first trace in more detail the adventures of one particular currency, the pound sterling.

Notes

[1] Even as late as the 1870s Bagehot (Lombard Street 7th edition, p. 60) says of the Bank of England that, though it 'more or less does its duty, it does not distinctly acknowledge that it is its duty'.

[2] Lombard Street was named after immigrant Italian merchants.

[3] *Macmillan Report on Finance and Industry*, p. 34. If anyone still doubts the banks' power to create money, they should consult R.S. Sayers, *Modern Banking*, pp. 12 and 13; J.K. Galbraith, *The Age of Uncertainty*, pp. 166–7; or, among earlier authorities, Eric Roll, *About Money*, pp. 159–60; and J.M. Keynes, *A Treatise on Money*, Vol. I, Ch. 2.

[4] As definitions change, it is difficult to give strictly comparable figures of the rise in bank deposits, even in the UK. In *The Pound Sterling* (p. 304), Sir A. Feavearyear shows 'Total bank deposits of Great Britain exclusive of Bank of England' as £8 million in 1796, £120 million in 1856, £1,061 million in 1914, and £2,231 million in 1928. London clearing bank deposits were £4,751 million in 1945 (p. 392), and £7,783 million in 1959. On 31 December 1983 'UK private sector deposits' are recorded as £89,997 million (*Annual Abstract of Statistics*). Whatever definition is taken, there has been a huge and continuous increase.

3

The Silver Pound

'He was required to define what he meant by the pound. His answer was "I find it difficult to explain it, but every gentleman in England knows it." The Committee repeated the question, and Mr Smith answered: "It is something that has existed without variation in this country for 800 years – 300 years before the introduction of gold." '

So said Sir Robert Peel in a debate in the House of Commons in 1819, quoting the evidence of Mr Smith, a London accountant, before the Committee on the Resumption of Cash Payments.[1] Peel, however, disagreed with the empirical Mr Smith, and declared dogmatically that the pound could only be defined as 'a definite quantity of gold bullion'. To which Mr Smith might have retorted that if so, how was it that the pound had been based on a silver standard for many centuries from Saxon times until the eighteenth century, and that contracts and debts had been continuously reckoned and discharged throughout that period in a money of account expressed in pounds and pennies, and later also in shillings.

In fact the pound began in pre-Norman times as the *libra* or Latin pound of silver: hence the pound, the French *livre*, and the Italian *lira*; and also basically, if not linguistically, the franc, the mark, and the ducat, though their later history varied.[2] To an Italian the pound is the *lira sterlina*. From the very start – indeed from the eighth century AD – the penny already existed in the Saxon kingdoms as one 240th part of the silver pound, a fraction not changed till the 1970s. Until the fourteenth century the penny was officially known by the Latin name, *denarius* (hence 'denier', a measure of yarn thickness, and the 'd' in £ s d).[3] It was also the silver penny, not the pound, which was first, in the twelfth century, called a 'sterling' – probably because some early Norman pennies were marked with a small star or *steorra*, though this derivation has never been conclusively established. But certainly because these pennies were regarded at home and abroad as of unquestionably good value, 'sterling' came to mean generally sound, of true value, staunch.

The shilling came later and was probably derived from the Old Saxon *scilling*, which meant a piece cut off. This word may have originally represented pieces of broken silver thrown into the balance and used to make up the due weight. At any rate when William the Conqueror and the Norman ruling classes took over, they naturally preferred their own basically Roman system of the *libra* (or *livre*) divided into 20 *solidi* (or *sous*), and the *solidus* divided into 12 *denarii*: hence again the '£ s d'. So to the ordinary English public in the Middle Ages the *solidus* naturally became the shilling, and the *denarius* remained the penny. Throughout medieval times the common people would hardly ever have handled any coin other than the penny or fraction of it. In the fourteenth century after the Black Death a farm labourer's daily wage would have been 3d. A sheep cost about 2s 3d, cheese was a little over ½d a lb, and eggs ½d a dozen.[4]

But though, during the Middle Ages, the English pound was supposed to be based on a pound of silver, governments and the Mint were far from operating anything like a modern 'silver' – still less gold – 'standard', which would have implied free movement of coin and metal in and out of the Mint and the country. Under a metal standard the central authority keeps the currency unit equal in value to a certain amount of the metal by offering to buy or sell the latter at a fixed price. What the Medieval English kings, chancellors and Mint conceived themselves to be doing was supplying the public with coins, seeking somehow to maintain their value in particular by outwitting the clippers (of whom more below); and sometimes, if needs must, helping to finance the government by issuing depreciated coins.

In these early times it was the use of money as a measure and store of value, rather than as a medium of exchange, which naturally dominated the mind of both the governed and the governments. The authorities could not, except perhaps by occasional intuition, have fully understood all the economic consequences of their own decisions, or the complex economic enigmas which were beginning to confront them.

One major economic problem of the future which began to

trouble currency managers from the late Middle Ages onwards was the difficulty of stabilizing the value of money by attaching it to the value of some metal if the value of that metal was itself changing. It will perhaps be helpful to sketch out at this stage in the story of the pound the nature of this central problem.

In order to provide a useful and reliable measure and store of value, it is desirable that the currency unit should be in some sense stable; and stability, in simple terms, means the power of the unit to buy the same quantity of goods and services. But if you attempt to achieve this by making the value of the money unit stable in terms of, say, silver or gold, you do not necessarily make it stable in terms of a representative sample of other things. All you do is to ensure (if you succeed) that the value of the money unit – for example the pound – varies in terms of goods generally at the same rate and in the same direction as gold or silver so varies. Suppose the value of the money unit is kept the same as that of the approved amount of silver or gold (for instance, 1 lb of silver), there are still several possibilities. If silver or gold become more plentiful relative to other goods, the value of silver or gold must fall relative to those goods, and if the value of the monetary unit is held equal to that of the metal, the value of the monetary unit must fall equivalently in terms of other goods; in other words the general price level for goods and services must rise. One pound of silver buys less wheat; and since £1 must then buy less wheat, the price of wheat in pounds must rise.

This happens in practice because the extra supply of silver, whether minted into coins or not, soon appears as extra effective demand which pushes up prices. The usual secondary effect is a general rise in employment and output of goods and services as idle or partially idle labour, land, and equipment are set to work. The final effect of this expansion process is likely to be a gain to those who have goods to sell or debts or charges fixed in money units to meet, and a loss to those who hold money as a store of value or are owed debts fixed in money terms. The lenders lose and the borrowers gain. But the expansion process need not always have this latter effect. In so far as expansion increases the total output of real goods and services, nobody need lose; and it is possible that almost everyone may gain. Historically, growth in the quantity of money has not always expanded real incomes, because there may be strong counter-pressures at work. But it will be a powerful force working that way.

If, on the other hand, silver or gold become more scarce relative to other goods, the process is reversed. The value of the metal rises in terms of other goods, and with it the purchasing power of the currency. Money is more scarce; demand flags; and prices fall. The creditor gains and the debtor loses or becomes insolvent, and many producers find they cannot cover their costs. Output and employment tend to fall, and with them the government's revenues. In this cycle of contraction or deflation, it is usually the property owner and creditor with fixed-money claims who are better off (until the point is reached when the debtor cannot pay, and then everyone is worse off).

The above are the two main possible outcomes on the assumption that the currency is successfully held stable in terms of the value of silver or gold. If thirdly, of course, silver or gold, or both, themselves remained stable in value for a long period, this particular problem would disappear; but history shows that this rarely happens. Suppose, however, that the controllers of the currency and holders of the metal reserve do not, for whatever reason, hold the currency unit stable in terms of silver or gold, then again two broad options are open to them. If they decide to lower the value of the currency unit in terms of silver – to decree, for instance, that the price of 1 lb of silver shall be not £1 but £2, then the quantity of pounds in circulation will be expanded; prices, output, and employment will rise; creditors will lose and debtors gain. But those who issue the new coins will also gain substantially, because until prices rise fully their stocks of silver will buy more and discharge debts more cheaply than before. On the other hand if the controlling authorities are rash enough to raise the metal value of the currency unit – to say that £1 in future will buy 2 lb of silver, then money will tend to become scarce, prices will fall, and general activity will contract. Creditors will be given a huge bonus, and debtors will loudly protest that they cannot pay.

Even this simple analysis shows that changes in the purchasing power of money have not merely economic and commercial, but also social, consequences; and that these consequences cannot normally be overcome by just gearing the value of the money unit to the market value of some precious metal. The basic dilemma arises from the fact that contracts and debts and fixed charges (such as rent) are normally expressed in money units, while these money units themselves are persistently changing in value, even if based on some metal.

The money controllers of the Middle Ages, however, faced another, lesser, but even more pressing, practical difficulty. It was easier to understand, but for many centuries much harder, and indeed impossible, to surmount: the clippers. Throughout medieval times these troublesome and ingenious persons clipped pieces of metal off the king's coins, used the metal for their own purposes, and passed on the debased coins so far as possible at their face value. After a period the authorities were usually forced to call in the inferior coins and recoin the metal; and the loss had to fall on somebody. Fierce denunciations and savage legal penalties were aimed at the clippers, but largely in vain. A final solution was not discovered till the seventeenth century.[5]

So a cycle set in meanwhile of new coinage, sporadic clipping and then recoinage, which supervened on the major cycles due to changes in the value of silver or later of gold, and of changes in the volume of output and trade which had to be financed. At least seven recoinages occurred in England between 1100 and 1300. But though clipping reduced the weight of metal in the coin, it did not necessarily increase the circulation or affect the level of prices generally. Unhappily, however, the clippers were accompanied in these times in England by the counterfeiters (and importers of base coins from abroad), who actually increased – sometimes substantially – the number of coins in circulation, and so must have reduced their value.

In the middle of the thirteenth century a major new economic force became pronounced throughout Europe: shortage of silver. Sources of supply which had been adequate in late Roman times had been lost in the Dark Ages and not effectively replaced. Imports of silver from the East were seldom sufficient in the thirteenth and early fourteenth centuries to keep pace with rising population and economic activity; though England, thanks to wool exports, was often able to attract a fair amount, but not enough, of the silver available. Money became scarce and prices tended to fall in the early fourteenth century. So the classic dilemma, not yet fully understood, confronted the English government. If the old silver value of the pound was to be preserved, prices generally would be lowered, and the wool merchants, already a vocal lobby, would protest. But if the silver value was not preserved, others, including property owners, would complain that the currency was being debased. A trade deficit caused by the start of the Hundred Years war in 1338 also made silver harder to acquire.

A parliamentary inquiry into the dilemma was held as early as 1343, after which Parliament itself came down on the side of 'sound money', to use the twentieth-century term, or as the 1343 Parliament put it: 'good sterlings, of the weight and alloy of the old sterlings, should be current in England and should not be carried out of the kingdom in any manner or for any cause whatever'.[6] But Edward III did not agree. Possibly, or partly, in order to avoid too violent a deflation of prices, by a series of measures in 1343–6 the King introduced what was in effect a reduction in the silver weight of the pound or a rise in the Mint price of 1 lb of silver to about 22s. The new coins, the King said, would be 'as good and of the weight of the sterlings current in the land, or better'.[7] This was a tactful way of saying: 'The pound in your pocket will not be devalued.' And indeed if the avoidance of deflation was among the King's motives, this must have been one of the earliest occasions on record in England when a government decided to prefer a change in the value of the monetary unit to the infliction of depression, losses, bankruptcies, and unemployment on the country. Even more interestingly, there was little public protest in the 1340s, although this was the first formal change in the silver value of the pound for 350 years. Parliament, wisely and characteristically, contented itself with a petition asking the King not to make further changes in the silver standard without their consent; and (after another cut by the King in the pound's silver weight in 1351) this was embodied in a formal statute the following year.

King and parliaments, however, may propose, but higher powers dispose. In 1348–50 the Black Death struck Europe, and the grisly economic experiment of a cut in the population by at least one third in two years was remorselessly imposed without the consent of anyone. Men and women caught the Black Death; but the coinage did not. And so by 1351, when the plague had for the moment nearly burnt itself out, the number of pennies in circulation had largely risen relative to the number of hands wanting work and to the volume of goods being produced. So demand in the short term pushed up wage rates and prices.[8] It is true that there were also fewer mouths to feed. But what counts, as will be emphasized later in this argument, is *effective* demand. In this case, since though there were fewer consumers they had enough money to pay higher prices, those prices would naturally have risen. At the same time those who had lost, or thought they had lost, by the King's action in previously devaluing the currency blamed the subsequent rise in prices on that devaluation.

Not long after the Black Death years, however, the underlying deflationary forces once more gained the upper hand. Output of food recovered more quickly than population. The European shortage of both silver and gold persisted right through the fifteenth century up to the discovery of silver and gold mines in America. So during that century the kings of England, in so far as they had time to spare from fighting the French overseas and the Wars of the Roses at home, were faced by declining stocks of silver, falling prices, more clipping and counterfeiting, and a pressing need to finance their armies. They responded partly by experiments in gold coinage, but mainly by imitating Edward III in further cuts in the silver value of the pound. Gold was no more than a sideshow in the history of the pound before the time of Henry VII, though Edward III had tried a gold florin (so called after the Florentine gold florin). But it was a failure.

Much more successful in the fifteenth century were further devaluations of the silver standard which both gave the king a profit and, whether intentionally or not, prevented a deflation of prices which would otherwise have been caused by the silver shortage. There were further major devaluations in 1411 and 1464. As a result, the effect of the shortage of silver in raising its value and that of the currency was just about offset by the change made in the quantity of silver equivalent to £1; and the sterling prices of commodities remained remarkably stable. Adam Smith himself remarked that from 1351 for a long period the average price of wheat in sterling remained almost unchanged. This exceptional good fortune should probably be ascribed mainly to luck rather than to wise government. But it must have been an immense blessing, nonetheless, to English agriculture and the whole English economy. In the fifteenth century, with a lower population and restored food supply, the actual standard of living was higher than it had been previously or would be for a long time afterwards. This was still a time when the standard of living largely depended on the ratio of population to food supply.

Notes

[1] Quoted in A. Feavearyear, *The Pound Sterling* (Second edition),p.1.

[2] As I write (1983) the pound sterling, despite its various depreciations, is worth about 12 French francs and 2,350 Italian lire.

[3] Though the word 'penny' does not derive linguistically from *denarius*. See *The Pound Sterling*, p. 7, and E. Victor Morgan, *A History of Money*, p. 18.

[4] I am indebted to Sir Henry Phelps Brown for these figures.

[5] See p. 39.

[6] Quoted in *The Pound Sterling*, p. 16.

[7] Quoted in *The Pound Sterling*, p. 17.

[8] Prices from 88 in 1346 to 160 in 1352 (1451–75 = 100). From Henry Phelps Brown and Sheila V. Hopkins, *A Perspective of Wages and Prices*, p.28. See Appendix.

[9] *Wealth of Nations* (1837 edition), p. 82.

4

Silver and Gold from America

The discovery of America very soon brought to Europe large new supplies of gold and even greater supplies of silver. Most historians used to believe this influx to have been the main cause of the sharp rise in prices, including sterling prices, and of the general economic expansion which appeared to follow. More recently, however, this has been doubted, and the rise in the price of food relative to other prices has been attributed to the population growing more rapidly than food supply. There is at any rate no doubt that the gold and silver did reach Europe and that prices generally did rise. Within twenty years of the discovery of America in 1492 gold began to arrive, mainly via Spain. The most massive silver influx came from the re-equipped mines of Potosi (in modern Bolivia) after 1545.[1] At first sight it is natural to suppose that such a wave of new money would have expanded demand and hence trade, production, and no doubt employment and investment throughout much of Western Europe; also, as an inevitable part of the expansion process, it would have raised prices.

The boom started in Spain when silver first arrived in bulk. Prices began to rise steeply from about 1520, and by the end of the century had reached levels about five times higher than they had been eighty years before. In France prices rose rather later, and were two and a half times higher at the end of the century than at the beginning – also a rapid rise compared with the previous century, if moderate compared with our own. England had escaped currency upheavals in the reign of Henry VII. He had come to the throne in the aftermath of the silver shortage and sterling devaluations of the fifteenth century and acted in his monetary decisions, as in other spheres, with caution and calculation. He naturally could not have known in his early years that within a generation ample supplies of gold and silver were destined to arrive from a still undiscovered continent. In 1489 he minted the first gold £1 piece, which be called a 'soveraigne';[2] and in 1504 the first silver shilling. Otherwise he refrained from either uprating or downgrading the silver value of the pound; and sensibly also refrained, unlike his predecessors and his son, from starting wars on the continent.

Some American silver was already arriving in Europe in the early years of Henry VIII's reign. But neither he nor his advisers could have been expected to grasp the full implication of these supplies: that money was likely to be plentiful for some years, and that further devaluation could not be justified as needed to avoid deflation. Those who attribute the sixteenth-century rise in prices to American silver and those who attribute it to rising population will no doubt both believe that in England this rise was already inevitable by the time Henry VIII became king. On either interpretation, what he in fact did was make the increase, without any real economic justification, more severe than it need have been. Even so, despite a rise in the sterling price of all gold coins in 1526, it was not till 1542 that the King, under pressure from his Exchequer's constant needs, issued a summary Royal Warrant to the Mint authorizing them to alter the sterling value of 1 lb of gold or silver whenever instructed to do so by the King and Privy Council.[3] In 1544[4] the Mint price of both gold and silver was substantially raised – the amount of metal equivalent to £1 was reduced – and the Exchequer secured a large profit on the gold and silver which it held. Shortly after Henry's death in 1547 a further major increase was made in the gold and silver price, in what seems to have been a rather desperate effort to meet the huge debts which the King had left.

Under the influence of these royal manoeuvres and the other economic forces at work, the English public experienced in the 1540s the steepest rise in general prices experienced for several generations. Such index numbers as are available for commodity prices generally suggest that between 1538–41 and 1551 the price level actually doubled.[5] The highest point for the time was probably reached in 1555–7, when bad harvests occurred, just before Queen Elizabeth's accession. The exchange rate for the pound in Antwerp and elsewhere fell heavily – by more than 50 per cent in Antwerp between 1510 and 1551.[6] Over the whole of what later became known as the 'price revolution' period – say from 1500 till 1650 – a more than fivefold rise occurred in the general price level in England.[7]

The young Queen Elizabeth, faced with unpopular coins and high prices, was remarkably fortunate in having, as two of her chief advisers, William Cecil and Thomas Gresham. After much learned and discreet debate a major recoinage was carried out, which at least got rid of the scandal of the debased coins. Their face value was reduced in 1560 to near their existing real value, and new coins issued in exchange. But though Elizabeth thus eliminated her father's debased coins, she and her advisers had the wisdom not to try to restore the real value of the pound to what it was worth in Henry VII's time.[8] This would inevitably have meant a severe deflation of prices and the quantity of money generally, which might well have devitalized economic expansion at the very start of the Elizabethan age. By 1562 the new measures had brought the sterling price of silver a little way down, but nowhere near to the level of 1542. And after 1562 the rapid rise in the general price level slowed down for the time being.

The net effect, therefore, of the Tudor monarchs' management of the currency was a steep rise in prices, followed by comparative stability at a high level; and a fall in real wages as money wages lagged behind. Population was also almost certainly rising faster than food supply. According to some authorities real wages, which had risen in the fifteenth century, were actually halved between 1500 and 1600.[9] What is at any rate probable is that the severe impoverishment and protest which this would have led one to expect were somewhat eased, at least among those wage earners who possessed their own vegetable plots. Risings did occur, however, in 1549 in Norfolk, Devon and Cornwall, and maximum prices were fixed for some foods. Much hardship must have lurked behind the conventional façade of Elizabethan enterprise and expansion, though considerable affluence, due to high food prices, among the more vocal farming and landowning groups no doubt contributed to the expansive spirit. ('Here's a farmer that hanged himself on the expectation of plenty,' said the porter in *Macbeth*,[10] first performed in 1606. The worst year in several centuries for food scarcity and high prices – 'dearth', as they called it then – was 1597).

It has been customary, of course, for historians to blame Henry

VIII for 'debasing' the coinage and praise Elizabeth for 'restoring' its probity. The extent of blame must mainly depend on whether you judge that Henry's wars were inevitable. And Elizabeth's 'restoration' really amounted, wisely, to little more than avoiding any further slide. Certainly the Tudor monarchs presided over a fall in real wages, but also a rise in population and probably in employment and economic activity generally. Despite the fall in real wages, the combination of rising population and agricultural affluence might well account for the Elizabethan atmosphere of growth and optimism. At least the Tudor governments abstained from a plunge into deep deflation, in pursuit of some ideal value of the currency, such as later proved so disastrous after both 1815 and 1918.

The question[11] remains, however, how far the great price rise of the sixteenth century, in England and elsewhere in Europe, was due to the influx of gold and silver, and how far to a major growth of population which exceeded the food supply. In Spain in particular the evidence is strong that rising quantities of money were a powerful influence. There is no *a priori* reason why the price movement should be attributed wholly to one factor or the other. Economic events have many causes, not one. Secondly, the mere fact that the rise in prices was different for different commodities does not prove that monetary pressure was not at work. A purely monetary inflation does not raise all prices equally, but tends to equalize the difference between the individual rises which occurred, and what would have occurred otherwise. On the other hand, the fact that food prices rose notably faster than most prices does suggest that the population–food ratio was a major factor. The price ratio certainly moved in favour of the food producers and against the rest of the community; and this must have favoured farmers and those who received farm rents which could be raised. But such a change in itself would not necessarily have raised the general level of prices if total money demand had not increased. It also seems reasonably clear that in England, Henry VIII's devaluations made the price rise more acute. For though living standards depended largely on the population–food ratio, the price level must also have been affected by the volume of money available to be spent.

In general it is probable that, in an age when money consisted largely of metal coins, if population was increasing faster than food production, and if supplies of metal for coinage also expanded, prices would rise, and food prices would lead the rise. If food had been scarce, and money supplies also scarce, more people would have gone without food (because fewer had full-time work such as in building), and prices would have risen less or perhaps not at all. In fact it is fairly evident that both population and the volume of money were increasing simultaneously. If so, it was a lucky coincidence for sixteenth-century Europe that the precious metals arrived in the same period as the growth of population, helping to ensure a wider distribution of scarce food and perhaps, through pressure of effective demand, a quicker expansion of the supply.

Notes

[1] A. Feavearyear, *The Pound Sterling*, p. 47.

[2] *The Pound Sterling*, p. 46.

[3] *The Pound Sterling*, pp. 50–1.

[4] *The Pound Sterling*, p. 53.

[5] *The Pound Sterling*, p. 68. This is approximately confirmed by the estimates made by Henry Phelps Brown and Sheila V. Hopkins, *A Perspective of Wages and Prices*, p. 29. See Appendix.

[6] *The Pound Sterling*, p. 68.

[7] See Appendix.

[8] *The Pound Sterling*, p. 84.

[9] According to the estimates made by Henry Phelps Brown and Sheila V. Hopkins, the index of prices of a package of consumables (1451–75 = 100) rose from 193 in 1548 to 459 in 1600; and the index of *real* wage rates of building craftsmen (also 1451–75 = 100) actually fell from about 61 to 44. If the years 1500 to 1600 are taken, the fall in real wage rates was from 106 to 44. See Appendix.

[10] Act II, Scene III.

[11] For the arguments on this issue, see Peter Ramsey, *The Price Revolution in Sixteenth-Century England*, and Brian Outhwaite, *Inflation in Tudor and Early Stuart England*.

5

The Paper Pound and the Bank of England

In the seventeenth century 'promises to pay' or paper money came into existence, as described in Chapter 2, in most parts of Western Europe including England. Up till then the common people in England had normally handled silver coins, but neither paper money nor gold. In those days, as Shakespeare put it, silver was the 'pale and common drudge 'tween man and man', as opposed to 'gaudy gold, hard food for Midas'.[1] But in the general turbulence of the seventeenth century, just before the credit system began its great leap forward, three major advances were made in the coinage structure supporting the pound sterling.

First, the clippers were finally defeated; even Queen Elizabeth, Cecil, and Gresham had previously been unable to outwit them. In the mid-seventeenth century, however, after various experiments, failures, and false starts, a Frenchman called Pierre Blondeau perfected the device of 'milling' the edges of the coin. After its adoption in France it was resisted for a time in England by vested interests whom some suspected of making profits out of clipping. But in 1663 the Mint officially adopted Blondeau's system, which signalled the end of clipping. The appearance of the new milled coins did not of course immediately remove from circulation the old clipped ones, which continued to cause trouble for some years. But it was only a matter of time, because the new coins could not be clipped. Seldom in human history can so stubborn a problem have been so completely and permanently solved by a single technical device.

Secondly, the silver supplies available for sterling coins were in this period rapidly increasing. Spain was still fighting to maintain her influence in Flanders, and was paying for these exertions from the only major resource available: silver from Mexico. Up till 1630 it was transported across the Atlantic in Portugese ships to Genoa, confronting many hazards, including pirates, and so to Flanders. In 1630 the English Ambassador in Spain, Sir Francis Cottington, negotiated a new agreement by which the silver should in future be brought in English ships to London, and payment then made to Antwerp. This was much safer for the Spaniards, and more profitable to the City of London and to Charles I. At least one third of this silver inflow was coined at the Mint for some years; though this far from solved all Charles I's financial problems or in itself guaranteed the quality of the coinage.

The third new venture in the evolution of the pound in these years was more picturesque, if less economically significant. In 1663, at a time when gold was appreciating in terms of silver, a gold 'guinea', marked with an elephant, was issued – so called from the place of origin of the bullion supplied by the then Africa Company. The guinea, when first coined, was supposed to be a 20s coin. But since the pound was not yet on a gold standard, the value of the gold guinea fluctuated with the market price of gold; and indeed, as the value of gold was at the time rising, the guinea also rose temporarily well above 20s.

These changes, however, did little or nothing to remove the need for banking and credit or delay its coming. The rapid development of the new forms of money in seventeenth-century England sprang mainly from two sources: the need of the late Stuart kings for money through some channel other than devaluing the coinage, and the advances in banking techniques made in Amsterdam earlier in the century.

Devaluation of the coinage had become unpopular as a method of raising revenue after what were regarded as Henry VIII's excesses. So the Stuart kings preferred, if possible, to borrow from the new merchant and banking interests which had flourished and expanded in England as well as on the continent after the inflow of silver and gold supplies from across the Atlantic. The Civil War had encouraged landowners and the wealthy generally to deposit their funds for safe keeping with the goldsmiths and bankers in London; and Cromwell as well as the kings borrowed at interest from them in return. But the question now arose: if one lent to the government, would it ever repay? In 1667 Charles II was authorized by Parliament to issue paper orders which were in effect claims on future revenue. These orders, issued for instance in £1, £2, and £5 units, were used by the recipients as money. They were the first government paper money in England. Naturally there was much suspicion about all this new paper whose value depended on somebody's promise to pay. In 1667 a rumour spread that Charles II would not honour his debts. Ironically the most successful banker of the period, Edward Backwell, had been believed two years earlier to be himself in trouble, and was rescued by the Exchequer – an early precedent for the 'Lifeboat' operation of 1973, when the Bank of England saved the so-called secondary bankers.

In 1672, however, the tables were turned. Charles II no longer had enough cash to pay his fleet. So he 'stopped' payment for twelve months of the Exchequer orders due, and instead used accruing revenue for his own immediate purposes. This rather desperate decision, which became known as 'the stoppage', naturally caused crisis and general distrust of paper money issued by the King. The panic was only checked when the King undertook to pay interest on his debts and honour the principal as soon as he could. Interest payments were in fact kept up, and ultimately became part of the National Debt Charge. The damage to the economy generally was not as lasting as might have been feared. Whether because the bankers had learnt from this misfortune to spread their risk, and not lend all or nearly all to one customer, or whether because the underlying expansion of incomes in the seventeenth century was still operating vigorously, both credit and public revenues improved in Charles II's later years.

But William III, at war with Louis XIV after 1689, needed money on an even grander scale than his predecessors. Thus the foundation of the Bank of England in May 1694 sprang from three origins: the King's need for funds, the experience and success of the Bank of Amsterdam, and the preference of the City merchants, after their experiences with Charles II in 1672, for lending to a private bank rather than to the King direct. And so as a chartered but private joint stock company (the first joint stock bank in England), the Bank was formed; and private it remained from 1694 till 1946. The original 'subscribers', or shareholders, were City men of the time. The Bank was given the power to accept deposits, to hold gold and silver, to issue notes, and to lend money to the British government; in effect to create and maintain the money the country needed. Its very first act, indeed, was to lend £1,200,000 to the government at 8 per cent. From the start the Bank's notes were treated with general confidence in the City of London and elsewhere; and the King found that he could pay his army and navy with an ease which would have surprised most previous monarchs.

William's government, however, having stumbled on the great secret of creating paper money, had also of course stumbled on the great problem: how much should you create? Naturally the full significance and difficulty of this was little understood in the 1690s. There was indeed an initial legal dispute about the limit, if any, restricting the Bank's liabilities. After some argument the Bank took a liberal view of its legal powers, almost certainly with immediate benefit to the King, the armed forces and the trading community. But before very long a marked credit expansion occurred, indeed something of a boom. It may seem surprising, almost shocking, that the foundation of the Bank of England should have led almost at once to what severe critics might call the first credit inflation in our history. But so it happened. By the middle of 1695 commodity prices had risen 25 per cent since 1691; sterling had fallen against Dutch currency by the same percentage; and the price of gold and guineas had risen 40 per cent.[2]

Notes
[1] *The Merchant of Venice*, Act III, Scene II.
[2] A. Feavearyear, *The Pound Sterling*, p. 131.

6

Locke, Newton, and the Gold Standard

Alarmed by rising prices in 1695, Parliament took notice and adopted a time-honoured remedy – indeed one destined to be even more honoured in the future. They set up a committee to ascertain what was happening to the pound and the coinage. Not for the first or last time, the report was shelved. But economic forces unkindly ignored these parliamentary dispositions, and the rise in prices obstinately continued. So later in 1695, and more fruitfully, the government invited the Secretary of the Treasury, William Lowndes, to give his views and to make recommendations. At about the same moment the philosopher John Locke joined in the argument, with profound and lasting consequences. The first of what was to be a long series of classic, learned and often fierce controversies about the future of the British currency thus began in 1695.

Lowndes, in his 'Essay for the Amendment of the Silver Coins' of 1695, written after discussion with Locke, made a remarkably penetrating contribution. The issue was this. The value of the pound had fallen: that is, the market price of silver was well above the nominal value of a coin containing that weight of silver. Did you accept that change (as, broadly, Henry VII and Elizabeth had done) and raise the face value of the coin to accord with its silver value – for example, issue new coins with a face value of, say, 6s containing silver, which would previously have had a face value of 5s? This would have benefited debtors generally, would arguably have imposed a loss on landlords and creditors if the debts owing to them were expressed in pounds sterling, but would have required no deliberate creation of a scarcity of money and fall in prices. Or did you deliberately create such a scarcity, and perhaps refuse to treat existing clipped coins any longer as legal tender, in order to restore the metal value of money to its previous level? This would have benefited landlords and creditors, damaged debtors, and starved trade and industry of money – in other words it would have forced a deflation. Lowndes favoured the first alternative, stabilization of the pound's value at the existing level; and Locke the second, deflation to restore its old silver value. At this point, however, the classic controversy was complicated by two special circumstances. First, a large volume of old clipped coins were still circulating, and had to be got rid of somehow. Secondly, both Locke and Lowndes believed that the fall in the pound's value was the result of the clipped coins, whereas it was in fact mainly due to the rapid expansion of paper money.

In his 1695 pamphlet, 'Further considerations concerning Raising the Value of Money, wherein Mr Lowndes' argument for it in his last Report concerning the amendment of the silver coin are particularly examined', Locke (who from 1696 till 1700 was a commissioner on the original Board of Trade, set up in 1696) took a simple, straightforward moral view. Money's function as a measure of value is paramount; the pound represents a certain weight of gold or silver and nothing else; and to lower this weight is to cheat and defraud creditors and all whose property consists of money claims. Locke thus became the standard bearer of all those since him who have believed that the value of money is something sacred, all 'sound-money' men, all deflationists, and all to whom William Jennings Bryan[1] addressed, two hundred years later in 1896, his famous peroration:

You shall not press down upon the brow of labour a crown of thorns;
You shall not crucify mankind on a cross of gold.

In retrospect it is the arguments used by Locke which are particularly striking. The decisive point for him was not the practical effect of the decision in promoting or impeding economic activity generally, but rather the need to do justice to creditors. The proposal to coin the new money at the depreciated rate would, Locke wrote,[2] 'deprive great numbers of blameless men of a fifth part of their estates beyond the relief of Chancery. . . . ' It would 'weaken, if not totally destroy the public faith when all that have trusted the public and assisted our present necessities upon Acts of Parliament in the million lottery, Bank Act and other loans, shall be defrauded of 20% of what those Acts of Parliament were security for'.[3] So, Locke said, the pound sterling was the value of 3 oz 17 dwt 10g of sterling silver, and an ounce of gold should be worth £3 17s 10½d.

Locke selected these values for historical reasons. In periods before the credit inflation of the 1690s they had been, for silver at least, the 'ancient right standard of England'. But his moral argument was a new one in its dogmatic purity. In the Middle Ages few, though they might grumble, had (at any rate up to 1352) questioned the King's right to alter the weight or value of the coins if he so decided, as he several times did. But Locke's prestige, strongly supported by Sir Isaac Newton, who became Warden of the Mint in 1696 and master in 1699, was so great that the figures quoted above acquired a sacrosanctity which they had not previously possessed. Locke's gold price, amazingly enough, survived till 1931 – one of the longest periods in human history for which a major currency has retained its value in gold or silver.

Locke's moral argument was in reality weak. It implied that in previous years, when anybody had made a contract in sterling, they assumed £1 sterling to be a certain weight of silver. But in fact they did not necessarily, or probably often, so assume. Probably in most cases they made no clear assumption; or if they did, they assumed sterling to be what the king said it was. It could just as well be argued, on the moral plane, that if one makes a contract in pounds sterling, one is entitled to be paid in pounds sterling, no more and no less.

This was the view held by Lowndes in his 'Essay for the Amendment of the Silver Coins'. He believed, as apparently had Henry VII and Elizabeth before him, that the damage of depreciation, if any, had already been done, and that the sensible course was to accept existing values and build on them. Since the market price of silver was 25 per cent above the Mint price, the face value of existing coins should be raised by that amount. The clipped coins should be purchased by the Mint and recoined as milled ones at the higher face value. It was right and reasonable, he maintained, that a pound's worth of coins should contain no more silver than a pound would now buy. The recoinage would admittedly inflict a loss on the Mint, but a smaller loss on the proposed new standard than on the old.

Locke and Lowndes discussed the matter, but could not agree. Newton, also consulted, is known to have supported Locke.[4] The bankers and City interests, unlike the landowners, favoured Lowndes. The King, discreetly, told Parliament that they should decide, and the government came down on the side of Locke. After several days of debate in November 1695, the House of Commons, which must have contained more landlords than tenants, backed Locke, Newton, and the government. The old standard was to be enforced; though few if any seemed to realize what a fierce deflation this would involve. Indeed the government made the disruption worse by first ordaining that the clipped coins could be used solely to pay taxes or make loans to the government, and even that only up to an early date. This caused panic and protest among those who could not get rid of their clipped coins in that way, and the date had to be extended. But even so the Mint could not issue the new coins quickly enough, and the rich and privileged found it much easier than the poor and ignorant to unload their clipped coins on the authorities. There were riots at Halifax and Kendal, a petition from Norwich, a threatened Derbyshire miners' insurrection, and finally a mob attack on the Exchequer which had to be protected by the Guards – not a good precedent for future advocates of deflation.

In the end the landowners, merchants, and prosperous middle classes came off well, because they could both pay taxes with the clipped money and buy up such coins at a discount from those who could not get rid of them otherwise. The wage-earning classes undoubtedly suffered. The deflation showed itself in late 1696 and 1697 in an acute shortage of coin and credit. In the summer and autumn of 1696 commodity prices fell, and the exchange value of the pound in Amsterdam climbed back to par. No doubt these latter upheavals caused most excitement in the minds of the public at the time. But seen as an episode in the history of the pound sterling, the lasting consequences of the whole episode were the canonization of John Locke's doctrine and, a little later, of the £3 17s 10½d official price for an ounce of gold.

The recoinage of 1696 did not, however, establish the gold

standard. Indeed the gold standard was never installed by a formal decision of government or Parliament, but became established, if not like the British Empire in a fit of absence of mind, nevertheless unintentionally. In the late seventeenth and early eighteenth centuries gold was falling in value relative to silver, partly because gold supplies were more abundant, and partly – in Britain – because silver was being exported to the East and elsewhere to pay for imports. Since gold and silver were changing in value relative to one another, the pound could not be attached to both a gold and silver standard. Up till now it had been based, if uncertainly, on a silver standard. The principal gold coin, the guinea, had varied in price according to the market price of gold. By Charles II's reign the guinea had become a popular and important coin, and was beginning to be generally used by merchants as a standard by the time of the recoinage in 1696. But what value should be attached to it? After the war with France ended in 1713 gold imports increased and silver exports continued. As this seemed to threaten the silver coinage Newton, now Master of the Mint, was again asked for his advice. He recommended in 1717 (as he had already done before the war, in 1701 and 1702), mainly in order to save the silver coinage, that the price of the guinea should be reduced. Parliament agreed, and later that year a maximum price of 21s for the guinea was established, which corresponded with the sterling price of £3 17s 10½d for an ounce of gold.

Neither Parliament, nor even Newton, to judge by his 1717 memorandum, intended or foresaw that a lasting switchover from a silver to a gold standard would be the result. But in fact, since no further change was made in the price of the guinea, and since gold supplies were available, and gold coins were being increasingly used by bankers as reserves, it came to be accepted by the middle of the eighteenth century that the pound was now based on a gold standard. As T.S. Ashton puts it, 'It was not by Statute but by what Liverpool[5] called "the disposition of the people" that the gold standard was silently established in England.'[6] Probably the change was inevitable, as gold became cheaper and more plentiful. The same conversion occurred in the other main European countries, though in most cases later and often more controversially. In Britain the change was none the less lasting because it had never been consciously or formally made. No doubt also, because the value of gold was tending to fall, its adoption as a standard had an expansionary rather than a deflationary influence on trade and industry generally for much of the eighteenth century. Money was on the whole performing its function as a medium of exchange, whether or not this had been foreseen, as well as that of a measure of value. If it had not been performing in this way, the new standard might not have been so readily accepted nor lasted so long.

Thus Britain embarked on the great economic expansion of the eighteenth century with the pound anchored to a fixed gold price and a rapidly growing paper money and banking system. The latter was almost certainly the more important, particularly when the Industrial Revolution, with its hunger for finance capital, began to dominate the scene. The supply of bank loans and paper money was more flexible than regulated or systematic, though the volume of small coins failed to keep pace with the general expansion. Various efforts at improvement were made in the middle years of the century. Engraved and watermarked bank notes were developed to outwit the forgers. Bills of exchange – another form of promise to pay, or of borrowing and lending – became common, as merchants and middlemen bought the produce of agriculture or the woollen industry and organized its distribution. These merchants usually kept their funds in London banks, and in the early part of the century very few banks could be found in England outside London. Local banks developed only when local manufacture spread in the latter part of the century. Edmund Burke stated, probably with truth, that when he came to England in1750, there were not twelve 'bankers' shops' outside London, but in 1793 there were four hundred.

Despite this general growth in the quantity of money, and perhaps because of the close grip of the property-owning and wealthier classes on Parliament and the government in the eighteenth century, the ordinary public and the mass of wage earners were less well supplied with means of payment – even on the modest scale needed – than the merchants and landlords. The small man could use only coins, because paper money of small denomination was rare until the latter half of the century. But coining had still not been refined to the point where counterfeiting was too difficult. The result was that, if coins were issued of a weight equivalent to their face value (as they were still supposed to be), they tended to be too scarce. If, however, a 'token', say copper, coin was issued, worth less than its face value, counterfeiting on a large scale was encouraged. This then created a glut and damaged the good coins. In fact copper farthing and halfpenny coins, worth only a little less than their face value, were first issued in 1672; and in 1703 Newton advised in favour of issuing more copper farthings and halfpennies containing their full face value in copper. From 1717 till 1754 copper coins were issued sporadically, but by the latter year about half of the coins in circulation were believed to be spurious; so their issue was totally suspended for forty years, and at the end of the century no way out of this dilemma had been found. The modern system of small coins, worth in metal much less than their face value, but not capable of being counterfeited, was still not feasible.

Notes

[1] US Democratic candidate for the Presidency in 1896 and later Secretary of State.
[2] A. Feavearyear, *The Pound Sterling*, p.134.
[3] Quoted in *The Pound Sterling*, p. 135 and pp. 147–8.
[4] *The Pound Sterling*, p. 134.
[5] Lord Liverpool (formerly Charles Jenkinson, President of the Board of Trade, and father of the future Prime Minister); see p.58.
[6] *An Economic History of England. The Eighteenth Century*, p. 177.

7

The Control of Banking

By the end of the eighteenth century the problem of deciding how much money ought to be issued, and then ensuring that that amount was issued, still remained unsolved. The Bank of England had learnt how to rescue the government from its financial difficulties, and it is arguable that without the Bank the Napoleonic Wars could not have been fought or won. But banks generally issued notes or other forms of paper credit when there was a demand from respectable customers. From time to time individual banks' creditors demanded more cash than the bank possessed, and crises or total failures followed. There were major crises in 1763 and 1772, in which the Bank of England came to the rescue of certain private banks. In 1765 Parliament stepped in, not in order to regulate the note issue, but to protect the public against banks which refused to supply the public with coin in return for that bank's notes. Similar Acts were passed in 1775 and 1777. In 1783 the Bank of England went further. Amid a speculative boom, which followed the end of the American War of Independence a year earlier, the Bank refused to give its usual support to other banks who had lent on a large scale, and the Bank did so on the ground that the trade balance and exchanges were moving against Britain. Later in the year, when the speculation eased, the Bank relaxed its squeeze and began to lend more freely again. This time the double manoeuvre succeeded, and came to be regarded as a classic model for the behaviour of a central bank faced by a speculative boom.

Next time, however, the difficulties were much greater. In 1793 revolutionary France declared war on Britain, and invasion scares very soon led to runs on banks all over the country. The Bank could not rescue everybody, and in response to appeals from the City the government issued interest-bearing Exchequer bills – forebears of the Treasury notes of the First World War – which for the time restored confidence. But throughout 1794 and 1795 the government demanded war loans from the Bank of England far beyond what the Bank wanted to grant. The Bank protested, but Pitt the Younger insisted. At this moment, in 1795, the final collapse of the French *assignats* – theoretically paper claims to land, which were issued almost without limit and became worthless – was bruited abroad, and alarmed all holders of paper money.[1] Pitt kept the ship afloat during 1796, in a manner which is now highly orthodox, by borrowing from the public rather than from the Bank. But in early 1797 invasion rumours, true or false, became so frequent that after the reported landing of French troops in Wales, Pitt, the Prime Minister, summoned the King as well as the Governor and Deputy Governor of the Bank to London on a Sunday (26 February); and the Bank was authorized by Order in Council to refuse 'cash' – that is, gold or silver coin – in payment of claims against it until Parliament had time to think. In what would later have been called the Dunkirk spirit sucessful appeals were made to the public to use Bank of England notes rather than cash. Paradoxically, the Bank's notes were still not legal tender, even though Parliament hurriedly and wisely authorized the Bank to issue notes of less than £5. Equally wisely, because there was little else to take, the public accepted the notes. In May 1797, by the Bank Restriction Act, Parliament fully authorized the Bank's new issue of notes and indemnified it against the consequences; and the Act was repeatedly extended throughout the war. Late in 1797 copper pennies and twopences, containing their full face value in copper, were issued, and copper halfpennies and farthings followed in 1799.

By 'stopping payment' in February 1797 the Bank and Pitt in effect 'went off gold', as it would have been called in the 1930s, or introduced a 'managed currency', in the language of the 1950s, or 'floated the pound', in the fashion of the 1970s. Of course prices rose; the sterling exchange rate fell; and the market price of gold, as against the standard price of £3 17s 10½d an ounce, rose in 1809–10 to £4 12s 0d.[2] Commodity prices shot up to peaks in 1801 and 1813, according to the estimates of Henry Phelps Brown and Sheila V. Hopkins.[3] But the battle of Trafalgar was won, and the future Duke of Wellington was dispatched to fight the Peninsular War. The

Duke might have said later – I have no evidence that he did – that the troops would not mind being paid partly in paper money, but they would not take kindly to not being paid at all. If the sound-money purists had had their deflationary way in these years, it is hard to see how the war could have been fought.

Meantime, while the troops and the humbler public were getting used to the new notes and copper pennies, a high-level, learned controversy not surprisingly once again broke out among those who professed to understand what was going on. Charles Jenkinson, the future first Lord Liverpool, wrote in 1798 and published in 1805 his *Letter to the King*, laying down the principles of a full gold standard. 'One metal only', he said, should be 'the principal measure of property', and that should be gold. Silver and copper coins were to be subordinate and were to contain metal worth their face value as determined by the metal markets. Jenkinson did not explain what was to happen if their face value and market value diverged. More significantly he was still, like Locke, conceiving of the pound merely as a 'measure of property', not a determinant of the output and real wealth of the whole community.

Jenkinson's letter provoked much debate. But it was only in 1810, after his death, that the issue came to a head. Amid greater optimism about the war, a speculative commercial boom broke out, fed by largely unregulated paper money from new private banks. Deposits in the Bank of England doubled; the pound on the foreign exchange market fell 20 per cent; and the market price of gold touched £4 12s an ounce. Disturbed by all this, and by the horrid spectre of the *assignats*, Parliament intervened once more in the person of Francis Horner, a young barrister and Member of Parliament who wrote articles on banking in the *Edinburgh Review*. On his motion, a committee of the Commons was unanimously appointed in February 1810 to inquire into the 'high price of gold bullion'. This was the famous 'Bullion Committee'. Besides Horner its other chief members were William Huskisson, later President of the Board of Trade, and Henry Thornton, a banker who was not merely regarded in the City as 'sound' but had written a textbook on banking theory. This formidable committee held thirty-one sessions between February and May 1810 and published its Report in June; a fine example of efficiency for all such bodies thereafter.[4] Its conclusions decisively affected the measures adopted when the Napoleonic Wars were over, and exerted a major influence on British economic policy throughout the nineteenth century.

The task before the committee was to explain why the price of gold and other prices had risen and the pound fallen to a discount of 20 per cent on the exchange market. Two views emerged in the evidence put before the committee. The first was that of the practical men (including directors of the Bank of England), who maintained that the gold price just rose because of increased demand, and the exchange moved against the pound because of a trade deficit. The second was that of Thornton: that a substantial issue of notes by the Bank had been responsible for the movement of both prices and the exchange rate. The committee's report cogently pointed out that gold prices had not risen on the continent, and that the trade balance appeared to have been in surplus in the relevant years. With illuminating naïveté, most of the practical bankers denied, probably in good faith, what they were really doing, and argued that their issue of more or fewer notes had no effect whatever on the level of prices, or the exchanges or economic activity in general. All they were doing, they said, was responding to public demand. One Bank of England director said he would have to alter his opinion 'materially' if he was asked to believe that changes in paper currency had any effect on the exchange rate. The Bank's directors generally, with less perspicacity than in 1783, in effect disclaimed any obligation or ability to control the quantity of money.

The committee, however, came down decisively on the side of Thornton. They concluded that the rise in the gold price and fall in the exchange value of the pound were wholly due to the quantity of notes issued; that the convertibility of notes into gold should be restored; and that the method of doing so should be left to the Bank and the timing to Parliament.

Before the parliamentary debate in 1811, a fierce public controversy raged over the Report. Pamphlets were issued by Huskisson (though a member of the committee himself) and also by David Ricardo, who broke into print for the first time with a tract called *The High Price of Bullion a Proof of the Depreciation of Bank Notes*. There were sensational leaks from the Bank of England, which regarded itself as having been attacked by the committee. Horner opened the parliamentary debate by moving resolutions affirming the conclusions of the committee and recommending a

return to cash payments within two years. He even observed about
the Bank (in language which Keynes might have used a hundred
years later): 'It was to have been expected that the Governor of the
Bank and the other directors should be acquainted with the plainest
maxims of political economy.' Horner also very candidly and
intelligently pointed out that the longer you preserved a depreciated
currency, the more uncertain became the argument from justice as
between debtors and creditors. Those who had lent in a depreciated
currency could not complain if they were repaid in one. Huskisson
supported Horner. Canning (later Prime Minister) agreed with the
reasoning of the Report, but opposed any return to cash payment
until the war was over. When put to the vote, all Horner's
resolutions were lost. A few days later opposing resolutions were
moved by Nicholas Vansittart, denying that the Bank's notes had
depreciated and opposing any return to gold payments until six
months after the end of the war. This was a not unsatisfactory, if
rather English, provisional compromise. Parliament had said, in
effect, 'Let us be pure later on – perhaps – but not yet.'

On the sheer question of fact, Thornton and the Bullion
Committee were of course right and the practical bankers wrong.
The large expansion of the note issue by the Bank, whether or not it
was necessary to fight the war, was the cause of the rise in the price
of gold and other commodities and the fall in the exchange rate. But
that does not mean that it should not have been undertaken. An
increase in the volume of money which leads to rising prices is a
form of taxation: and victory in war, among other things, cannot be
achieved without taxation. (Pitt had, after all, also perfected the
income tax.) Secondly, the fact that an expansion of the note issue
depreciated the value of the currency does not in itself establish that
the process should be reversed; still less that gold payments should
be resumed at the price prevailing before the expansion. It was in
drawing these two latter fallacious inferences from a correct
statement of the facts that Thornton's followers and post-1815
governments went wrong.

Notes

[1] The moral story of the *assignats* was regularly and tediously set out in 1930s' economic tracts by 'sound-money' men who wished to imply that all paper money, if not all reflation, would end in similar 'inflation' or disaster.

[2] A. Feavearyear, *The Pound Sterling*, p. 194.

[3] See Appendix.

[4] Compare, for instance, the inquiries into the Third London Airport between 1960 and 1984, which have debated intermittently for twenty-five years and reached no conclusion.

8

The Great Deflation

The debates and parliamentary votes on the Bullion Committee
Report in 1811 left only one thing clear: there was to be no
resumption of 'cash payments' by the Bank in return for its notes
until after the war. But the controversy went on while the country
did most of its business in notes which were not even legal tender;
the arguments of the Bullion Report made headway; and the sound-
money men again took heart. Among them was Lord King, one of
those enterprising but eccentric individualists who have always
enlivened the British Parliament. He announced that he would no
longer accept payment from his tenants in notes because the notes
were depreciated and were not even legal tender. He demanded an
increased payment proportionate to the rise in the price of gold since
before the war, and proved his honesty by offering to pay the same
extra amount to his creditors. The weak point in Lord King's case
was that he based what he called the 'intrinsic' value of the currency
not on its value in commodities generally, but on its value in terms of
gold. To which it could be unanswerably replied that many people,
both before and after the cessation of gold payments in 1797, had
made contracts in the pound sterling, not gold. Lord King's critics,
Sir Albert Feavearyear records:[1]

> 'held to the time-honoured principle that a man who contracted to
> receive a pound, whether his contract were a long or a short one, must
> take whatever was by general consent called a pound when payment was
> made. This was the principle which had been followed for a thousand
> years in spite of all the many changes of form and value, some of them
> very rapid, which the pound had undergone.'

But Lord King had put the government on the spot all the same. For the Bank's notes were indisputably not legal tender. So the government hastily introduced a bill, which became law in July 1811, making the Bank's notes virtually full legal tender.

Nevertheless for the rest of the war the note issue remained largely uncontrolled. The market price of gold rose further, and commodity prices fluctuated but with a rising trend. Gold prices reached a peak of £5 10s 0d an ounce in 1813[2] (compared with Locke's sacred £3 17s 10½d), and went up again to £5 7s 0d in the Hundred Days before Waterloo. Commodity prices reached their final peak in 1813.[3] After Waterloo, though prices generally fell headlong, the gold price, though it had dropped substantially, was still above the old Mint price. There were prolonged hesitations before the government and the Bank decided what to do next. The government asked the old Privy Council Committee, originally appointed in 1798 with the first Lord Liverpool as member, for a report, which was received in 1816. In it the committee accepted the first Lord Liverpool's views, and recommended in effect the establishment of a full gold standard. Gold should be declared the only standard, and silver coins should be 'representative' and only legal tender for limited amounts. The Prime Minister in 1816, who happened to be Lord Liverpool's son, the second Lord Liverpool, adopted these proposals and an Act was passed that year to enforce them. Gold was to be the standard of value, and legal tender for any amount; a gold 'sovereign' of 20s was to be issued; and the old ratio of gold to the pound sterling, implying Locke's price of £3 17s 10½d, was to be restored. The latter was, of course, the crucial decision. For the full gold standard paraphernalia could have been re-established, but with a higher gold price nearer to the existing market price.

Very few voices seem to have been raised at the time to recommend the latter alternative, even though industry and agriculture were already acutely depressed by the sudden ending of the government's heavy war expenditure, and even though many people now realized that the note issue must be contracted if the gold value of the pound was to be thus raised. Hudson Gurney, a Norwich banker and MP, was one of the few exceptions, and showed remarkable prescience. He declared in the House of Commons in May 1818 that 'the pound of account in 1818 is not the pound of account of the days of Mr Locke, and to the pound of account of the days existing you must adjust your coinage, or, on resorting to payments in specie after so long a cessation, your embarrassments would be unbounded'. Protests from the commercial and industrial world about shortage of cash were already reaching the Bank and the government, and the Bank at least realized that it could not relieve business distress and contract the note issue at the same time. But there seems to have been no thoroughgoing examination of the effect on industry and employment of restoring the old gold price. Probably the general dislike of high wartime prices was the reason for the easy victory of the sound-money party. Locke's moral argument about 'honest money'[4] may well have influenced many, too: it was simple and easy to understand. As Keynes[5] said of a similar argument a hundred years later, it had the advantage 'of economising thought'. Thus in the event the savage deflation of the 1820s was made inevitable by a government which simply did not intend or foresee the consequences of its own decisions. The ruling attitude on economic policy in the years immediately following Waterloo can perhaps best be described as: ' *Fiat John Locke, ruat caelum.* '

Even so, several more hesitant moves were made before the skies actually fell. The 1816 Act had not specified the date on which cash payments were to be resumed. This was left to the government and the Bank, and the government for a time extended the Restriction Act. The Bank tried a partial resumption in 1816, but lost so much gold overseas that it had to abandon the attempt, rather as with 'convertibility' in 1947 (see page 121). Merchants and manufacturers, acutely depressed, petitioned Parliament against further deflation; and so in February 1819 Parliament appointed yet another committee with an even more formidable membership. It included Castlereagh, Canning, Huskisson, Vansittart, now Chancellor of the Exchequer, and Peel. Ricardo appeared as a witness and advocated a compromise designed to ensure a less severe deflation by making small notes legal tender instead of coin. But the only outright advocate of a higher gold price before the committee was Mr Thomas Smith, quoted at the opening of Chapter 3, who did not regard Locke's formula as God-given and incurred the ridicule of Peel for saying, when asked what the pound was: 'I find it difficult to explain it: but every gentleman in England knows it.' History would seem to have vindicated Mr Smith; but the committee came down on the side of Peel. Locke's triumph was complete. The committee recommended a return to the full gold standard, but by gradual steps until £3 17s 10½d[6] was reached in May 1823. In 1819 Peel introduced the bill carrying this into effect, and though Gurney and a few others bravely spoke against it, the House approved it without a division. The bill became law[7] in July that year, and by what was no doubt a coincidence, though a grim one, the tragedy of Peterloo[8] occurred on 16 August that year. Cash payments were fully resumed by the Bank in 1821.

Thus was launched the most brutal deflation in British history. The Bank's deposits and note issue were at once contracted. Commodity prices fell heavily;[9] and severe distress emerged in industry after industry. Prices would have fallen somewhat anyway as production recovered after the war; the monetary deflation intensified the fall. Those lucky enough to be in work naturally gained from falling prices, but unemployment was certainly widespread and severe, although there were then no figures with which to measure it. As prices[10] appear to have fallen to their lowest point of the decade in 1822, when they were 40 per cent below the level of 1813, unemployment was probably at its worst in about 1822. For records made in the second half of the nineteenth century show that unemployment was usually highest when prices were at their lowest. Human hardship must have been as acute as in almost any years in modern British history, since there was no unemployment benefit nor any form of public relief other than the Poor Law. It may well be that more distress was caused in the 1820s and 1830s by the deflationary decision of 1819 than by the ruthlessness of employers, the *laissez-faire* doctrines then fashionable, and the appalling working conditions about which we hear so much. If more people had been employed, incomes would at least have been better spread. The country was being deprived of the medium of exchange without which production and distribution cannot be carried on – which is indeed what deflation means.

After a 35 per cent drop between 1818 and 1822–3 prices levelled out, and there was even a mini-boom in 1825. But they did not regain the 1813 level until 1917![11] The deflationary trend in the 1820s hit agriculture as well as industry so severely that protests in Parliament – always sensitive to the landed interest – began to be raised almost at once. Prices had fallen so far that fixed rents and tithes could not be paid. It was in these years that the Corn Laws (in force since 1816) were stubbornly maintained – interesting early evidence that deflation is often the father of protectionism. In 1821 one Member of Parliament, with the reassuringly orthodox name of Alexander Baring, joined Gurney and said bluntly in the House that the value of money had been raised too rapidly and too high. He supported Ricardo's suggested compromise. The real burden of the National Debt, swollen by the war, had of course been still further increased by the uprating of the pound. In the debates of 1822 some speakers pointed out that it was equally unjust to make the post-war debtor pay his debts in upvalued currency as it would have been to repay the pre-war creditor in a devalued one. These protests continued till the early 1830s, but without much effect. Parliament still took the view that if Locke, Newton, and Peel all agreed, they must be right.

Although the rate chosen was wrong, the attachment of the pound to the gold standard as such in 1821, regarded in retrospect, and its stubborn retention at the same gold rate for nearly a hundred years, probably had some long-term advantages. In terms of general commodity prices the pound in 1913 was worth much more than in 1819, and just about the same as it was in 1822 after the great deflation of 1819–22.[12] This record of value maintained over a hundred years, almost unrivalled in the history of currencies, gave the pound great strength, particularly in the second half of the nineteenth century. It assisted, though with fits and starts, the vast expansion of British trade in that century. It made London the world's financial centre, and enabled an ever-growing volume of international trade to be financed in sterling. But there was a very high internal price to be paid, in recurring depression, lost output and heavy unemployment, for these external gains.

In the short term, while the long depression of the 1820s and 1830s dragged on, interrupted by brief upswings, it also became ever clearer that no effective system for regulating the quantity of money had yet been devised. Either too little money was available for productive capacity to be fully employed, or panic doubts about the convertibility of the paper money into metal led to periodic crises. The system was dogged by the horrid spectre that underlies all banking: the thought that a bank is only sound if people believe it is sound. The Bank of England still formally maintained that it had no power to control the volume of paper money. Its own power to issue notes was limited and supposed to be temporary. But a growing number of private banks could issue as many notes as they liked, which were theoretically convertible on demand into coin or gold. In 1825 a paper boom developed in shares of new companies, largely financed with notes newly issued by private banks; and when a Bristol bank had to admit that it could not supply gold in return for its notes, there was a general run on the private banks. In three weeks over sixty private banks collapsed, causing great hardship; and the Bank of England did not know what to do. First it sternly refused help, believing that to be the only way to deter paper speculation. This, however, caused such distress that it later gave way, lent more freely, and issued all the coin physically available. As William Cobbett pointed out at the time, the Bank was then blamed both for issuing paper and for not issuing paper.

In an attempt to learn the lesson of this crisis, Parliament legislated again in 1826. Since Scotland had survived the 1825 crisis better than England, partly because joint stock banking was allowed there, an Act was now passed to enable joint stock as well as private banks to operate in England. This permitted the development of larger and stronger banks, and they were also given a limited power to issue notes. But the more lasting effect of the crisis was a change in attitude and practice in the Bank of England itself. Up till the 1830s the Bank had discounted bills – that is, lent to the money market or other customers – in competition with other banks. But it was bound to lend at interest rates normally not exceeding 5 per cent, because – believe it or not – rates above this were still forbidden by usury laws dating from the Middle Ages. Throughout this period interest rates were at levels so low that they would astonish people used to those of the 1980s, and the 5 per cent maximum was not generally abolished till 1854. When conditions were difficult, therefore, and the Bank was pressed for help, it could only either lend indiscriminately and excessively at low rates, or stop lending altogether and cause a crisis.

John Horsley Palmer, however, who became Governor of the Bank in 1830, proposed a new system. The Bank, he thought, should not normally compete with private banks in discounting private bills. But when credit was scarce, and the exchange rate was adverse to sterling, it should be prepared to lend, though only at rising rates of interest. It should thus be able to choke off excessive expansion by raising interest rates without causing a banking crisis. It would become, in effect, a lender of last resort. Once the Bank's discount rate had been exempted from the legal 5 per cent maximum by the Bank Charter Act of 1833, Palmer's system was in effect adopted. Thereafter the Bank was prepared to lend on bills when other credit was not available, but normally only at rising rates. The same Act also made Bank of England notes of over £5 legal tender, and limited the power of other banks to issue notes.

No sooner had this advance begun to be put into practice than a railway finance boom broke out. It started with a speculative rise in security prices, followed by the usual fallback which threw several banks into serious difficulties. The Bank tried to operate its new system. But partly because it still tended to regard itself as a private bank, not responsible for the nation's currency, it did so this time half-heartedly and too late. In 1839, with bank rate at 6 per cent, a number of country banks again suspended payment. The Bank was blamed for this new failure, and some blamed the new system also. The controversy led to the Bank Charter Act of 1844, and also to yet another historic controversy about the best way to manage the currency: the contest between the so-called Currency School and Banking School.

The central question which now emerged has a familiar ring in the 1980s. For purposes of currency control, what *is* 'money'? Is it the total of coins, or coins and notes, or what? Up till the 1840s any paper promise to pay (notes, bills, or deposits) had usually been regarded as in an equal sense money. The Bullion Committee, however, had concentrated attention on the note issue, and Peel had been particularly impressed by this way of looking at it in the 1819 committee of which he was chairman. On this approach, therefore, were based the ideas of the Currency School, which included several influential bankers, among them George Warde Norman, a director of the Bank from 1821 till 1872 and grandfather of Montagu Norman, Governor from 1920 to 1944. They believed that the volume of coin and paper money (by which they meant notes) in circulation should not be allowed to differ from what it would be if the currency consisted entirely of the metals actually available. It would then rise and fall as gold moved in and out of the country.

This was simple, but unfortunately more simple than the facts. It ignored the existence of bank deposits (which Norman called merely 'means of economizing money'), though such deposits were very soon to become a major part of the public's means of payment. All that mattered, in the eyes of the Currency School, was the control of notes. So this school tended to argue that the control of the Bank of England note issue, being a crucial national responsibility, should be separated from its ordinary banking business – an idea which came originally from Ricardo.[13]

The Banking School denied that changes in prices could be explained by changes in the note issue alone, and argued that it was absurd to try to regulate the price level solely through the note issue when this was already becoming little more than half of the total circulation.[14] This school included Thomas Tooke, who by 1838 had published his monumental *History of Prices*, and James Wilson,[15] who in 1843 founded *The Economist*. The Banking School, however, made a mistake in trying to maintain that an issue of inconvertible notes by a government could have inflationary effects on prices, while a similar issue of notes by a private bank could not (a fallacy shared by crude monetarists in the 1980s). It was also a weakness in the views of some members of this school that if they were really right, it seemed that neither Parliament nor the Bank of England had very much power to influence the volume of money available to the public or the level of prices.

As a result of the 1839 banking crisis a new committee was set up, of which Peel was again a member. The Currency School had by this time devised a plan to divide the Bank of England into two separate departments: the Issue Department and the Banking Department. The idea was to emphasize the difference between the national function of providing a note issue, and the more private commercial business of ordinary banking for the government and others. Peel swallowed the Currency School's ideas almost whole, and embodied them in the Bank Charter Act of 1844, often regarded as a landmark in the history of the pound. More importantly, the 1844 Act laid down that the Bank might only issue £14 million of notes over and above an amount equal to the coin and bullion in the Issue Department.

Even the existence of this £14 million 'Fiduciary Issue' was really an admission by the Currency School that the pure milk of their theory could not be applied in practice without an intolerable scarcity of notes. The Fiduciary Issue was to be backed by securities and could be reduced but not increased. The profit made on it – from the yield of the securities – was to accrue to the Exchequer and not to the Bank's shareholders, as remained true right up to the nationalization of the Bank in 1946. It is one of the ironies of banking history that this provision (based on the perfectly valid assumption that the power of creating money confers a profit on the creator which ought to accrue to the public as a whole) should have been applied to the Bank's Fiduciary Issue in 1844, but never to the vastly more important power of banks generally to create money in the form of deposits.[16] It seems to have been as a result of the Currency School's already antiquated belief that only coins and notes are money that private and joint stock banks have been permitted ever since not merely to create money on a huge scale (as was of course necessary), but also to keep the profit for themselves. Hence the consistently high level of bank profits, both in boom and slump.[17]

The 1844 Act, however, also secured the gradual extinction in England and Wales of the issue of bank notes by anyone other than the Bank of England. This section of the Act was certainly a step forward, since it prevented uncontrolled expansion of the national stock of notes by small banks, which too often had ended in collapse and repudiation. But this restriction was not applied to Scotland, where the banks had acted more prudently in the 1820s and 1830s, and were now merely required by the Act to have their future note issues limited more or less on the basis of the status quo. The 1844 Bank Charter Act as a whole became a pillar of Victorian orthodoxy, a bulwark of the pound in its finest hour, and remained the Bank's legal framework until 1914 and to some extent beyond. But it is doubtful whether the division of the Bank into two departments and the strict limitation of the note issue, based as they were on a crudely oversimplified theory, were really of much value. The modern illusion that altering institutions or formalities necessarily solves real problems[18] seems to have been to some extent shared by the authors of the Bank Charter Act. In fact the new organization of the Bank did not, as the Currency School theorists had naïvely hoped, prevent banking crises; and when the crises came, the Bank's power to help ailing banks was restricted by it.

Indeed in the first years after 1844 there was even a tendency for the Bank to assume that, as the note issue was now taken care of, it need not worry too much about other forms of credit control. In these early years the Act's operation had in fact more than once to be suspended to enable the Bank to withstand crises. The first suspension came in 1847, after speculation in railway shares, and more particularly in grain prices, had caused a paper boom, followed by the repeal of the Corn Laws and a collapse in prices. In the early stage of the 1846–7 crisis the Bank's gold reserve was steadily falling because the rail boom led to reckless borrowing to buy shares, and the high price of grain led to heavy imports – which were indeed acutely needed. The Bank protected itself for a time by raising the discount rate. But in 1847 better harvests, coming on top of the repeal of the Corn Laws, brought grain prices crashing down, and City firms which had been speculating in grain with borrowed money suddenly found themselves unable to meet their debts. As usual the panic spread from the borrowers to the lenders, and the Bank was urged to help by discounting bills. But it could not do so, the Bank argued, because this would mean a rise in the circulation of notes which was forbidden by the 1844 Act.

The threat became so acute to the whole banking system that the government was forced reluctantly to suspend the working of the Act and promised to legislate if necessary to indemnify the Bank. The Bank thereupon lent, though at 8 or 9 per cent; the crisis was surmounted; and few notes were actually withdrawn from the Bank. Disaster had been avoided, but at the price of admitting within three years that the simple principle of the Bank Charter Act did not work. Neither in the longer term did the strict limitation of the Fiduciary Issue work. Even though bank deposits rather than notes were increasingly to be the money of the future, the Fiduciary Issue had frequently to be increased. By 1928 it had reached £260 million, by 1954 £1,575 million, by 1961 some £2,350 millions and by 1984 some £13,500 millions[19]. The framers of the 1844 Act were no doubt unlucky both in having to start from the deflation of the 1820s and 1830s, and also in being confronted within a few years with wild share speculation, the potato famine, grain shortage and the sudden repeal of the Corn Laws. Nevertheless, in the end the Act was probably more valuable in the breach than in the observance.

Notes

[1] A. Feavearyear, *The Pound Sterling*, p. 206.

[2] *The Pound Sterling*, p. 209.

[3] See Appendix.

[4] See Chapter 6.

[5] *A Tract on Monetary Reform*, p. 68.

[6] This was the official buying price. The selling price was £3 17s 9d.

[7] The House of Commons approved it in May.

[8] Large crowds, who had assembled to demand reforms, were savagely dispersed by the military.

[9] Even Ricardo underestimated the fall that would occur. See J. Clapham, *The Bank of England: A History*, Vol. II, p. 74.

[10] See Appendix.

[11] See Appendix.

[12] According to the Brown Hopkins index. Layton and Crowther's index of wholesale prices gives an even higher rise in the pound's value between 1819 and 1913 (*The Study of Prices*, p. 237).

[13] *The Bank of England: A History*, Vol. II, p. 172.

[14] See, for instance, *The Pound Sterling*, p. 304.

[15] Wilson became a Liberal MP in 1847, and was at one time both editor of *The Economist* and Financial Secretary to the Treasury. He was also the father-in-law of Walter Bagehot, who in 1859 succeeded him at *The Economist*.

[16] The total of bank deposits other than those in the Bank of England was already £50 million in 1844. For later figures see p. 25, note 2.

[17] See also Chapter 26. Bagehot (Lombard St. 7th edition, 1878, p.247) says that even in a period of losses and bad debts 'banking is a trade profitable far beyond the average of trades.'

[18] A recent example of this illusion was the decimalization of sterling currency in 1971.

[19] By the currency and Bank Notes Act of 1954 the Fiduciary Issue was limited to £1,575 millions, or more if agreed by the Treasury, and this was raised to £13,500 millions by the Currency Act of 1983.

9

Trade Cycle

In the second half of the nineteenth century the pound sterling, though anchored to gold, was swung this way and that, rather like an anchored boat swinging in the tide, by a rhythmic cycle of booms and slumps. Not merely were the British, and other, economies rocked by these successive and compulsive swings, but the minds of professional economists were troubled by an enigma which orthodox theory did not predict or explain. A sort of trade cycle can be shown to have existed in the first half of the nineteenth century and also even earlier, in the eighteenth[1] century (interrupted by wars and harvest failures). But after 1850 it became more visible, more regular, more recognized, and more dominating. The facts are these. A short-term cycle of two or three years' duration, connected with accumulation and then dispersal of stocks, had been familiar before the nineteenth century. But as the nineteenth century wore on, and both the banking system and large-scale industrial invest- ment developed rapidly, the older short-term 'stocks cycle' came to be superseded by a longer eight- to nine-year fairly regular cycle that became clearly apparent first in Britain, but gradually grew international in its scope. A period averaging eight or nine years tended to separate one boom from the next and one trough from the next. The value of the pound in terms of goods and services moved up and down with this cycle. For prices fell from the top of the boom to the trough, where they tended to stagnate for a time before rising with the upswing of the next boom. Production and employment rose with the upswing, and unemployment increased again from boom to trough. Both wages and profits in money terms rose in the boom and fell in the depression, though the fall in wages was slight except in 1874–80. Real investment – particularly industrial investment – rose in the upswing faster than production generally, and in the trough or depression the drop in output was almost always greater in the industries producing capital goods than in those producing consumer goods. Rates of interest also regularly fell in the downswing to depression, and rose again to a near-crisis level (usually 5 or 6 per cent in Britain in the nineteenth century) at the top of the boom. In the depression the standard of living of those thrown out of work suffered severely, but those lucky enough to be still employed gained by lower prices. In the boom those finding work gained partly at the expense of those already employed.

This general cyclical pattern has long been recognized, and the main historical facts are not seriously disputed. In the early nineteenth century the cycles have to be traced mainly by price movements, and in Britain by changes in the bank rate, because no other accurate figures are available. But in the later years of the century trade union unemployment percentages help to fill in the picture. If one takes the statistical researches into the cycle made by such authorities as W.W. Rostow in *The World Economy* (1978), in particular Chapters 10–22, Henry Phelps Brown and Sheila V. Hopkins, partly reproduced in the Appendix of this book, and Layton and Crowther in *The Study of Prices* (1938); and compares them with earlier accounts such as Beveridge's *Unemployment* (1909 and 1930), a fairly clear outline of the nineteenth-century cycle emerges. Cyclical troughs occurred in 1820–1, 1832–3, 1844, 1850, 1863, 1870, 1879, 1886, 1894, 1902, and 1908–9; and peaks in 1825, 1839, 1847, 1860, 1866, 1873, 1881, 1890, 1900, and 1907.

It was once argued by some economists that these movements do not require explanation, on the ground that, as prices, production, employment and so on can only move up or down or stand still, it is not surprising that they all sometimes move up, sometimes move down, and sometimes stand still. This argument, however, is not statistically valid because the movements in question have been conclusively shown to be not random, like some phenomena, but governed by a regular rhythm. What then was the cause of this persistent economic cycle? It has never been hard to understand why both the upswings and the downswings, when once started, tend to duplicate themselves. A cumulative movement plainly sets in. In the upswing greater employment generates higher incomes, higher incomes greater expenditure, greater expenditure higher prices and profits, and so still higher employment and output. Thus, after the boom breaks, the shrinkage of employment deflates spending and so in turn prices and output. This has always been clear in both theory and practice. But why does either cumulative process come regularly to an end? Why does the boom abruptly break, and the stagnating depression, rather more gradually, pick up?

Economists and others have been perplexed by this question for a long time, and have not yet reached a generally agreed answer. In the nineteenth century, and indeed later, the debate was clouded by the notorious Say's Law. At the start of the nineteenth century the French economist Say (1757–1840) argued that since economic activity is essentially an exchange, all goods produced represent a demand as well as a supply, and an overall lack of demand as compared with overall supply cannot occur. If this was really true, there could never be an overall surplus of productive capacity (only imbalances between one trade and another); and the trade cycle could not occur either. For the cycle was essentially an oscillation between full employment and underemployment of overall productive capacity. But plainly the cycle did occur. The fallacy was, of course, that there *can* be an overall shortage of *effective* demand, that is, money spending, as compared with physical productive capacity. And on the face of it this was precisely what most ordinary people, whether employers or wage earners, thought that the slump periods looked like. From the time of the enunciation of Say's Law for almost a century, some optimists tacitly assumed that an overall shortage of demand could not exist, and that therefore all productive capacity was normally fully employed. Since on these assumptions the existence of the trade cycle could not be convincingly explained, various economists tended to seek explanations which were strictly outside the range of economic argument; of these perhaps the most sophisticated was A.C. Pigou's surmise that fits of alternating optimism and pessimism in the minds of the business world were the operating cause. Many businessmen must have been surprised to be told that their optimism or pessimism was the cause, and not the consequence, of the economic tides surrounding them.

Popular explanations were even more unsatisfying. Boom phenomena, and rising prices and profits, tended at the time to be

ascribed to fits of profiteering, to excessive speculation, to price
rings, or (perhaps nearer the mark) mismanagement of the currency.
The depression of the 1880s was attributed by some (the
'bimetallists') to the failure to use silver as well as gold as a currency
standard. A British commission was set up in 1886 to examine this
major depression, but failed to agree.[3] And then, following the
general recovery after the 1890s, this explanation faded out. Slumps
were also regularly attributed to growing imports,
'overproduction', trades union restrictive practices, managerial
inefficiency, other countries' tariffs and – most popular of all –
technological advance. Unfortunately these theories could not
explain why the process in question was reversed every few years.
For instance, the cry that technical progress was causing ever-
growing unemployment was heard in most Victorian depressions,
again most vociferously in the years 1930–4, and is still with us even
in the 1980s. It has always been proved wrong, or at least grossly
exaggerated, within a few years.[4]

Because these theories of the cycle were so unconvincing,
economists of the present century, having at last liberated
themselves from the intellectual paralysis of Say's Law, have
evolved two distinctly more sophisticated types of explanation. The
first regards the cycle as being generated somehow by the process of
saving and investment and the production of capital goods, and the
inter-relation of these processes with the rest of economic life. This
inter-relation is inevitably complex, since a rise in investment
generates higher incomes and employment (a process known as the
'multiplier'), and higher incomes and employment in turn generate
higher investment (the 'accelerator'). This type of interpretation was
launched by Keynes among others, and elaborated with great
mathematical ingenuity by, for instance, R.F. Harrod[5] and J.R.
Hicks.[6]

The second general type of explanation attributes the cycle mainly
to the management of the monetary machine by the central bank or
government in control. In the upswing of the cycle, according to
this view, the central bank watches the quantity of money steadily
increasing as incomes and employment rise; finding, after a point,
that prices are also rising and currency reserves declining, the bank
raises interest rates ever higher. Certainly this is the way the Bank of
England operated in the nineteenth century when sterling was on

the full gold standard. It was loss of gold which usually prompted a rise in the bank rate. At some point, according to this explanation, that rise discouraged both new investment and the holding of stocks, and the consequent cut in incomes then started the cumulative downswing. Similarly, during the depression, increasing supplies of unused savings and money in the banking system led to lower and lower interest rates, until these in turn stimulated new investment and the holding of larger stocks.

Neither of these general explanations of the cycle can be conclusively proved unsound, nor on the other hand has either won universal acceptance. There could well be elements of truth in both, for they are not incompatible. An attempt at a full explanation is made later, in Chapter 23, since it is better sought after the rest of the historical record has been traced. What is reasonably certain, meanwhile, is that in the period from the mid-nineteenth century till 1914, during which the modern industrial economies were largely left to *laissez-faire* forces, guided almost solely by the maintenance of a fixed gold parity for the currency, the system developed a wobble which gradually became more pronounced and which powerfully influenced the real value of the pound as the general price level rhythmically rose and fell.

Although Britain and many other countries enjoyed a huge expansion of output and international trade during these years, the wobble inflicted on them a major loss of output and therefore a reduction in living standards, as compared with what they might have been enjoying if all available productive capacity had been fully used. Unemployment in Britain between 1850 and 1914 varied between about 2 and 11 per cent,[7] and owing to the trade cycle stood for two or three years out of every ten between 5 and 11 per cent. It is evident, therefore, that if unemployment had remained consistently at the minimum throughout these sixty years, at any given time the level of real national output and income would have been very much greater than it was, and living standards at the end of the period very substantially higher.

In addition to the eight- or nine-year trade cycle, the value of the pound sterling was influenced between 1850 and 1914 by another longer-term, and in some ways more curious, cycle. From 1820 to about 1850-1 the trend of sterling prices (and world prices) was downwards. After 1850 the trend changed, and the general level of prices tended to rise till the boom of 1873–4. In this latter phase the recessions were relatively mild and the upswing of prices stronger. From 1873–4 till 1895–6 the process was again reversed, and sterling prices gradually fell to their lowest point of the century. The pound, according to the estimates of prices made by Henry Phelps Brown and Sheila V. Hopkins,[8] reached its highest value in terms of commodities in 1893 – higher of course than ever since. Measured by *The Economist* index of wholesale prices, the peak in the pound's value was 1895. Depressions in the deflationary eighties and nineties were intense and peaks very much weaker. The country abounded with talk of 'trade depression', particularly in agriculture, and interest rates fell to the lowest levels yet known. Finally, after 1896, a general rise in prices emerged again which persisted until 1914.

What was the cause of these successive twenty-year upswings and downswings in the late nineteenth century? Here again two major explanations have been put forward, the one mainly concerned with monetary forces and the other with the real economy. The traditional view, lucidly expounded, for instance, in *The Study of Prices* by Layton and Crowther,[9] attributes the swings to changes in the world output of gold and therefore in the volume of money available to support trade and industry. It is similar to the explanation, mentioned in Chapter 4, that the great sixteenth-century rise in prices was due to newly discovered American supplies of silver and gold. According to this view production of goods was outstripping new supplies of gold from the end of the Napoleonic Wars until the mid-century, and so prices fell. But in the seven years after 1846 the world's gold production, mainly from Australia and California, increased sevenfold and continued at a very high level. Most of this gold found its way first to Britain, France, and the USA. The gold holdings of the Bank of England and the quantity of gold coins in circulation in Britain certainly grew very rapidly in the few years after 1846; and prices rose over the next twenty years. By the mid 1870s, according to this explanation, expanding output of goods had caught up with the new gold supplies which were no longer expanding; and more countries (including Germany in 1873 and the USA in 1878) had adopted the gold standard, thus increasing the demand for gold. Prices again turned down until the late 1890s. At this point gold mining was being rapidly developed in South Africa and South African gold in quantity first reached the Bank of England in 1893. From then on world gold supplies rose dramatically till 1914, thus expanding the world's money stocks once more. So, it is argued, a rise of prices would naturally be expected in these last years.

The alternative explanation, favoured for instance by W.W. Rostow,[10] finds the answer in the waves of nineteenth-century investment (particularly in railways), in population changes, and in the fast-growing supplies of grain and other foods available in the later part of the century. According to this scenario, wars in the 1850s and the great railway-building booms between 1850 and 1870 in North America and western Europe, financed largely by capital exports from Britain, tended to increase money incomes in all these countries and so push up the price level. After the 1870s a period of international peace, the opening up of North American, and later Argentine, grain-growing areas, and a halving of shipping rates caused an exceptional fall in world wheat prices. Between 1867 and 1894 world wheat prices fell by over 50 per cent.

Certainly as a result of that fall this was a period in which the real wages of the British working population rose substantially (if the figures of Henry Phelps Brown and Sheila V. Hopkins are accepted, the biggest rise since the fifteenth century); Britain admitted free imports of North American grain, while France and Germany shut it out under pressure from agricultural vested interests. These twenty-five years were notably a time in Britain when real incomes rose, due to a fall in import prices and not to monetary expansion. But it does not necessarily follow from this that the fall in grain prices was the main cause of the general fall in prices. After the 1890s, according to W.W. Rostow's account, the growth of grain output in Canada, Russia, and India failed to offset the levelling off of US output, and grain prices again turned upward. For grain output was no longer running ahead of rising world population.

On balance, on the evidence we have at present, it seems to me probable that in the second half of the nineteenth century changes in the flow of money, generated by changes in gold output, were one strong force launching the swings of the general price level, and so the value of the pound, up or down. It would, first of all, be a remarkable historical coincidence if very large discoveries of silver or gold were followed in more than one century by major upswings in prices, but yet there was no connection between the two. Indeed in the case of the years 1850 to 1914 the conformity of dates is so close as to make it hard to question the view that gold discoveries were one main influence operating on price trends. Anyone who doubts this should look, for instance, at the chart of price movements and world gold output in the nineteenth century compiled by Layton and Crowther.[11] Gold output rose steeply in the late 1840s and 1850s, drifted down in the 1870s, and rose steeply again from the 1890s onwards. Prices followed. And the fact that most other primary product prices moved with grain prices, though not so sharply, is itself some evidence that monetary factors were operating. An increase in the supply of one commodity – such as food – need not necessarily produce a general fall in prices, since it normally releases purchasing power to be expended on other things and so raises their prices. A general fall in prices suggests either a general fall in money spending or a general increase in supplies of goods, or both. In some circumstances it can reasonably be argued that the demand for money itself elicits the supply, rather than vice versa. But this is more likely to be true of an expansion of bank deposits or notes than of gold, unless we assume gold discoveries to be prompted by high gold values.

That does not mean that in the nineteenth century any more than in the sixteenth[12] silver or gold supplies were the only force at work. Indeed, to say that anything in either century was the 'cause' of something else merely means that, if all other forces had been unchanged, that factor would have produced the relevant effect. But since other forces are always in fact changing, in practice the effect is inevitably blurred. As for instance in the 1870s it was true both that gold supplies were not rising, *and* that world wheat output was expanding rapidly, it is not surprising that wheat prices fell. In any case, if in the expansive period from 1850 to 1873–4 the more copious gold supplies were lowering the value of gold in terms of other commodities, then, since the pound was tied to the value of gold, it follows indisputably that the value of the pound in terms of commodities must have fallen. And that is the same thing as a rise in sterling prices. In other words, in the sixteenth century and from 1850 to 1873–4 the flow of money demand was rising faster than the flow of goods; and so prices rose. From 1874 to the 1890s the flow of goods was rising faster than the flow of money demand; and so prices fell. Before, however, this issue is further pursued,[13] it is best to trace the historical record more fully.

Notes

[1] See T.S. Ashton, *An Economic History of England: The Eighteenth Century*, pp. 196-200.

[2] G.N. Clark, *The Wealth of England*, p. 76.

[3] A. Feavearyear, *The Pound Sterling*, p. 310.

[4] See Chapter 24.

[5] R.F. Harrod, *The Trade Cycle*.

[6] J.R. Hicks, *Trade Cycle*.

[7] See Layton and Crowther, *The Study of Prices*, Appendix E, table 1; and W.H. Beveridge, *Unemployment: A Problem for Industry*, pp. 42 and 43.

[8] See Appendix.

[9] Chapters VII, VIII, and XI.

[10] *The World Economy: History and Prospect*, Parts 2 and 3.

[11] *The Study of Prices*, p. 288.

[12] See pp. 37-8.

[13] See Chapter 23.

10

Nineteenth-Century Crises

The story of the pound in the later nineteenth century, however, was by no means confined to the wobbles and swings caused by either the eight- or nine-year or the twenty-year cycle. The problem of controlling the huge expansion of bank money which occurred in this century, and which was necessary to sustain the unprecedented growth of production and trade, was far from solved by the 1850s. After the 1847 crisis, surmounted by suspension of the Bank Charter Act as described in Chapter 8, the Bank of England was still struggling with the problem of supplying industry and trade with sufficient funds to support a major expansion, while at the same time rescuing insolvent banks and other City firms, and protecting its own gold reserve. The system was always haunted by the knowledge that if a bank was believed to be unsound, it became unsound, because its liabilities always greatly exceeded its cash reserves. In 1857 the next test came. Large sums had been lent from Britain to finance a rail-building boom in the USA, which had otherwise been financed so recklessly by unstable US banks that in August 1857 the price of railway securities crashed, American banks failed, and the losses spread to London investors who called for help which the money market could not supply. Only when bank rate was raised to 10 per cent in November 1857, and the Bank of England authorized by the government to suspend the 1844 Act, was the Bank able to lend freely. When it did, the panic subsided, even though the Bank's own reserve had fallen to the desperately low level of under £1 million.

After this crisis the Bank induced discount houses to keep more adequate reserves of their own, and attempted to avert crises in advance by more frequent changes in bank rate. Nevertheless further crises occurred in 1866 and 1890, both peak years in the trade cycle. The notorious Overend and Gurney crisis was the most dramatic. This leading bill-discounting firm, which had rescued others in the 1825 panic, began to lend rashly in the 1860s. When it was forced to appeal to the Bank of England for help in May 1866 the Bank refused; Overend and Gurney collapsed, unable to meet its obligations. A mob surged up and down Lombard Street on 11 May – the original Black Friday – hearing and spreading dark rumours; but the panic was largely unfounded. Again, as soon as the Bank Act was suspended, and the Bank of England, with Treasury support, had again raised bank rate to 10 per cent and supplied large quantities of notes and coins to any reputable bank that needed them, the ferment quickly subsided. Following this eruption, the Bank tightened its hold on the bill-discounting market by being unwilling in future to lend to most customers other than at bank rate and in special circumstances.

The Baring crisis of 1890 – another cyclical boom year when money was tight – is usually quoted as evidence that the Bank of England and the City had learnt from their previous panics. Then, as in the present century, Baring Brothers were a famous private bank which lent extensively abroad, particularly in South America. Unable to realize mainly sound but long-term investments in South America, Baring's asked for help from other City firms, and knowledge of their request began to spread general alarm. This time the Bank of England agreed to help – but only after a hectic dash to Whitehall by the Governor, William Lidderdale, and the agreement of the Prime Minister, Lord Salisbury, in person for the government to share the risk. A City committee was set up (a precedent for the 'Lifeboat' of 1973) which arranged support for Baring's until their substantial long-term assets could be realized.

In this emergency the Bank had established the principle that since the panic threatened all, as one lender tried to borrow from another in a chain reaction, a co-operative effort should be made by others as well as by itself to restore what the City would call 'confidence' – that is, a belief that those who owed money would be able to pay if they were asked to. Nevertheless after the Baring crisis the question was again raised whether the Bank itself was maintaining a large enough gold reserve to sustain its now vast responsibilities. It was therefore something of an historical irony, or a piece of good luck, that in 1893 South African gold began to reach the Bank in large quantities, and not merely relieved these worries, but preceded, whether or not it caused, the twenty-year economic upswing of prices from 1896 to 1914. In 1894 the reserve in the Banking Department of the Bank reached 67 per cent of liabilities, higher than ever before, and bank rate fell to 2 per cent. Between 1890 and 1896 the Bank's total bullion and coin reserve doubled. The mid-1890s were the years, not merely of the highest real value of the pound, but also of the lowest short-term and long-term interest rates, and of the highest gilt-edged prices, in the whole of the nineteenth century and for a long time afterwards.

During the twenty years between 1894 and the outbreak of the First World War further banking panics were successfully avoided; interest rates remained low; and production, trade, and employment (though not real wages) were broadly rising, despite a cyclical downswing from 1900 to 1904, when unemployment temporarily rose to over 6 per cent. Meanwhile, over the century a vast expansion of sterling money in the form of bank deposits had occurred, helped greatly by the cheque system, the development of the central clearing house, and the concentration of banking in a few strong joint stock banks instead of in numerous small private firms. Deposit banking developed much more rapidly in England than on the continent. The number of banks in Great Britain declined from 550 in 1819 to sixty in 1913. But over the same period the total of bank deposits outside the Bank of England rose from £12 million to £962 million.[1] Here, incidentally, was proof – if any were needed – that banks must be able to create money, even though respectable bankers had not yet come to admit this publicly. For the total of coin and bullion in the Bank of England had risen over the same years only from £4½ million to £37½ million,[2] less than a tenfold rise, while total outside bank deposits had risen eightyfold. It was indeed remarkable that the Bank of England was able to maintain, on the foundation of so small a gold reserve, not merely so huge a mountain of national bank money, but to some extent an international money system as well. For sterling by this time financed a major proportion of the world's trade and the pound had become in truth the international currency. These were years when London could rightly be called the financial capital of the world, and when the Bank and the City were disposed to congratulate themselves on the marvellous system they had created. Part of the credit, however, as Susan Strange has pointed out,[3] was due not to the City but to Britain's naval and military power. It was the Napoleonic Wars, for instance, which eliminated Amsterdam as a serious rival to London. In addition, throughout most of the Empire sterling had been established as the effective currency. In turn, in Susan Strange's words, 'acceptability of sterling was one of the two trade secrets of Britain's imperial success and her rapid rise, as a minor European power, to world power status in the 19th century.'[4]

The whole impressive system, however, rested on certain basic assumptions. Internally the first assumption, taken for granted rather than argued, was that when overall money demand fell, pay rates in money terms could in the last resort be reduced. Another general assumption was that the system would last almost for ever. So also, it seemed, would the ruling dollar–sterling exchange rate. For since the dollar was also now fixed in terms of gold, the exchange rate between the two was immutably established at $4.86 to £1. Nobody in the financial any more than in the political world expected Britain's declaration of war on Germany on 4 August 1914 until almost a few days beforehand.

Notes

[1] A. Feavearyear, *The Pound Sterling*, p. 304.
[2] *The Pound Sterling*, p. 304.
[3] *Sterling and British Policy*, pp. 42 and 45.
[4] *Sterling and British Policy*, p. 46.

11

1914–25: Boom and Slump

It was not until 28 July 1914 that the full crisis hit the City of London, and the rush for cash made securities unsaleable on the Stock Exchange. Bank rate was raised to 10 per cent on Saturday 1 August, and the Bank Holiday, which should have taken place on 3 August only, was extended to three days to give the government and the Bank time to act. On 1 August the government had relieved the Bank of restrictions on the note issue under the Bank Act, so that it could discount bills and pay out notes to any legitimate borrower that needed them. A month's moratorium on bills of exchange was declared on 2 August. Since some new and less restrictive note-issuing system was needed, Parliament passed the Currency and Bank Notes Act on a single day, 6 August, and empowered the Treasury to issue £1 and 10s notes without any formal reserve. These were printed in great haste and lent to the Bank. The notes were formally convertible into gold at the Bank, but a patriotic appeal was made to the public not to ask for gold; and it was successful. Immediate confidence was thus established in the new Treasury notes; trade and industry were kept running; and from 6 August the bank rate came down.

All available gold was concentrated in the Bank of England, but the gold standard was not formally or legally suspended. By its control of shipping, the government in practice prevented any gold leaving the country without its consent. After a time the South African government agreed to compel its gold producers to sell the whole of their output to the Bank of England at the traditional buying price of £3 17s 9d an ounce. By this means the dollar–sterling exchange rate[1] was maintained throughout the war not far from the previous $4.86, and from the end of 1916 the Bank of England used dollars to support the rate whenever it fell below 4.76^7/_{16}$ – thus foreshadowing the managed exchange rate of post-1931 and the 1970s and 1980s. It was from this moment in 1914 that the value of the pound came to be generally thought of in terms not of its gold price, but of its exchange rate with the dollar. Similarly the French franc was pegged at 27.50 to the pound. As the war went on, the overseas cost of it to Britain mounted; the South African gold supplies were not adequate to meet the bill; and American and Canadian securities held by UK residents had to be mobilized, and later (in 1917) requisitioned outright, as in the Second World War.

In mobilizing the internal economy for war purposes, though the change was much slower and less drastic than in 1940–5, nevertheless, after an initial period of hesitation and delay, almost all the cherished *laissez-faire* shibboleths of the nineteenth century were abandoned one after another. The shining virtue of freely moving prices, and the sacred right of the business community to do what it liked, were very soon forgotten. 'Business as usual' became almost a mark of shame.

In the first two years, however, the government was too slow in raising taxation, and revenue fell to only 27 per cent of expenditure in 1915–16. As a result large-scale government borrowing from the public was necessary, and the Bank of England also lent to the government direct, mainly by Ways and Means Advances. New money was in fact created by the banking system on a major scale. Prices rose. In the last two years of the war greater increases in taxation were imposed; more effective controls were applied; and the rise in prices moderated. British governments of 1914–18 proved – a lesson that still does not seem to have been learnt – that borrowing of newly created money on this scale, though it is bound to raise prices, and did in fact enable unemployment to fall below 1 per cent,[2] need not inevitably push the economy into collapse if adequate measures of control are enforced at the same time.

Not merely were essential foods rationed in 1914–18 and then prices controlled after the initial hesitations, but a whole range of other safeguards against uncontrolled price inflation were gradually introduced. Rents were controlled. The government bought the entire supply of essential imported commodities; fixed the price of others and paid a subsidy if costs rose; and allowed controlled prices to rise when this was unavoidable.

The practical effects of price control and subsidies are not always understood. Such controls are not a magic by which the laws of arithmetic are suspended. It remains true despite controls that the total money spent by the public on all goods and services bought must equal the total value of the goods and services they buy. Nor do control measures suspend economic laws. But they do alter the way in which those laws work. Price control and subsidies keep down necessities such as food and rent, and thus restrain the increase in wages and salaries which would otherwise generate a secondary uprush of prices. But the money thus released to the consumer must either be saved by him, or drawn away in taxation, or spent on ever dearer less essential goods. This became partially understood in the First World War; and so, though there was a steep four-year rise in prices, runaway price inflation was successfully avoided. And the cost of living (retail prices) rose much less than wholesale prices.

Between the end of 1913 and the end of 1919 the total of paper bank notes in existence in the UK rose from £57 million to £459 million, and of bank deposits from about £1,006 million to £2,300 million.[3] The total stock of money at the peak in 1920 was about 250 per cent of that in 1913. Wholesale prices rose to a peak in March 1920 of 300 per cent of the 1913 level. The probable reason why this price rise exceeded the rise in the volume of money was the shortage or entire disappearance of many types of goods during the war period. But more strikingly the cost of living index, based on retail prices, even in March 1920 reached only 230 per cent of the July 1914 level. This partial success was the result of the controls already described. Interestingly enough, the biggest rise in bank credit occurred after the main rise in prices.[4] Pay rates of course rose steadily, and roughly as fast as the cost of living, until 1919 and 1920, when they advanced ahead of it. Real wages in Britain were higher in 1920 than they had ever been before, and in addition the labour force was fully employed. It is indeed a notable irony of British economic history that in the words of Layton and Crowther: 'the war years and the immediate succeeding boom will long be remembered as a period of astonishingly rapid advance in improving the conditions of life and work of the poorer classes of society'.[5] Though this may not be the ideal way to do it, the years 1914–20 proved that a great expansion of money and credit, supported by the necessary controls, need not lead to hyper-inflation and chaos, but can contribute to the winning of a Great War and an unprecedented rise in the living standards of the mass of the population.

But unfortunately the post-war government of 1919, unlike that of 1945, simply did not know what to do next. A recklessly hurried dismantling of almost all major controls contributed to the intensity of the 1920 boom and subsequent collapse. The only planning for the country's post-war economic life had been done by a committee consisting largely of bankers. The chairman was Lord Cunliffe, Governor of the Bank of England, and while Professor A.C. Pigou, the Cambridge economist, was a member, of the other eleven members nine were bankers. Although the grievous effects of the deflation of 1820 to 1830 were plainly written on the record, this committee, as is the habit of those who live and work among and understand financial figures on paper rather than real economic life, recommended in August 1918 another sharp deflation and a return to the gold standard at the old parity. In that month the pound was still pegged at the old parity, but it was expected to fall if unpegged after the war, as in fact happened. Even as sober an authority as Sir A. Feavearyear[6] says of the Cunliffe Committee that 'the possible effects upon industry and trade of a sudden rise in the value of money do not seem to have been considered'. Peel's committee in 1819 had at least known clearly what was the gap between the existing and recommended gold value of the pound when they made their recommendation. When the Cunliffe Committee published its first report, in August 1918, it had little or no idea what the gap would be when the old standard was restored. Yet the committee recommended that the state should 'live within its income' and repay out of revenue a large part of the government securities held by the banks; and that the note issue should also be reduced.

Though most of these sharp deflationary measures were adopted over the next few years, the government was not quite so rash as to try to enforce them all at once. The immediate response of the British economy to the Armistice on 11 November was, perversely, a four-month *fall* in prices – until March 1919. Probably this was caused by the initial drop in the government's direct military and munitions expenditure. But individual spending picked up again, and prices started to rise from March 1919. A speculative boom then developed, and in the thirteen months up to April 1920 wholesale prices actually rose 50 per cent. In March 1919 the government sensibly ended the wartime pegging of the sterling–dollar exchange rate at a minimum of 4.76^7/_{16}$, which was clearly out of touch with economic realities. American prices, though they had risen, had not done so nearly as fast as sterling prices. Left to market forces, the pound fell to a minimum of $3.19½ in February 1920. At this moment, as a free market in gold had been restored, the sterling price of gold rose to £6 7s 4d as against the traditional price of £3 17s 10½d.

In November 1919 the authorities made their first effort to restrain the speculative boom which was now in full swing on the Stock Exchange as well as the commodity markets. Bank rate was raised to 6 per cent. This had no visible effect. But in December 1919 the Cunliffe Committee issued a final report with a firm recommendation for an outright and steady cut in the size of the note issue; and this the government put into force a month later. In April 1920 bank rate was raised to the then crisis rate of 7 per cent; and suddenly and violently the collapse set in. For two years prices fell almost headlong, industry contracted, and unemployment rose to record levels. It was the worst deflation since that of the 1820s, and, together with those of 1929–32 and 1979–84, the worst ever suffered by the British people. The wholesale price indices, which in the spring of 1920 had stood at about 300 per cent of the pre-war level, had fallen by March 1921 to 200 per cent and by early 1922 to 150 per cent of that level. Retail prices fell, but with a time lag after wholesale prices, and wage rates with a further time lag after retail prices. By 1923 wage rates had fallen as far since 1920 as retail prices.[7] Unemployment rose from an average of 2.4 per cent in 1920 to about 15 per cent in 1921 and 1922, or about 2 million.

Was the collapse directly caused by the action of the Bank and the government in 1919 and 1920? Or did the boom, in the popular but muddled phrase, 'carry within it the seeds of its own collapse'? In fact the government approved the restriction of the note issue as from 1 January 1920; bank rate rose to 7 per cent in April 1920; and in the same month the Treasury, no longer borrowing from the Bank directly, allowed the interest rate it paid on Treasury bills to rise to crisis levels. And the collapse of prices started in that very same month. But it would be too simplistic to regard this as a plain example of economic cause and effect. The cut in the note issue operated gradually, not immediately. Bank deposits actually reached a peak in 1921, not 1920. And signs of the world boom breaking were visible in the USA, western Europe and Japan before the British government pulled its own deflationary levers in the spring of 1920.

There is probably one sense in which the speculative element in a boom does predispose it at some point to collapse. Here again the picture has been blurred by those who take refuge in the traditional metaphors: the drunkard who after the revel inevitably and *consequently* suffers a hangover; the bubble that bursts; or the sudden flash of lightning followed by the thunderclap and chilling downpour of rain. The facts are more prosaic. But it remains true that if in commodity and security markets a fair proportion of buyers are acquiring goods or shares, not because they wish to hold or use them, but because they wish to sell them at a higher price, then the price will rise until the moment when there are not enough people left who expect it to rise higher. And at this point most of them will want to get out fast. The reversal will then be sudden and sharp. In *The Great Crash 1929* J.K. Galbraith has brilliantly described how this drama was enacted first in the Florida land boom of the 1920s and then, with all its world-shaking consequences, in the Wall Street boom of 1929. The speculative element, the optimists who are simply buying 'for a rise', are of course only the froth on the surface of the real economic forces of demand and supply. But the losses of the disappointed speculators inflict on them a genuine loss of purchasing power, which can itself, when large enough, tip the balance of a whole economy into deflation if counter action to maintain demand is not taken quickly enough. This, I would judge, is the morsel of hard truth underlying the facile metaphors so often used to describe booms and slumps.

On the evidence, it would certainly seem that a speculative movement of this kind was operating, not merely in Wall Street in 1929, but in Britain in 1919 and 1920. The real underlying problem was how to switch the economy over from war to peace production without either letting the price rise get out of hand or cutting purchasing power too quickly and causing extreme depression. This problem was then made even more difficult by the speculative froth on top of the initial imbalance between high demand and limited supply. The government, by its deflationary measures of 1919–20 which were an attempt to remove that froth, hit a fragile economy much too hard, and caused a needless depression of the real economy by maintaining these measures much too long and failing to restore the public's purchasing power when that became necessary. The 7 per cent bank rate was enforced until April 1921, when unemployment was 15 per cent. If anyone argues that on the contrary the full depression of 1921–2 was for some mysterious reason made inevitable by the boom of 1920 – that the hangover followed as the day the night – he can very easily be proved wrong. It did not happen in 1945–6. In those years both the speculation and the post-war collapse were avoided by deliberate policy. For once the lesson had been learnt.

Notes

[1] Paradoxically, in the first few days of August the dollar–sterling rate rose to the all-time record of $6.50 because of a rush from overseas to repay debts owing to London.
[2] From 1915 onwards the trade union unemployment figure was below 1 per cent.
[3] Layton and Crowther, *The Study of Prices*, pp. 121–5.
[4] A. Feavearyear, *The Pound Sterling*, p. 346.
[5] *The Study of Prices*, pp. 129–30.
[6] *The Pound Sterling*, 1st edition, p. 318.
[7] *The Study of Prices*, p. 145.

12

Churchill, Keynes, and the Great Depression

The post-war downward slide of the British economy ended in 1922. But it was followed by stagnation, not recovery. The Bank and Treasury regarded the lull as an opportunity, not for restoring high production and employment, but for enforcing the whole Cunliffe Committee medicine and returning yet again to the full gospel of John Locke, the pre-war gold standard and the mystical price of £3 17s 10½d for an ounce of gold. By 1924 the rise in living costs compared with 1913 was 78 per cent and in average money wage earnings 94 per cent.[1] To this extent the pound had depreciated in terms of goods and services. On the face of it a much larger gold reserve should have been needed to sustain this higher level of prices and higher money national income. The gap was partly and sensibly covered by concentrating all available gold in the Bank of England, and so permitting a higher pyramid of paper money. But the heavy unemployment showed that the gap was not wholly covered and that total demand and hence, probably, the money stock, were too small. There also still remained at the beginning of 1922 an uncomfortable gap between the actual dollar–sterling exchange rate of $4.25 on the exchange markets and the traditional $4.86. This gap implied a depreciation of 12½ per cent, which fairly closely coincided with a 15 per cent excess of sterling prices over dollar prices at the existing rate of exchange.

Two separate issues required decision from the government. First, should the gold standard be restored: in other words should a fixed parity be established between the pound on the one hand, and gold and the dollar on the other? And secondly, if so, what parity?

The first question did not arouse much disagreement, since it was then generally assumed that some return to gold would be made. It was the second question that mattered. For it would have been perfectly possible to re-establish the gold standard, at least temporarily, at the existing rate of $4.25 to the pound; and if this had been done, much subsequent trouble would have been avoided. But the Cunliffe Committee appears never even to have considered this. So the government in 1922 decided to wait and see whether the gap would close of its own accord over time, and the first Labour government under Ramsay MacDonald in 1924 continued this cautious policy. But in the latter half of 1924, when American prices were rising, the market rate of exchange moved up to $4.70; whereupon the new Conservative government, with Baldwin as Prime Minister and Churchill as Chancellor, advised by a small Treasury committee, decided to take the plunge. Bank rate was raised to 5 per cent in February 1925; the return to the old gold parities of £3 17s 10½d and $4.86 were announced by Churchill in his budget speech on 28 April; and the Gold Standard Act 1925 became law on 13 May. Thus, after more than two hundred years, John Locke triumphed yet again, for the third – and last – time.

This decision was probably the most fateful of the three. It arguably did more long-term damage to Britain as an economic power than any decision taken by a twentieth-century British government until the 1970s. At the time, however, in the eyes of orthodox observers and experts, it did not seem unreasonable to overvalue the pound on the exchanges by something like 5 per cent in order to re-establish a standard on which it had rested and thrived for two hundred years. At least gold was to be economized by being kept wholly in the Bank of England; which meant in effect that something like the compromise suggested by Ricardo a century before was adopted. The note issue was also to be amalgamated under the control of the Bank, though this was not done till 1928.

But all this was no longer enough. Seen with the benefit of hindsight, it is plain that three crucial mistakes were made in taking the 1925 decision. First, little or no allowance was made for the fact that over a million workers were already unemployed and the economy was working well below capacity. Secondly, American prices, which were expected to rise, actually fell from the moment of the change, thus accentuating the overvaluation. The American retail price index (1913=100) dropped from 150 in the spring of 1925 to 137 by 1927. Thirdly, most fundamental of all and most significant for the future, the time had passed when wage rates in money terms could be actually and materially *reduced* without industrial struggles which would wreck economic stability. The Treasury committee did not allow for the growth of trade union power, which made all previous economic doctrines on this issue out of date.

One critic, however, did not require hindsight to understand what was happening and foresee the consequences: J.M. Keynes. And so in the 1920s the classic dispute between Locke and Lowndes at the end of the seventeenth century, and Peel and his critics after 1815, was fought once again between Keynes and Churchill. The main difference was that in 1925 Churchill, as later became known, did not really believe in his own case, but had been persuaded by pressure from the Treasury and the Bank.[2] In a letter of February 1925 to Sir O. Niemeyer, Churchill even made a simple calculation of the loss of national income due to unemployment and concluded: 'I would rather see finance less proud and industry more content.'[3] Keynes wrote his pamphlet 'The Economic Consequences of Mr Churchill' in 1925, after the return to gold, but *before* the General Strike and disastrous coalminers' strike of the spring and summer of 1926. He argued that by the second half of 1925 sterling at $4.86 was overvalued by 10 per cent against the dollar, owing to further falls in American prices; that British exports had been made to that extent too dear; and that unemployment and industrial strife had already been generated and would get worse. 'Deflation', he said, 'does not reduce wages automatically. It reduces them by causing unemployment. The proper object of dear money is to check an incipient boom. Woe to those who use it to aggravate a depression!'[4]

To those of us who have known the 1970s and 1980s with their wildly fluctuating exchange rates an overvaluation of the pound by 10 per cent may not sound very alarming. But it was enough in 1925–6 to throw the whole precarious British coal industry, then employing nearly one million men, into deficit. Churchill, as Chancellor, in reply to Keynes, had felt bound to say publicly that the return to the gold standard was 'no more responsible for the state of affairs in the coal industry than is the Gulf stream'; which Keynes described as a 'statement of the feather-brained order'.[5] Within a few months of the publication of 'The Economic Consequences of Mr Churchill' the miners' strike began, and persisted for six months of long, bitter, tragic struggle, which was never forgotten, before the miners were forced to accept the wage cut which deflation required.

Nor of course was the tragedy in the coal industry the only trouble caused by the enforced return to $4.86. The whole of Britain's export trade was affected, and bank rate was kept on average at what was then considered the high rate of over 4 per cent. Unemployment, even in the world boom years 1928 and 1929, never fell below 9½ per cent (or over a million), whereas in pre-1914 booms and in 1920 it had stood at 2 or 3 per cent. Real capital investment was too low, and the ability of the pound and the British economy to meet the coming catastrophe of the 1929–33 Great Depression was further needlessly weakened.

That depression finally wrenched sterling off the gold standard and ended for ever the £3 17s 10½d price of gold. The story of this world upheaval has been told many times,[6] but some popular misconceptions still survive and they are worth exposing. First, it is not demonstrably true that the boom of 1928–9 itself inevitably caused the depression, in any sense other than that the speculative Wall Street share boom did provoke its own collapse. It is not true that the Wall Street collapse of October 1929 was the first sign of a downswing. It is not true that growing protectionism caused the depression. On the contrary, deflation itself led to protectionism.[7] The famous US Hawley-Smoot general tariff, for instance, was not imposed till June 1930, and only after this could it have accelerated the downward slide. It is not true that the depression ended of its own accord. It was only ended when Roosevelt in effect devalued the dollar in relation to gold in the spring of 1933. It is not true that Hitler was the product of the German inflation of 1922–3 rather than the deflation after 1929. His electoral support was trivial in 1929, and only began to rise in 1930. And finally it is not true that it was a depression of the 1930s. A very substantial general recovery occurred between 1932–3 and 1937 in the UK; a gain of 2 million jobs and 50 per cent in manufacturing output.

Certainly in the late 1920s a number of special forces were predisposing the world economic upswing to waver, quite apart from the normal factors, whatever they were, which brought the pre-1914 cyclical booms to an end. The futile attempts of Germany to pay reparations, and the various loans from the USA and Britain to enable her to do so, caused growing strain and fears of default. The drain of gold mainly to two gold hoarders, the USA and France, created a scarcity everywhere else. It is an illuminating comment on this period that the gold holdings of the main gold-hoarding countries turned sharply up, and the rest of the world's holdings down, at the end of 1928, six months before the general collapse began.[8] (China, which stuck to a silver standard, was almost the only non-Communist country to escape the world depression.) The efforts of Britain to defend its overvalued gold parity led to high interest rates and deflation. Meanwhile the US Federal Reserve Board was caught in two minds, between fear of allowing the Wall Street boom to get out of hand because of low interest rates, and causing a business downswing by raising them.

All these forces were tending to pull back effective demand in the world below the level needed to support the high level of output, employment, and prices. But right into 1929 the ever-rising share prices and profits on Wall Street fed enough purchasing power into the hands of the American public to maintain general demand at least in the USA. It was in the summer of 1929 that the first signs of a reversal appeared, little noticed by the public at the time. British bank rate had been raised to 5½ per cent in February 1929. World commodity prices started to edge down during the summer, and the US manufacturing production index began to fall in June. The Federal Reserve Board, still uncertain what to do, raised its re-discount rate in August to 5½ per cent. The Wall Street share index began to fall gradually on 3 September, exactly ten years before the day on which, as a result of the long chain of misfortunes generated by the crash and its aftermath, Britain declared war on Germany.

Which if any of these summer omens was the psychological straw which toppled Wall Street over in October can never be known. But, as argued earlier here, it seems reasonably clear that when people in the mass are buying shares not to hold, but to sell at a higher price, and when most of them are borrowing the money to buy the shares, it is highly likely that at some stage the sellers will outnumber the buyers. This, for whatever immediate reasons, was almost certainly what happened on Wall Street on 21, 24 and 28 October 1929. Panic struck the American investor and speculator in the greatest market crash of modern history, and all the wise words of reassurance from eminent persons ranging from President Hoover himself to Professor Irving Fisher were contemptuously ignored – and proved wrong within days. (As it happened I myself, then a very raw sub-editor on *The Times*, had the job of sub-editing some of these horrifying stories from New York. I had no idea what it all meant, but assumed that there were wise men in high places who did. Unfortunately there were not.) Between 3 September and 13 November the share index fell 50 per cent, so that the value of all the shares quoted must have been approximately halved. Some mild recovery, which encouraged false hopes, emerged later and continued up to the spring of 1930, but prices then fell away to even lower depths. The stream of Wall Street profits which had sustained the American public's purchasing power for months turned now to shattering losses, and deflation spread throughout the Western world. The downward vicious spiral remorselessly set in. The more governments and firms and individuals cut their expenditure to meet their deficits, the more other people's incomes fell; and the more other people's incomes fell, the less they spent, and the greater the producers' losses became.

For there can now be no serious dispute that it was steadily shrinking effective demand – money – in the hands of an ever-widening circle of the population in one country after another which in 1929–33 created the ludicrous and tragic spectacle of, side by side, vast unused world productive capacity and millions of impoverished consumers unable to make use of it. Even economists like Lord Robbins, who questioned this at the time, have since admitted that they were mistaken. Writing in his *Autobiography of an Economist*, published in 1971, he most candidly withdrew his rather extreme judgement of 1934:[9]

> 'Whatever the genetic factors of the pre-1929 boom, their *sequelae*, in the sense of inappropriate investments fostered by wrong expectations, were completely swamped by vast deflationary forces sweeping away all those elements of constancy in the situation which otherwise might have provided a framework for an explanation in my terms. The theory was inadequate to the facts.'

This is surely a reason for amending the theory rather than denying the facts. How strange, nevertheless, that so many deflationists of Lord Robbins' school, having denied that lack of demand was to blame in 1929–33, and admitted it forty years later, should then have denied it again in 1979–83 when very largely the same 'vast deflationary forces' were swamping us all. Always deflation yesterday, but never deflation today!

Being wise after the event, we can all now see that the Federal Reserve Board got their timing wrong. What they probably should have done was to tighten credit in 1928 and early 1929 to check purely speculative buying of shares 'on margin' for a rise, and then, when the turndown came at the end of 1929, to ease credit liberally and check the vicious spiral at the start (very much as the Bank of England learned in the nineteenth century to avoid crises by checking speculation at the start, but supplying generous support if the crisis came). What the Federal Reserve Board actually did, however, being human and fallible, was to hesitate to put on the brake beforehand, and then, when faced with the horrifying crash, to try to atone for its guilt by keeping interest rates too high for too long. Then in the third stage, when it did try to expand credit, the deflationary forces proved too strong; interesting evidence again that changes in the money stock do not automatically affect incomes and output.

And so, after the false dawn in early 1930, the weaker economies in the outside world began to suffer from the icy wind of contracting demand blowing from the USA. Trade balances became adverse, as exports shrank; and gold was lost. Budget deficits grew as unemployment rose. France suffered least at first, for three reasons. Unlike the pound sterling, the French franc had been deliberately *undervalued* in terms of gold; high protection in France had been maintained against imports, particularly of food; and a large gold hoard, much greater than Britain's, had been accumulated. Germany and Austria were most vulnerable. Germany, still under obligation to pay reparations in currencies not her own, could only do so by borrowing dollars and sterling through the Dawes and Young Plans, and other devices, because she had no chance of earning an export surplus. Fears, threats, and predictions of default now began to alarm the banking and financial world.

At this stage of an international deflation a secondary shudder sets in. The losses made by business firms and traders of all kinds turn the loans made by the banks into bad debts from the banks' point of view. Then the knowledge that the banks may themselves be making losses, and are short of cash, may at some point prompt their depositors to ask for cash which is not there. And then the whole house of cards begins to shake. Similarly governments of debtor countries find themselves unable to service their loans and are compelled to appeal for help. This is exactly what happened in Mexico, Brazil, Argentina and other countries in the great deflation of 1982 and 1983, which so closely repeated the blunders and disasters of 1929–33, because there had been just enough time for the lesson of these blunders to be forgotten. But at least in 1982–3 the world had an International Monetary Fund, set up largely by the prescience of Keynes, which, with all its faults, was able to help. In 1930–31 no such longstop existed.

The second round of trouble in 1930–31, this time in the banks rather than the Stock Exchange, broke out in Germany and Austria. Germany's Chancellor then was Dr Brüning, a sincere, conservative Catholic, who not just honestly but devoutly agreed with President Hoover and Montagu Norman, Governor of the Bank of England, that the slump had largely been caused by financial profligacy, and that the only way for the sinners to atone for their misdeed was to cut their spending, honour their debts, balance the books, and stick to the gold standard. This Dr Brüning faithfully did, and as a result by July 1930 unemployment had reached 2 million (giving the Nazis their first substantial vote in the election in September), on its way to the final calamitous total of 6 million in January 1933. Walter Layton, then editor of *The Economist* and a friend of Brüning, told me a few years later of a conversation he had had with Brüning in 1932. Layton urged Brüning to soften the severity of his deflationary measures, and Brüning's final words, expressed with deep feeling, were: 'I believe Germany can only find salvation through suffering.' Sadly, the parable of the sinner expiating his guilt, and the drunkard requited with a hangover, would seem to have played a real part in inflicting on mankind the tribulations of 1929–33, and 1979–83.

In May 1931 the pressure on the German and Austrian banking systems became so great that something had to snap. The fall in world prices had raised the value of debts in money, and reduced the funds with which debtors could pay them. Germany had maintained reparations by short-term borrowing, mainly from the USA, which was no longer possible. The oldest and most respected Austrian bank, the Credit-Anstalt, failed,[10] with losses exceeding its total capital. This was the jolt which by a chain reaction threw the pound off its historic parity later in the year. First, anxieties spread about other Austrian banks, which all turned for cash to the National Bank of Austria, which in turn ran out of foreign exchange and appealed for help abroad. The French, for the moment in a strong position, characteristically made political conditions which the Austrians could not accept; so the Austrian government turned to London.

At this moment Britain's international economic policy was still being conducted, not by the government, but by Montagu Norman, Governor of the Bank since 1920. Ramsay MacDonald, the Prime Minister, had little idea of what was going on and even less of what could be done about it. Snowden, the Chancellor, believed that until the capitalist system was transformed, its classical rules were best followed. So in effect he supported Norman. The latter's views on currency and banking, though impeccably orthodox, were not narrow. They included the vision of a stable, all-European, and indeed international, system of banking and trade. Unfortunately Norman tended to pursue this without too much thought for the effect on the internal economic life of the UK. He also profoundly believed that all these matters were only understood by central bankers and that the politicians should not interfere. (Before 1925 he had discussed the whole issue of the pound's return to gold with the US Federal Reserve Board before any consultation with the British government.)[11] In the summer of 1931 Norman's international system was clearly imperilled, and he came to the temporary rescue of Austria with an interim advance of £4½ million. Predictably, the French were so incensed at Austria being let off the hook that they joined in the attack on the pound a few weeks later by selling more of their sterling holdings. Susan Strange[12] shows that ever since France, wisely, had reattached the franc to gold at an undervalued parity in 1928, the Bank of France had been selling sterling; and that the Governor of the Bank of France saw himself as fighting for French against British influence. Norman, however, put British interests second to the creation of an ideal international system.

The troubles of the Credit-Anstalt switched the pressure for cash on to the German banks, which were in much the same plight with locked up assets, depreciated investments, and bad debts – the equivalent in the banking world during a deflation to unemployment in the real world. As in Austria the German banks sought help from the Reichsbank, the German central bank, which, being itself short of reserves, also turned to the Bank of England.

At this moment, on 20 June 1931, President Hoover proposed a one-year moratorium on all international political debts, including in particular German reparation payments and Allied war debts to the USA. This remedy, though nominally temporary, was the same in some ways as that adopted by the International Monetary Fund in similar circumstances in rescuing Central and South American debtor countries in 1982–4: the debtor promises not to default on his debts provided the creditor does not ask him to repay them. It was a bold and generous gesture by the otherwise baffled Mr Hoover. The bankers backed it up with a similar 'standstill'. A year earlier all this might have saved the situation. But now it was too late. All those who could not recall their loans from Germany turned to the British banks, who also had large funds now locked up in Germany. Pressure on the Bank of England mounted. Since its reserve was too small, temporary advances were obtained from the United States and even France.

By a strange coincidence, while this pressure on the pound gathered force, in June and July 1931 two major British official reports were issued: those of the Macmillan Committee on Finance and Industry, and the May Committee on Public Expenditure. The Macmillan Committee, of which Keynes and Ernest Bevin were both members, made a number of proposals for improving the supply of finance for industry, but also published figures showing the short-term weakness of sterling. Keynes did not recommend devaluation of sterling; Bevin and Thomas Allen alone did. But Keynes had changed his mind by 5 August when he wrote a letter to the Prime Minister accepting devaluation as inevitable with the words: 'The game is up.'[13] The majority of the May Committee, relying mainly on accountancy arguments, recommended drastic cuts in government expenditure, including 20 per cent cuts in teachers' pay and unemployment benefit. A minority of two out of seven members dissented.

In these circumstances, not surprisingly, Montagu Norman told the bewildered MacDonald and his doctrinaire Chancellor, Snowden, that 'confidence' in the pound sterling could only be restored if drastic budget economies were made, including the cuts in unemployment benefit proposed by the May Committee. This led in August to the resignation of most of the Labour cabinet, and the formation of MacDonald's National Government. That government duly and hastily made the cuts which Norman demanded as the condition for securing the loan in New York to save the pound. These cuts included a sharp reduction in naval pay, which provoked much-publicized protests by naval ratings at Invergordon, reported round the world as a 'mutiny'. So 'confidence' was not restored. On 21 September 1931 the Bank gave up the struggle and, to the horrified amazement of the financial world, the pound's historic gold parity was nominally 'suspended' but in truth abandoned. John Locke's proud banner, inscribed for over two hundred years with the legend '£3 17s 10½d', was hauled down for the last time.

Contrary to a myth which has never quite died, it was of course the National Government, and not the previous Labour government, which took the pound 'off gold' in September 1931. What had really happened was that an untenable economic position had been abandoned, because there was no choice, and the British economy had been relieved from a painful burden. Such fearful warnings had been given in the previous few weeks about the catastrophe that would follow 'abandonment of the gold standard', as it was then called, that many ordinary citizens were relieved to find that everything seemed to go on as before. 'They never told us we could do that,' one ex-member of the Labour cabinet was supposed to have said. Ramsay MacDonald's response was to call a general election, and win an enormous majority. More prosaically, in early 1932 the Bank of England and the Treasury created the Exchange Equalization Account, which was to hold at the Bank large amounts of sterling and foreign exchange, so that the Bank could steady the sterling exchange rate by buying or selling when it judged this necessary. Thus the violent fluctuations feared were normally avoided, and this improvized system has survived in substance right up to the present day. Immediately after 21 September the dollar value of sterling fell to $3.94, and by February 1932 to $3.46, around which it fluctuated till the spring of 1933.

This 35 per cent depreciation of the pound on the foreign exchange market immediately relieved the deflationary pressure on Britain. To many people's surprise, the 'pound in their pocket' was not devalued. The price of imports did not rise anything like proportionately to the fall in the exchange rate. There were many reasons for this. First, when a currency depreciates, exporters from another currency area – for example in this case meat exporters from Argentina – do not necessarily raise the price of their produce in the depreciated currency proportionately, because they may fear loss of their markets, and may prefer to lower the price somewhat in their own currency. In the case of the pound in September 1931 this tendency was enforced by the fact – unforeseen by some economists and bankers – that British imports of many foodstuffs and raw materials formed so large a share of world demand that overseas producers in acute slump conditions were compelled to hold down their own prices to retain their market in Britain. Secondly, a large group of Commonwealth and other countries decided, since Britain was their major trading partner, to link their currencies with the pound rather than with gold and, as compared with gold or the dollar, to depreciate to the same extent as the pound. This group included not merely Australia, New Zealand, India and the British colonies, but also Denmark, Sweden, Norway, Eire, Egypt, Iraq, Argentina, Colombia, and Bolivia. The Commonwealth members of the group became the embryo of the sterling area, which assumed so much importance later. France, Belgium, Holland, and Switzerland were left marooned in the 'gold bloc', which continued to suffer acute deflation until Belgium finally devalued in 1935 and France in 1936.

Thirdly, and even more important, in these years Britain most wisely maintained under both the Labour and National governments the free and unrestricted entry of almost all food and raw material imports, which had been the foundation of the country's comparatively high living standards for a century, and which was so recklessly and gratuitously thrown away in 1972. According to Layton and Crowther, in their dispassionate *Study of Prices*,[14] throughout the worst period of the Great Depression Britain 'continued to import most of our foodstuffs and raw materials without restriction, and consequently reaped the benefit of the extremely low prices prevailing on the world market'. As a result

The Economist wholesale price index, which rose four points from August to October 1931, began to fall back in January 1932, and by June that year reached its low point for the whole depression years at five points *below* the pre-depreciation month, August 1931. Thus in the nine months following the abandonment of the gold link the real value of the pound actually *rose*.

The sterling cost of living, as opposed to wholesale prices, also fell several percentage points between the third quarter of 1931 and the second quarter of 1932. The index number of the sterling price of a 'composite unit of consumables' prepared by Henry Phelps Brown and Sheila Hopkins and set out in the Appendix of this book, shows a marked fall between 1931 and 1932, and a nearly 30 per cent fall between 1929 and 1932. Layton and Crowther[15] conclude that, even though unemployment doubled between early 1929 and the middle of 1932, the 'average real income of the working class as a whole' – in effect, that is, the total real consumption of goods and services by the employed and unemployed together – actually rose by about 1½ per cent over these three and a half years. This is not of course a precise statistic, and it does not alter the fact that the unemployed suffered severely.

What it does mean is that, largely thanks to our free import of food, the real purchasing power of the British people was better maintained than those elsewhere. Germany, in particular, suffered far more severely. By the winter of 1932–33, the depth of the slump, the luckless Brüning's unrelenting deflation – in pursuit of 'salvation' – had not merely removed him from office, but had probably cut the real living standard of German wage earners as a whole by something like 50 per cent: in all likelihood a steeper fall than in any other great country in modern history. For Brüning had also maintained high protection against food imports to please the Prussian landowners, and German wheat prices were double those on world markets: a foretaste of the Common Agricultural Policy. The contrast between the British and the German experience in 1932–33 is sharp. It fully explains the huge vote for the Communists and Nazis in that winter which brought Hitler (who had had little support in 1929) to power. The economic plight of the USA in 1932 was only a little better. Prices of farm products had fallen 40 or 50 per cent. Some 12 million people or nearly 25 per cent of the working population of the USA were unemployed and there was no general or effective unemployment insurance. It is perhaps surprising that democracy and law and order survived in America. But it is in no way surprising that, luckily for the world, in the presidential election of November 1932 Franklin Roosevelt won an overwhelming victory.

The last two years of the depression, 1931–32, were those in which protectionism took hold in one country after another. Deflation always breeds protectionism for the simple reason that, when total demand falls sharply, imports can plausibly be blamed for unemployment. Indeed in these conditions they do cause unemployment; and that is why pious exhortations to allow free trade from pundits who are not willing to reverse deflationary policies have little effect on governments or electorates. But there was an even more powerful motive reinforcing the slide into protectionism in 1931–32. In face of a world scarcity of gold the weaker countries, with their currency reserves disappearing, simply could not pay. Unless they could borrow, they were bound to shut out dispensable imports by tariff, quota, or exchange devices; and this did of course have a cumulative effect. In Germany the notorious, crafty Dr Schacht, head of the Reichsbank, was only the chief wizard of the tortuous art of import exclusion, to which he gave his name, but which many others copied. At the end of 1931 France and Canada imposed special duties on countries whose currency had depreciated – that is, those linked with sterling. Partly to support the pound, Britain herself introduced in 1932 the first general tariff (though with exemption for goods from the Empire) on imported manufactures for nearly a hundred years; and this was probably (as argued later in this book) desirable and far-sighted from the British point of view. But it is instructive, nonetheless, that it was introduced in the extreme deflationary year, 1932.

The release of the pound from gold in September 1931 had eased the actual downward swing a little in the British economy and in the whole sterling-linked area, and in some other countries by the late summer of 1932. But the general world depression was still at its deepest in January 1933 when Hitler took power in Germany and in March when Roosevelt took over in the USA. It is part of the implicit, unargued assumption (or faith) of the old sound-money economics that depressions somehow end of their own accord, like day after night or spring after winter. Why the nineteenth-century depression did so will be examined later in this book. But the greatest of all depressions, in 1932–33, did not. It only ended when the new American President took active steps to end it. In January–March 1933 there were nearly 3 million unemployed in Britain, 6 million in Germany and 13 million and still rising in the USA.[16] *The Economist* index of wholesale prices was still falling in March 1933; in other words, world prices were still falling when Roosevelt assumed office. Even UK unemployment reached its actual maximum in January 1933 at 2,955,448 or 22 per cent; and such measures of general industrial activity as existed touched their low point in 1932 and did not turn upwards till 1933.[17] W.W. Rostow records:[18] 'The depression after 1929 hit the US with peculiar force. The decline in incomes it induced sent the industrial system into a spiral which was not self-correcting, as such spirals had been in the pre-1914 world.' In Germany, production in January 1933 was barely half what it had been in 1928. Arthur Salter[19] wrote at the time: 'The World's economic mechanism has lost its self-adjusting quality.' The record of the Great Depression lends no support to the theory, at any rate in the post-1918 world, that some mysterious economic force automatically at some point reverses the slide.

Notes

[1] Henry Phelps Brown and M.H. Browne, *A Century of Pay*, Appendix 3, table headed 'UK 1913, 1920–1938'.

[2] See Martin Gilbert, *Winston S. Churchill*, Vol. V, Chapter 5.

[3] *Winston S. Churchill*, Vol. V, p. 98.

[4] J.M Keynes, *The Economic Consequenses of Mr Churchill*, p. 19.

[5] *'The Economic Consequences of Mr Churchill'*, p. 8.

[6] See, for example, J.K. Galbraith, *The Great Crash 1929*, Lionel Robbins, *The Great Depression*, Goronwy Rees, *The Great Slump*, and Arthur Salter, *Recovery*.

[7] Lord Robbins admitted in retrospect that protectionism at this time was a reaction to 'general deflation' (*Autobiography of an Economist*, p. 161).

[8] See Layton and Crowther, *The Study of Prices*, chart on p. 189.

[9] *Autobiography of an Economist*, p. 154.

[10] A director had asked that the true value of its depreciated assets should be shown in its published balance sheet!

[11] Susan Strange, *Sterling and British Policy*, p. 50.

[12] *Sterling and British Policy*, p. 54.

[13] Susan Houson and Donald Winch, *The Economic Advisory Council 1930–39*, p. 89.

[14] p. 194.

[15] p. 195.
[16] For percentages see W.W. Rostow, *The World Economy*, p. 220.
[17] W.H. Beveridge, *Full Employment in a Free Society*, p. 313.
[18] *The World Economy*, p. 219.
[19] *Recovery*, p. 208.

The Pound and the Dollar

In the USA in early 1933 the deflationary rot spread from the industrial world to the banking system. Again, as business losses turned one loan after another into a bad debt, and governments defaulted, suspicion grew that individual banks were insolvent, and a rush for cash began. In the traditional manner, as one bank called for cash from another, the crisis spread; and on 4 March, the day Roosevelt took office, almost all the banks in the USA were closed. Unrestrained cumulative deflation had reached its logical conclusion. For a few days economic activity was nearly at a standstill. Roosevelt's first acts were to declare a Bank Holiday until the Federal Reserve system could ensure that ample supplies of notes were available to overcome the short-term wave of panic, and secondly to prohibit exports of gold: in other words to suspend the gold standard and sever the link between the dollar and the existing price of gold. The dollar immediately depreciated against gold (that is, the gold price in dollars rose), as the pound had done in 1931. From the point of view of the pound the exchange rate, which had been $3.27 in December 1932, began to rise.

Roosevelt's clinching decision, however, the one which turned the tide, came a few weeks later. He was a man who held no economic theory, and was attached to no single panacea. As a discerning reader of his 1932 campaign speeches, published under the title *Looking Forward*, could have perceived, he believed amid this desperate predicament in trying any plausible remedy that was proposed, and seeing which one worked. Roosevelt decided to alter the dollar price of gold from time to time by presidential fiat, and started by raising it. This procedure had its comic aspect. The President was believed to be advised weekly by one of his advisers, Professor Moley, known in Wall Street as 'Moley, Moley, Moley, Lord God Almighty'. But it worked. The US financial and business community, acting on the accepted classical principle that a higher gold price meant more currency and easier credit, expected a rise in commodity prices, and began to buy stocks. From that moment prices began to rise in commodity markets, as one purchaser after another tried to get in first. Gradually, through the summer months of 1933, the ripple spread round the world. In these months it happened to be my job on the staff of *The Economist* to record these market movements; and it was fascinating to watch the turning tide influence almost every creek, gully, and estuary throughout five continents. Cause and effect can seldom if ever be decisively proved in economic affairs, and no doubt the end of the deflation in Germany, contrived by the grim and ruthless methods of Hitler and Schacht, at least stopped the vicious spiral in that area. But judged by the dates, Roosevelt's decisions in the spring of 1933 were the world turning point.

The regular changes in the gold price were given up later. In early 1934 Roosevelt *de facto* stabilized the dollar price of gold at $35 an ounce, which meant a 41 per cent cut in the gold value of the dollar, compared with the previous parity. But the general economic upswing, once started, ran on, even though it was years before the 1929 level of activity in the USA was regained, and though a major expansion of the money stock had a gradual effect. Virtually all indices of world prices or business activity or trade values turned upwards in 1933. *The Economist* price index showed a three-point rise in April. Indices of production and business activity in Britain also rose in the first half of 1933 and kept on rising.[1] Unemployment started falling in 1933 in Britain and in most of the sterling countries, but it reached a peak in the USA in 1934. The dollar value of the pound continued to rise regularly in the summer of 1933, as the dollar gold price was raised. The pound even passed the old $4.86 rate for a time, and at one time in 1933 touched $5.20. After this, as the changes in the dollar price of gold were discontinued, the rate settled down for the next few years not far from $4.86. But though this level was regained, John Locke's £3 17s 10½d had gone for ever. Both the pound and the dollar had depreciated about equally in terms of gold, but were for the time once more 'looking each other in the face'. (Only in 1939 did the pound fall back to $4.03, where it stood at the outbreak of war.)

Throughout 1931–33, in both Britain and the USA, numerous articles and books were written maintaining (as in 1982–3) that owing to rapid technological progress unemployment would rise indefinitely, that the 'problem of production was solved', and that the only solution was to cut down working hours and for workers to retire earlier. A textile factory in West Virginia was constantly adduced in evidence, where – so we were told – you only had to press a button and the whole factory ran for a fortnight with only one employee. So numerous were the propagators of this doctrine that they came to be known for a year or two as 'technocrats'.[2] No sooner, however, had they achieved notoriety than, after the severance of the dollar from the gold link in March 1933, they were proved wrong, as their predecessors had been in every nineteenth-century cyclical upswing. From 1933 to 1937 both production and employment, in the USA, Britain, and elsewhere, gradually and unsteadily but nevertheless progressively moved upwards. And unemployment fell.

The pound was now a 'managed currency' not tied to gold. Fluctuations in the exchange rate against the dollar were smoothed out by the Exchange Equalization Account, and the rate tended to remain not far from $4.86. The market price of gold in London had risen to about 140s an ounce. The Board of Trade index of production in Britain (1924=100) rose from 95 in the first quarter of 1933 to 141 in the fourth quarter of 1937. The then *Economist* Index of Business Activity (1924=100) rose from 97 in early 1933 to 126 in 1937. Unemployment fell (annual average) from 22.1 per cent in 1932 to 10.8 per cent in 1937. The total number employed, of course, rose very substantially, and in 1937 more people were employed in Britain than in 1929. Unemployment in the USA fell from 26.7 per cent in 1934 to 14.3 per cent in 1937.[3] The net national product[4] of the USA and Canada, which had plunged by about 30 per cent between 1929 and 1933, had recovered to 8 per cent above the 1929 level by 1939. Western European countries had largely the same experience, except for France and the other gold bloc countries, where overvalued currencies delayed recovery till France devalued under the Blum government in 1936.

Thus, though the 1933–37 recovery was incomplete, and there were still over a million unemployed in Britain in 1937, the picture of continued depression throughout the thirties is misleading. Certainly the policy of letting the pound find its natural economic value on the exchange markets assisted the recovery. It is sometimes sweepingly stated that the recovery of the thirties was mainly the result of rearmament. This also, except for Japan and Germany, is a falsification; as is shown by the fact that from 1937 to 1938 there was a major relapse in production and employment in Britain and the USA, and in most industrial countries other than Germany. The upswing from 1932 to 1937 was much more closely associated in Britain and the USA with the rising motor industry and house building.

One initial reflationary force was the effect of the sterling and dollar devaluation in writing up the sterling and dollar value of the national gold reserves and so generating a rise in the stock of money, and also making gold production more profitable. The total coin and bullion gold holding in the Bank of England rose from £125,401,728 in December 1931 to £195,228,035 in December 1933. Total gold coin, bullion, and certificates in the USA rose from $3,918.6 million in 1932 to $7,856.2 million in 1934. Two other decisions powerfully contributed to UK recovery in these years. First, bank rate was reduced to 2 per cent in June 1932 and held there continuously till 1939 – and, indeed (after a brief rise in 1939) till 1951. The great conversion of 5 per cent War Loan to 3½ per cent in June 1932 brought long-term as well as short-term interest rates down. These changes undoubtedly stimulated a major house building boom, which in turn expanded purchasing power and general public spending. The decline in the level of understanding in these matters is starkly shown by the contrast with the early 1980s when, with similar levels of unemployment and unused capacity, interest rates – even 'real' interest rates, allowing for rising prices – were held at much higher levels. The other stimulating influence on British manufacturing industry in the 1930s was the imposition in 1932 of a moderate tariff[5] on imports of manufactured goods. There can be little doubt that this tariff, supported by a 2 per cent bank rate, had a substantial effect in expanding British manufacturing output, and real growth in the British economy generally in 1932–37. In these five years steel production (behind a tariff varying between 30 and 50 per cent) rose from 5 million to 13 million tons a year, and the general level of manufacturing production rose by 48 per cent. Without this rise, particularly in steel, it is doubtful if British industry could have fought the Second World War.

One should not allow theoretical or doctrinaire assumptions about free trade or protectionism to blind one to realities. This whole issue has been bedevilled by a belief that one system or the other must be the best for all countries at all times. The truth is very different. Universal free trade would be preferable in a world where all countries pursued expansionary and full employment policies and were willing to allow their overseas deficits or surpluses to be adjusted by changing exchange rates. Expansionary policies are thus the best road to freer trade. But in a world where such policies often do not prevail, much depends on the individual country and commodity and the particular circumstances. Certainly various major industrial countries, including the United States, Australia, Canada, and later Japan, could not have built up their modern industries without industrial tariffs. Almost certainly the right policy for Britain since the mid-nineteenth century – and one which would have strengthened the pound sterling – would have been a combination of free entry for food and raw materials, and a moderate tariff on manufactured goods.[6]

In the years when Britain followed this intelligent policy – from 1932 to 1937 and from 1945 to 1972 – real growth was achieved, despite short-term fluctuations; industry expanded; and living standards rose. Since 1972, when high protectionism was applied to food imports and all tariffs removed on manufactured imports from most of continental Europe, Britain has slid into the first deficit on trade in manufactures for at least 150 years. Possibly, though this is more debatable, it was a similar mistake to maintain free entry for imports of manufactured goods after the middle of the nineteenth century. Up till then Britain had a head start in industrial manufacture, and unrestricted imports did not matter much. But from the mid-century others, notably the USA and Germany, began to compete. And they did so from the shelter of a protected home market, while Britain maintained free imports, with some exceptions in the 1920s, up to 1932. It was in these sixty or seventy years that Britain fell back *relatively* in industrial strength compared with the USA and Germany. (The one British industry which strikingly expanded in the 1920s and 1930s, motor vehicles, was one of those specially protected.)

Much controversy has emerged about the cause of the relative weakening of British industry since the mid-nineteenth century. I would judge on the evidence that the greatest single (not the only) cause was the inability of a national industry faced with unrestricted imports to keep up with other national industries sustained by a protected home market. For instance, as Professor Peter Mathias[7] has expressed it, speaking of the late nineteenth century:

> 'Tariffs in Germany, France and the US, by shutting equivalently priced British steel from those markets, meant that these steel industries could grow much faster than the British. This in turn meant that they could gain technologically as a consequence of fast growth: the incremental capacity in their industries could incorporate the latest technology and the "age structure" of their plant would be younger.'

This was equally true of other manufacturing industries.

The whole hundred years' debate in Britain has been muddled by the false assumption that, if you adopt some measure of protection, you have to apply it to all imports indiscriminately – manufactures, food, and materials. Yet, in the end, with much too little reflection, in the 1970s we chose the worst of both worlds and embraced high protectionism for food imports, and free entry for continental manufactures; with predictable, and predicted, results. It is relevant to the strong recovery of 1932–7, and the strength of the pound sterling, which this permitted, to sketch briefly in this way the background of the tariff controversy, but to review it further in Chapter 25 in the light of later history.

In the early 1930s recovery had lagged in France and the gold bloc countries because their currencies had been left high and dry, overvalued against the pound and dollar ever since the latter had left the gold standard. This lasted until the French franc was devalued in September 1936. As part of that devaluation, a Tripartite Agreement was reached between the American, British, and French Treasuries to refrain from competitive exchange depreciation, and to assist one another in smoothing out erratic jumps in the various exchange rates. This did not prevent the French franc falling from 105 to the pound at the end of 1936 to 178 in June 1938.

From 1937 a major cyclical relapse occurred in most of the main industrial economies, including the American and the British. This, as has already been observed, shows that rearmament cannot have been the main cause of the 1933–37 upswing in Britain. For rearmament here was expanding, not contracting, in 1938. The 1938 recession, like the 1929 collapse and 1933 recovery, began in the USA which, W.W. Rostow says, 'led the way in both the recession of 1937–1938 and the recovery from it'.[8] In Britain the relapse was sharp. For instance, Sir W. Beveridge's index of industrial activity in the UK fell back more than 10 per cent from the peak of 1937 to little above the 1933 level in 1938.[9] In dollar value the pound sterling, having stood near $5 in the first half of 1938, fell to $4.67 by the end of the year; it recovered briefly in early 1939. But as rearmament took increasing hold of the British economy, and war fears of the public mind, the rate began to fall again. From $4.68 in July it plunged, with the Exchange Equalization Account standing aside, to $4.03 on 3 September 1939, when exchange controls were introduced. And there it was pegged for ten years. This time $4.86 had also gone – in all human probability – for ever.

Ironically it was in 1938 that the word 'recession' was first generally used to describe an economic relapse. And it is a wry comment on the history of words that this euphemism, first selected to escape the dread word 'depression' by then irrevocably associated with 1929–33, should later have been universally used to describe the world deflation of 1979–83, which was fully as intense and unnecessary as that of fifty years earlier. W.W. Rostow's final conclusion on the 1929–33 disaster and the flagging recovery of the later 1930s is this: 'It was the lack of sufficient stimulus to effective demand, not exhausted investment opportunities, that caused the chronic high levels of unemployment in the 1930s':[10] a clear verdict fully justified by the evidence.

Notes

[1] Layton and Crowther, *The Study of Prices*, p. 270.
[2] See Chapter 24.
[3] W.W. Rostow, *The World Economy*, p. 220.
[4] *The World Economy*, p. 221.
[5] It was basically 10 per cent, but could be varied by special orders.
[6] See also pp. 240–1 for further discussion of this issue.
[7] *The First Industrial Nation*, 2nd edition, p. 380.
[8] *The World Economy*, p. 332.
[9] W.H. Beveridge, *Full Employment in a Free Society*, p. 313.
[10] *The World Economy*, pp. 336–7.

14

The Pound in the War Economy: 1939–45

In the Second World War British economic policy treated the pound as it should be treated: as a means, not an end. And as a result the economic management of the war effort, and the mobilization of resources, were from the start more successful than those of 1914–18, and also more successful than those in Germany. The pound sterling in 1939–45 performed its proper and essential function as a unit of account and a medium of exchange. Policy in those years was not allowed to be dominated by the aim either of stabilizing the value of the pound or of regulating its quantity in circulation. Still less was there alleged to be some mystically determined quantity of currency and credit, beyond which money could not be made available even though unused productive capacity existed. The essential principle of the economic war effort was that the nation could 'afford' what it had the physical capacity to produce. And the practical method of applying this principle was to identify all labour, materials, and plant which could possibly contribute to the war effort, and then to create and allocate the money needed to mobilize those resources. Wherever manpower or other capacity could be found, a concerted attempt was made to absorb it into the productive effort; and anyone in those days who thought the nation could benefit by paying people to do nothing would have been laughed out of court. Indeed in the latter stages of the war production programmes were based on a 'Manpower Budget', which started by ascertaining the number of active men and women available, and then planning production programmes accordingly. Unemployment, still a million in early 1940, was by these means reduced to 73,561 or less than 1 per cent by July 1944. The active mobilization of manpower was turned into a fine art. Work was steered to immobile workers, and mobile workers were steered to immobile work. An area's resources were only treated as no longer expansible when no more beds existed for building workers who would build hostels for imported workers to occupy. This was 'real' economics in every sense of the term.

The pound was thus for the time almost invisible. Sterling, one might have said:

> Throughout the war
> Did nothing in particular,
> And did it very well.

This did not mean, however, that no financial problem existed, or that a balance did not have to be kept between the total flow of spending by the public and the government and the total supply of goods and services available. On the contrary, it meant that that balance did have to be kept, and was broadly kept by deliberate restraints and controls. The total deposits of the London Clearing Banks actually rose from £2,277 million in June 1939 to £4,751 million in June 1945 – it more than doubled, in other words. But few complained of 'inflation'. Prices and living costs rose very much less than in the First World War. The cost of living index (1 September 1939=100) had reached 129 by 1941, mainly because of dearer imports; but it rose only another three points in the whole of the rest of the war. Yet the 'money supply' had more than doubled, and the government had borrowed, largely from the banks, on a huge scale, though proportionately less than in 1914–18. Between 31 March 1939 and 31 March 1946 the National Debt rose from £7,247 million to £23,742 million. The economic experience, therefore, of 1939–45 rather weakens the doctrine that some direct and inescapable relationship exists between the quantity of money, government borrowing, and the cost of living.

How then was it done? It was achieved mainly by restricting price rises to levels required by genuine costs, and by subsidies where needed; by higher taxation, which absorbed surplus spending power; by rationing; by encouraging the public to lend to the government; by concentrating productive capacity on essential output; and above all by persuading the organized pay groups severely to moderate their pay demands, provided living costs were effectively controlled. In particular interest rates, in sharp contrast to the First World War, were deliberately held at exceedingly low levels. Bank rate, after a brief and largely ineffective rise to 4 per cent in August 1939, came back to 2 per cent in October and stayed there. Nobody maintained that interest rates had to be decided by 'market forces', or supply and demand. On the contrary they were decided by the government, and the banks were requested to lend what the Treasury could not borrow elsewhere, and to curtail their other lending accordingly. In this way, for instance, some £3,400 million worth of National War Bonds were raised at 2½ per cent, £2,780 million worth of Savings Bonds at 3 per cent, £3,530 million worth of Treasury Bills at 1 per cent (largely from the banks), and £1,560 million worth of Treasury Deposit Recepts at 1⅛ per cent (wholly from the banks). By this policy of controlled low interest rates the financial cost of the war – again in contrast to 1914–18 experience – was drastically reduced, both during the war and afterwards. And the scandal of high wartime profits amassed by money-lending bodies – including the banks who were creating the new money – was successfully avoided. Geoffrey Crowther in '*An Outline of Money*' estimates that 47 per cent of the cost of the 1939–45 war was met by taxation, 7 per cent by other public revenues, 36 per cent by genuine saving, and only 10 per cent by creation of new money.

Naturally all this could only be done because the main sections of the community, from the banks to the industrial workers and the armed forces, were prepared, for the common purpose of winning the war, to accept severe discipline and sacrifices; and also because all sections were represented in the wartime government. But the public *did* accept all this. And it *was* done. Nobody can reasonably argue, therefore, that economically it *cannot* be done, or that some immutable economic law prevents it being done. What one can legitimately ask, in drawing more general and long-term morals from this exceptional experience, is whether the gains of submitting to market forces are, or are not, so great that they outweigh all that can be achieved by moderating or suspending them. For instance, the reason why Britain has had 10 per cent interest rates in 1983–5, and had only 1 or 2 per cent rates in 1943, is not that low interest rates are economically impossible, but rather that, if we choose to leave them to market forces, naturally market forces will determine them. The real issue is not whether market forces can be moderated or suspended, but how much interference with them is worthwhile to achieve a given objective. The argument should therefore be conducted, and the choice made, on this rational basis. But we should also remember that if in 1939–45 Britain had refrained from moderating market forces, and had treated the pound sterling or its value as an end rather than a means, we should probably have lost the war.

The maintenance of the internal value of the pound by direct controls was also of course one crucial instrument in the Second World War for preserving the living standards of the public as a whole. It is arguable that, as in the First World War, thanks to the fall in unemployment the real living standards of working people as a whole were as high at the end of the war as at the beginning, if not higher. It is at any rate certain that there had been a major improvement in the equality of distribution of incomes. 'The big reduction in the inequality of incomes, after taxation, as compared with the thirties', G.D.N. Worswick says, 'was brought about during the war.'[2]

In the internal economy in 1939–45, when the government, supported by the public, had full authority, a thoroughgoing control of the pound's value and of economic activity was thus perfectly possible. However in Britain's dealings with the outside world the problem was much more complex. Where supplies had to be bought from overseas, they had to be paid for by exporting, by running down reserves, or by borrowing. In the first months of the war an attempt was made to pay by exporting (and excluding inessential imports); but after 1940 that became no longer practicable as the main support. At least by this time effective exchange control had largely prevented actual loss to the authorities of reserves and foreign exchange through conversion of sterling by British individuals or firms into foreign currency. But this direct control applied only to UK residents. The very large amount of sterling held by overseas residents – 'non-resident' accounts – was much more difficult to control.

In the early months of the war the pound sterling in these accounts fell to a large discount compared with the official rate, particularly after the military disasters of 1940. Faced with this difficulty the pound was protected in two ways. First, in the sterling area itself payments remained free from one country to another; but such sterling could not, without exchange control approval, be converted into other currencies. Hence the huge 'sterling balances' built up during the war by major sterling countries, such as India and Egypt, supplying Britain. After the war debts owing by Britain to these countries constituted a major problem. Nevertheless during the war and after it the existence of a free payment system covering a substantial part of the world was a definite source of economic strength to Britain and the Allies. For most of the period the sterling area consisted of the whole Commonwealth apart from Canada and Newfoundland, with the addition of Egypt, the Sudan, and Iraq. Its value was great, mainly because it enabled large war supplies to be bought by Britain with paper sterling at a crucial time when other means of payment were scarce. Secondly, leakages threatening the pound from sterling balances held by non-sterling area overseas residents had somehow to be prevented. This was done by special 'payments agreements' between Britain and each individual country, which ensured that such payments were made only through special accounts that could be monitored and controlled. The leakage was in this way reduced to a trickle, and an open black market in depreciated sterling, which might have become a standing inducement to evade the control, was in practice averted.

Payment for current wartime supplies from countries outside the sterling area was also naturally an acute problem until Roosevelt brought Lend-Lease into force; and Britain also had somehow to finance the current deficit of the whole sterling area with the outside world – mainly the United States. In 1940 and 1941 all marketable British investments in the USA were requisitioned by the British government and sold for £200 million. Compensation was paid in sterling to the British holders. Another £225 million worth was sold in Canada; and a further £425 million was borrowed from the official Reconstruction Finance Corporation in the USA against the collateral of those British investments that remained, including the business of British insurance companies. In spite of all this, the gold and dollar reserve supporting the pound – now held at the Bank of England by the Exchange Equalization Account – which had totalled £605 million at the start of the war, had fallen to £74 million at the end of 1940 and to a negligible level by the time Lend-Lease came into effect. From 1941, however, at the end of which the USA entered the war, until 1945 Lend-Lease and Mutual Aid largely solved the problem. In effect the USA supplied the dollars required; and the pound, supported by all these props, stood firm at a somewhat nominal $4.03. Indeed by mid-1945 the reserve had edged up again to the respectable figure of £453 million. But the spectre of having to repay Lend-Lease, or a part of it, was meanwhile left to confront the first post-war government of Britain.

Notes

[1] p. 172.

[2] G.D.N. Worswick and P.H. Ady (eds), *The British Economy in the Nineteen-Fifties*, p. 16.

15

From $4.03 to $2.80

Winston Churchill had described Lend-Lease as the 'most unsordid act in history'. Roosevelt had introduced it to the American public by saying that if your neighbour's house catches fire, you do not bargain with him for a fee before lending him your fire extinguisher. But unhappily the magnanimity and genius of Franklin Roosevelt died with him. President Truman cancelled Lend-Lease in August 1945 without consultation and without warning. He acted not out of malice but out of hurry, genuine misunderstanding, and bad advice. He had actually signed a previous order cancelling Lend-Lease on 8 May without reading it, but rescinded it later[1] when he realized what it meant. The order of August 1945 was not rescinded. Thus the new British government under Clement Attlee, pledged by its electoral mandate to far-reaching social reform, found itself in the first fortnight with the pound high and dry and the sterling balance of payments completely uncovered. At least it started with two countervailing advantages. First nobody – not even the City – suggested, as after 1918, that the pound should be painfully levered back from $4.03 to $4.86. That lesson had been learnt. Secondly, in the last year Keynes had been busy preparing plans for meeting the sort of immediate external crisis which in fact emerged in August 1945. The Attlee government was rightly determined to treat the pound in internal planning as a unit of account and not a mystical symbol. But the overseas value of the pound had to be maintained in order to pay for imports; and this could only be done by borrowing dollars in the immediate emergency and building up exports in the longer run. Preparations already made enabled a British delegation headed by Keynes to be sent to Washington in September 1945, just a month after Lend-Lease was cancelled by Harry Truman, with concrete proposals for help from the American government.

The economic gap to be covered on external account was huge. Britain had sold most foreign investments; switched most of industry from exporting to the war effort; lost a major proportion of its shipping fleet; incurred enormous new debts overseas; and retained only a modest currency reserve. Since the pound was still pegged at $4.03, the economic pressure naturally showed itself in the form of a shortage of the Bank of England's holding of gold and dollars to meet essential demands. Keynes estimated that we needed £1,700 million worth of dollars so as to break even by 1949, and hoped to raise £1,250 to £1,500 million ($5 to $6 billion) from the US Treasury,[2] a large part of it as grant rather than loan. After three months' negotiation, in which the American authorities became less and less helpful, the British delegation were able to raise only $3.75 billion, the whole of it as a loan or 'line of credit' bearing 2 per cent interest, and a special further loan of $650 million. Canada later added another £281 million on similar terms.

Two damaging political conditions were also attached to the loan by the American authorities, despite strong British resistance. First, sterling was to be made freely 'convertible', in other words exchangeable into foreign currencies, within one year of Congress ratification of the Loan Agreement; and secondly, it was not to be used simply to pay off Britain's wartime sterling debts. American insistence on these conditions sprang mainly from doctrinaire *laissez-faire* beliefs in free convertibility, and a suspicion that the sterling area was a device for favouring British at the expense of American exporters and overseas creditors. The convertibility arrangement was to apply to current earnings, as opposed to existing holdings, of both sterling and non-sterling countries. This required complicated agreements with non-sterling countries distinguishing between current earnings and existing balances. The Americans also attempted to insert in the Loan Agreement a promise by the British government not to repay fully the £3.5 billion of wartime debts in the form of blocked sterling balances which Britain owed to very poor countries such as India and Egypt; but this was successfully resisted by the Attlee cabinet.

It is ironic that the Americans in 1945–6 should sometimes have regarded the sterling area as a sinister device for promoting British interests at the expense of others, when in later post-war years some internal British critics deplored the sterling area and the sterling balances as being a major handicap on the British economy, only to be removed by dissolving the sterling area and – in the view of some critics – all Britain's special economic links with the Commonwealth. These were both extreme views. The sterling area, as recorded in Chapter 14, sprang largely out of the blocked wartime sterling balances. In the years immediately after the war the area grew greatly in importance because the dollar was scarce and because a high proportion of British trade was conducted with sterling countries and vice versa. The post-war sterling area consisted mainly of the group of Commonwealth countries already mentioned[3] which kept most of their currency reserves in sterling in Britain, and between whom payments could be made and capital (and to a large extent trade) could move freely without controls. The gold and dollar reserves of the whole area were thus in effect pooled, which in a period of acute dollar shortage was an advantage to all. To Britain the advantages were that payments and trade were unimpeded by currency obstacles in this very large number of countries; and that if the whole area showed a surplus with the dollar area and the outside world, the reserves of the Bank of England, as in effect central banker of the whole area, would be strengthened. The disadvantage was that if the sterling area was in deficit the reverse would happen, and the Bank of England would be pressed beyond its capacity to supply hard currencies in return for sterling.

It is not easy to say for certain whether Britain was in the end the gainer or loser. Glib talk about the 'burden' of the sterling area and sterling balances was not always based on serious argument. Certainly in the crucial early post-war years British exporters gained by the existence of the sterling area, for purchasers of much needed goods over a large part of the world held a currency which had to be spent within the area, including Britain; and Britain bought a high proportion of the goods it needed most from sterling countries. The main conclusion of the Brookings Report compiled by American economists in 1968[4] was that 'the Sterling Area permitted real gains for all its members, including Britain, compared with what would have been likely in its absence, but that the gains to be shared have diminished over the course of time'. The main disadvantage to Britain, the Report thought, was the need to maintain higher interest rates to protect reserves. On balance I would also judge that

Britain gained materially in the 1940s and 1950s by the area's existence, and that its too hasty dissolution after that period contributed to the country's difficulties in the 1970s and 1980s.

However arguable that may be, it is now reasonably certain that the 1945 government took the right decision on the wartime debts owed by Britain to sterling countries. The attempt to 'adjust', in other words partially cancel, them as the Americans had proposed was abandoned as politically impossible in the very first negotiation (with Ceylon, as Sri Lanka was then called) in 1948. The spectacle of Britain defaulting on its debts to some of the world's poorest countries would not have been a very good start to the post-1945 sanguine new world. Only Canada, Australia, and New Zealand agreed to waive part of the debt voluntarily. Britain repaid the poorer countries in full. An arrangement was made with each country for a certain slice of its balance to be released from blocking each year; a small part of it was to be convertible into dollars and the rest taken in sterling. This compromise enabled Britain to foresee its total liability each year to repay sterling or dollars; it permitted the creditor countries to meet their most urgent needs by buying some dollar and sterling goods annually; it assisted the growth of British exports with the area, as sterling was spent on British goods; and it maintained the principle that Britain was repaying all its wartime debts to poorer countries. Seen in retrospect, it was the first post-war experiment in 'aid' to a needy Third World. And it turned out in practice, as the wartime debts were paid off, that sterling balances as a whole, contrary to the prediction of those who wanted to adjust, cancel, fund, or somehow get rid of them, began to grow naturally and not to disappear. From a low point of £3,143 million in 1949, after repayment had started, the balances had actually risen to £3,883 million in 1960.[5] They increasingly became in later years not wartime debts or currency reserves but – whether bank accounts, Treasury Bills, or other securities – the commercial holdings of traders from all over the world (including eventually the Organization of Petroleum Exporting Countries (OPEC)) who preferred to keep them in this form. These it was neither desirable nor possible to eliminate, though naturally reserves had to be kept against their sudden withdrawal.

In 1946–7, however, the obligation of convertibility forced on a reluctant British government by the Americans as the alternative to breakdown of the loan talks, proved impossible to bear. Most British negotiators thought that convertibility could not be long sustained, but concluded that, if the Americans could not accept this in theory, it was wisest to let them discover it from the practical outcome. At first, in the course of 1946, the known availability of the loan encouraged confidence in the pound; the external pressure on the British economy relaxed; and some understandably false hopes of easy recovery were born. Hugh Dalton called it an '*annus mirabilis*'. At the same moment, in early 1946, Britain had adhered to the Bretton Woods Agreement (formulated at the July 1944 UN Monetary and Financial Conference at Bretton Woods, New Hampshire) and assumed further obligations to keep its exchange rate normally fixed, and in effect only to alter it after consultation and with good reason. The Bretton Woods plan and the setting up of the International Monetary Fund were largely the product of Keynes' reflections and of Anglo-American talks on the best way to avoid in future the vicious spiral of retaliatory trade restrictions forced by deflation in the early 1930s. (Keynes had himself proposed a more thorough-going and effective plan, which provided for the creation of new international money.) But the principle of Bretton Woods was sound. Since the deficit of one country necessarily implied the surplus of another, the downward spiral could be avoided if, by means of a central mechanism and reserve, the creditor at some point in effect lent to the debtor. But mounting American pressure, based more on a simple nineteenth-century faith in fixed exchange rates than on serious economics, grafted on to the scheme the new exchange rate regime as a sort of modern refinement of the old gold standard. The basic idea of the central reserve, and aid to the temporary weak economy, was undoubtedly a huge step forward in world economic policy, and a major contributor to the immense economic advances achieved in the first twenty years after the war. But in the end the exchange-rate obligation proved too hard – even for the United States – to bear.

For the pound sterling in 1946 the immediate impact of Bretton Woods was the promise of new last-resort international reserves to back up the temporary American loan. But seldom has there been a more false dawn. The British internal economy was knocked sideways in the North-Easterly blizzard of January–March 1947, which brought coal supplies to a halt. In the first half of 1947, though British exports had recovered rapidly from about 40 per cent of the 1938 volume in 1945 to over 100 per cent, imports were also increasing rapidly, owing to the recovery of world supplies. Britain's own deficit on visible trade was £103 million in 1946[6] and over £361 million in 1947. The total current account deficit in 1947 was £381 million.[7] At the same time the general world scramble for dollars exerted pressure from all sides which squeezed the sterling reserve. As soon as convertibility of current sterling earnings was established, in July 1947, the loan began to melt away. Sterling was virtually the only currency at least partially convertible into dollars; and the Bank of England appears to have failed in some cases to distinguish clearly between current earnings and previously held balances. Without much doubt some capital outflow worsened the dollar losses.[8] The first announcement of Marshall Aid in June 1947 was too late to stem the rush, and convertibility had to be abandoned – as some of the British negotiators had always feared and indeed foreseen – on 20 August 1947.

From this moment the British economy achieved a remarkable recovery. The basis of it was a drastic policy, under Stafford Cripps as Chancellor, by which priority at all points was given to exports and real investment rather than consumption, and a whole array of financial restraints and direct controls were used vigorously to ensure that those priorities were honoured. Simultaneously Marshall Aid came into effect in 1948 and relieved the intense pressure of dollar shortage in Britain and the rest of western Europe. Without it Cripps' internal policy could not have succeeded as it did. To this day Marshall Aid remains the most far-sighted, constructive, and successful measure taken by any great power in the post-1945 world; and this should be remembered to the lasting credit of the United States. It set both Britain and the rest of western Europe on a course of long-term recovery and growth which they could not have achieved alone.

For Britain, recovery in the next few years moved in a series of jerks and swings – much shorter-term than the pre-1939 trade cycle – as one lurch after another from the outside world hit the pound sterling and the British economy. In 1948 potential demand inflation was held back by Dalton's highly disinflationary budget of November 1947. Contrary to impressions sometimes given, this budget with its large surplus was slightly more disinflationary than the later budgets of Stafford Cripps, who broadly maintained the budget balance which Dalton had established. Even more important, an effective pay restraint policy or, as it would later have been called, incomes policy, was introduced by agreement with the trade union leadership in early 1948. It saved the country and the pound sterling from cost inflation with remarkable success between the end of 1947 and late 1951. In 1948 pay rates rose only 4.2 per cent and unemployment remained at 1.5 per cent. The volume of industrial production rose from 108 per cent of the 1938 level in 1947 to 117 per cent in 1948. The volume of exports, the most crucial part of the recovery effort, actually increased by 27 per cent between 1947 and 1948. On the current balance of payments Britain just about broke even in 1948 – and this in only the third year after the end of the war. The economic strategy which had produced these early results (later published) was formally set out and presented to the Marshall Aid authorities in October 1948 as *The Long-Term Programme of the UK*. It contained targets over the proposed four-year period of Marshall Aid, particularly for real output and export volume, which were in the event very largely achieved.

Meanwhile in 1949 financial disturbances, less vital but perhaps more visible than the real progress which they temporarily obscured, pushed the pound off the $4.03 peg where it had been rather precariously perched for just ten years. The first post-war recession in the United States reduced the total dollar earnings of the whole sterling area at a time when imports into the area were increasing. And on top of this real threat to the pound's dollar value, in February the US Secretary of the Treasury, Mr Snyder, made before a Senate committee an incautious public remark suggesting that sterling might be devalued (an interesting example of 'open government'). This added the usual speculative flurry to the underlying economic forces. Weekly gains for Britain's gold and dollar reserve – the crucial signpost at this time – turned into losses in the early summer of 1949. But more solid reasons convinced the Chancellor's advisers at this time that the exchange rate must be altered, as was in fact inevitable. The rate of $4.03 had been reached, largely by market forces, in September 1939, and held there by the Bank for ten years. But Britain's economic weight in the world – her share in world production, exports, productive capacity, real capital, and currency reserves – as compared with that of the United States had drastically changed. Indeed in 1949 US real national income was nearly 50 per cent of that of the whole world. So $4.03 was already out of date, as was indeed equally true in 1945. But in 1945 Britain's physical capacity to export was still too small to satisfy the demand for exports which prevailed overseas. Nothing would therefore have been achieved by devaluing – it would merely have raised import prices and living costs. The object of lowering an exchange rate is to restrain imports and to cheapen one's exports so as to increase the latter enough to keep the trade balance under control. By 1949 not merely were British exports too expensive abroad, but Britain now had surplus capacity to produce them because her industry had expanded and export markets had become competitive. Everything was to be gained, therefore, by bringing the dollar–sterling rate into line with existing economic realities.

These were the arguments which convinced Cripps' economic advisers in July 1949; and since under the Bretton Woods settlement Britain was in effect bound to make a sharp change, and then refix the rate, rather than 'float' without control, in that month the decision was taken to devalue despite the reluctance which Cripps felt largely on non-economic grounds. The proposal for a new rate of $2.80 came on this occasion from the economists in the government (mainly R. L. Hall and Edwin Plowden) rather than the politicians.[9] Planned over a period of six weeks, the whole of this major financial operation, including the obligatory consultation with the IMF, was carried out with great skill and secrecy (standards were high in those days) by Treasury and Bank of England officials. On 18 September 1949 the pound sterling became worth $2.80.

The operation was more successful than even the most sanguine of its planners had predicted. Immediately the weekly dollar outflow turned into a weekly gain. The balance of payments on current account, in heavy deficit in 1946 and 1947, and barely balanced in 1948 and 1949, swung round to a £300 million surplus in 1950. And none of the predicted evil consequences of devaluation, such as 'runaway inflation', in fact occurred. Most remarkably, there was only a 2 per cent rise in retail prices for nearly a year after devaluation. This gratifying result was due partly to strong restraint of money demand by budget measures, partly to direct controls, and most of all to the effective incomes policy of these years. It is indeed a notable tribute to these measures that almost the sole ten months between 1945 and 1984 when only a very small rise in the cost of living occurred were the ten months after the exchange value of the pound had depreciated by 30 per cent. Between June 1949 and August 1950 the retail price index rose less than 2 per cent. In the whole of 1949, as against 1948, the index rose only 3.3 per cent and in 1950 by 3.0 per cent.[10] Exports in volume, which had stood at 127 per cent of the 1947 level in 1948 and 140 per cent in 1949, rose to 162 per cent in 1950.[10]

Sir Alec Cairncross sums up the effects of the 1949 devaluation with these words:

> 'Whether we start from the composition of British trade or from the American current account, there is evidence of a change in the balance between the dollar and non-dollar world [that is, a cut in the non-dollar world's deficit with the dollar world] that persisted into the 1950s and was an indispensable element in post-war reconstruction.'[11]

Thus 1950 started with the British economy again set fair. The pound stood in the exchange markets at near its true economic value, and so was a help and not a hindrance to exports. The economy was fully stretched, but the currency reserves were replenished by both a payments surplus and Marshall Aid. The gold and dollar reserve actually rose by £575 million during that year. As a result Britain was able, by voluntary agreement with the USA, to dispense with Marshall Aid by the end of 1950, two years before it had been contemplated. It was a major national achievement. But early optimism based on this did not take account of the effects of the Korean War, which had started a few months earlier in June 1950. It was not the outbreak of war itself, but the USA's resulting decision to buy war stocks of raw materials on a huge scale, which wrenched world prices into a new upward spiral. Rearmament in Britain and the USA, also resulting from the war, reinforced this effect. 'The Korean War', G.D.N. Worswick writes,[12] 'had a profound effect upon the economy of the US, an economy whose influence upon the rest of the world was especially great in 1950 and was to remain great throughout the Fifties.'

In the winter of 1950–51 a worldwide scramble for raw materials was another blow to Britain's recovery. For instance, between

March 1950 and March 1951 rubber prices more than trebled, wool prices nearly trebled, and tin prices doubled.[13] By February 1951 British import prices were 50 per cent higher than in 1949. The total UK import bill for 1951 was £1,100 million higher than in 1950, and only one third of the increase was due to greater volume. Even so, the main cause of the 1951 sterling crisis, as became known later, was the sharp swing of the outer sterling area into dollar deficit.[14] By the spring and summer of 1951 the upsurge in world prices had slackened off, and by the time the new 1951 government took power in the autumn the long-run slackening of demand pressure on world prices, which lasted from 1952 to 1954, had already begun. The balance of payments deficit for 1951 as a whole, though £369 million, was not large as a proportion of gross national product, and the reserve still stood at £834 million at the end of the year. A moderate round of import restriction by the sterling countries generally was enough to stem any further loss of gold and dollars.

In the six years after 1945, regarded as a whole, Britain had achieved a remarkable – and indeed by later standards, spectacular – rise in real output and exports: far greater than in any later period. National output – gross domestic product – in real terms had risen nearly 4 per cent a year between 1947 and 1951. Industrial production in 1951 was 44 per cent in volume, and manufacturing production 50 per cent in volume, above the 1946 level. Exports in volume in 1951 were 67 per cent above 1947. From a level in 1945 which was barely 50 per cent of the 1938 level, they had now risen to 70 per cent above it, thereby achieving the post-war target set by the government in 1944–5, which few people thought could really be attained.[15] Throughout the period unemployment nationally stayed close to 1.5 per cent and in 1951 fell to 1.2 per cent, lower than the authors of the famous 1944 White Paper on Employment Policy had thought possible. Nor had this impressive record of real growth and full employment brought the 'inflation' – meaning presumably an accelerating rise in prices – which later was alleged to be the inevitable effect of such high employment. Retail prices rose 5.9 per cent in 1948, 3.3 per cent in 1949, 3.0 per cent in 1950, and in 1951 (the year of the uprush of world prices caused by the Korean War) by 11.8 per cent.[14] The rise in wage rates averaged only about 3 per cent from 1947 to 1950.[16]

This record of a rapid increase of real output, exports, and investment, plus a very low level of unemployment, combined with a moderate rise in the general price level, is impressive and instructive by the standards of pre-war years and those of the late 1950s and 1960s – and by those of the 1970s almost miraculous, a golden age, though we hardly thought so at the time. And whether or not you approve of the methods by which it was done, the fact that it was done at least proves that in this way it *can* be done. Certainly one would expect, after the industrial dislocation of the war, a rapid recovery, and it is also true that later in the 1950s other countries, notably Germany and France, achieved a similar spurt with the help of Marshall Aid. Nevertheless the speedy reconversion of industry, at a time of acute material shortages and dollar scarcity, involved special obstacles as well as opportunities. Those who say that it was made easy by high demand pent up during the war are confusing real demand with effective (money) demand. It is effective demand which impinges on the economy, and effective demand can normally be created by budget and monetary policy when a government wishes. Plenty of pent-up demand existed in 1918–19; but, thrown to the mercy of *laissez-faire* policies, it produced not the high employment and steady real growth of 1946–51, but a hectic boom in 1920, as recorded in Chapter 11, followed by a sharp relapse into unemployment. Some argue that a great need to rehabilitate run-down capital existed in 1945 and that this maintained employment. But capital was run down in 1918; and it did not generate twenty-five years of full employment then.

The comparison with other periods, and the figures themselves, really leave no serious doubt that the economic successes of 1946–51 were mainly the result of a government policy of encouraging rapid rises in output, giving clear priority to exports and investment over consumption, and ensuring the fulfilment of these policies by whatever measures, financial or otherwise, proved most practicable. As soon as that government's one major failure – stumbling into the fuel crisis of 1947 – had been overcome, recovery went progressively forward. In fact in the prevailing circumstances, the most effective measure for ensuring this were budget restraint of spending, restraint of imports, and voluntarily accepted moderation in pay demands. The latter, some people may claim, was only possible because of the survival of wartime public spirit or confidence in such leaders as Attlee, Bevin, and Cripps. If there is some truth in this, that is instructive in itself. It is also illuminating that, while price increases were kept so low, very little attention was given by anyone at the time to the quantity of money created by the banks, or to its rise and fall. Indeed some of us then believed that a little more thought should be given to this question, since the commercial banks were pressing all the time to expand their profitable advances, often to private persons for personal consumption. Again it is a comment on the swing of fashion that in 1945–51 it was hard to get people to agree that a rising quantity of money was *one* factor influencing total demand, and that in the 1980s it is equally hard to explain to them that it is not the *only* influence; the simple truth being, of course, that it has always been one factor among many others.

It would be equally misleading to criticize Hugh Dalton, Chancellor from 1945 to 1947, for letting loose a flood of money and forcing up prices by his low interest rate policy. Neither the quantity of money nor the level of investment demand was materially affected by interest rates in these years, because as in wartime the banks accepted Treasury Bills, Treasury Deposit Receipts or other government securities at very low interest rates as the government requested, and kept their private advances – more or less – within agreed limits. The volume of both public and private investment was mainly decided by direct controls, not by interest rates. Though Dalton probably exaggerated the importance of cheap money, its principal effect, as in the war years, was to keep down the cost to the nation of the national debt – another marked improvement on 1914–18 wartime policy which left the taxpayer with a huge debt burden accentuated by subsequent deflation. The nationalization of the Bank of England by Dalton's Act in 1946 was no revolutionary innovation either. For the Bank's spiritual parent, the Bank of Amsterdam, when created in 1609, was owned by that city.

The 1945–51 record is therefore a standing refutation of the theory that full employment is incompatible with a controlled price level, or that the price level can only be controlled by juggling with the quantity of money. Some may possibly argue that the methods used in this period are in themselves so undesirable that they should never be used – or perhaps never be used in peacetime. But this is to argue, not that unemployment is economically inevitable, but that it is *less* undesirable than the measures necessary to prevent it. If this is the argument, it should be clearly expressed as such. One other equally outstanding lesson can be drawn from the 1945–51 experience. That period is equally a refutation of the theory that progressive direct taxation is a major disincentive to national output, and that cuts in tax on high incomes are likely to stimulate growth. Those who believe in practical experience rather than theory will note that the 1945-51 period happens to cover the years of both the highest taxation on large incomes in British peacetime history and the highest rates of expansion in the volume of national output in the last forty years. If it is argued that there was little connection between the two, that in itself would be an interesting moral from these years.

Notes

[1] H. Truman, *Year of Decisions*, p. 145.

[2] The detailed story of the US loan negotiations can be found in Hugh Dalton's memoirs, *High Tide and After*, Chapter VIII.

[3] See p. 114.

[4] Brookings Report: *Britain's Economic Prospects*, p. 184.

[5] *Britain's Economic Prospects*, p. 184.

[6] As estimated in 1980. These figures are periodically re-estimated as the years go on. They tend in most cases to turn out better than was thought at the time. See Alec Cairncross and Barry Eichengreen, *Sterling in Decline*, p. 145.

[7] *Sterling in Decline*, p. 145.

[8] See J.C.R. Dow, *The Management of the British Economy 1945–60*, p. 24.

[9] For further details of these events, see my *Change and Fortune*, Chapter 9. According to Sir Alec Cairncross, Bevin made the final choice of $2.80 (*Sterling in Decline*, p. 131).

[10] Official figures quoted in *The Management of the British Economy 1945–60*, p. 39.

[11] *Sterling in Decline*, p. 154.

[12] *The British Economy in the 1950s*, p. 6.

[13] *The British Economy in the 1950s*, p. 8.

[14] *The British Economy in the 1950s*, p. 9.

[15] See *Economic Surveys 1951, 1952*, and *1953*; and *Annual Abstract of Statistics 1955*.

[16] Official figures quoted in *The Management of the British Economy 1945–60*, p. 39.

The Easier Years

The fortunes of the pound sterling since 1945 fall into three phases. First was the struggle, already described here, to overcome the losses of the war and balance Britain's transactions, visible and invisible, with the outside world. Then came the easy years from 1952 until the early sixties. After 1951 world conditions turned in Britain's favour and British governments continued to pursue broadly sensible policies. Thirdly, serious mistakes of policy were made at the end of the fifties which unsettled the pound again in the sixties and were aggravated by even worse mistakes, of internal and external policy, in the seventies and eighties. Whereas most of the pressures and difficulties hampering the British economy up to 1959–60 came from outside and were unavoidable, many of those suffered since 1959–60 have been self-inflicted.

In the second, easier phase, that of the fifties, the new Churchill government, with R.A. Butler as Chancellor, started with two great advantages. First, the pound had been drastically devalued to $2.80. As soon as the acute Korean boom of mid-1951 was over, the pound at this level was probably no longer overvalued; and the new rate continued to assist exports and restrain imports. But, even more important, the slackening both of post-war shortages and the Korean boom brought a prolonged and substantial fall in world prices of raw materials and food which was highly beneficial to Britain. This fall persisted from mid-1951 for nearly three years. Britain's import prices and the terms of trade progressively improved. The import price index (1953=100) fell from 112 in 1951 to 99 in 1954. As a result, balance of payments surpluses were earned in 1952, 1953, and 1954. Reserves rose in the latter two years, and the pound at its new rate was secure. For not merely were world conditions easier; but the government was pursuing policies calculated to secure the main benefit from them.

It has already been remarked in Chapter 13 that the right basic commercial policy for Britain is to import food and materials without restriction at the lowest possible world prices and to maintain some restraint on manufactured imports. This policy, pursued from 1932 to 1937, achieved an industrial revival. Similarly in the 1950s it enabled in most years a balance of payments surplus to be combined with a rise in real gross domestic product and industrial output, and with a high level of employment (unemployment was at barely 2 per cent). The government continued to accept responsibility for controlling total demand, and this high level of employment was found compatible with reasonable price stability. The average rise of retail prices in these years was under 5 per cent, and in every year from 1953 to 1959 wage rates rose faster than retail prices. Real living standards rose in every one of these years (which no doubt can be seen with hindsight to explain the results of the 1955 and 1959 general elections, which some found puzzling at the time). This period shows that, given sensible policies and tolerably favourable conditions, it is not impossible to combine full employment with reasonable price stability, since it was in fact done not merely in the first few years after the war by direct controls, but also without many of them for nearly ten years afterwards.

This comparative success does not mean, of course, that there were not many defects in the British economy, that there were not minor deflationary or reflationary swings in the 1950s, or that no mistakes were made. One major mistake, intimately affecting the pound, was only very narrowly averted. As soon as the new government was formed, in November 1951, a school of thought emerged in the Bank of England and Treasury which advocated once again convertibility for non-resident sterling. This entire episode – code-named ROBOT[1] – contains elements of melodrama if not of farce. Almost no informed person would now doubt that if convertibility had been established in 1952 or 1953, the collapse of 1947 would have been repeated, and the whole of Britain's recovery set back. Nevertheless, a huge amount of governmental or bureaucratic time and effort, to the accompaniment of mysterious and embarrassing leaks, was devoted to this occult chimera on and off from 1951 to 1955. Butler, as Chancellor, appears to have been converted, at least temporarily. There were even secret talks with the US Treasury and the IMF. The pressure must have come from the Bank of England, certainly not from the economists in the Treasury. J.C.R. Dow, who in these years was working in the Economic Section of the Cabinet Office and later in the Treasury, says: 'It was evident from the beginning that the Bank of England strongly advocated speedy convertibility; and it was almost as much a matter of public knowledge that many Treasury officials took much the same view.'[2] Even at this late date it seems that, though Montagu Norman's ancient, solitary reign had ended in 1944, his vision of the pound ruling the world as *the* international currency still survived at least in Threadneedle Street. His spirit went marching on, even though the politicians now interfered. The whole episode indeed threw some retrospective light on the 1947 convertibility crisis, when the Bank failed to warn Dalton that convertibility could not work, or alternatively to make it work when the time came. More happily in 1951–4, though some technical loosening of exchange control was carried out to meet Bank of England sentiment, the main battle was in the end won by those who opposed convertibility, led reputedly by Sir Arthur Salter, Lord Cherwell, and Sir Donald MacDougall. It was not, however, till July 1955 that Butler finally silenced the rumours by affirming emphatically that the government would maintain the rate of $2.80 'either in existing circumstances or when sterling is convertible'.[3] Nothing but harm had been done by the whole escapade.

Meanwhile, on the plane of economic realities the fifties appeared to show that, owing to the more rational economic policies being pursued, the old pre-1939 eight- to nine-year trade cycle had been scotched but not killed. A rather uncertain three- to five-year wobble seemed to have replaced it. The new pattern was also more of a tremor in the rate of growth than an alternation of upswing and actual downswing in economic activity.[4] It was still, however, an international movement. A mild world recession in 1952 followed the Korean boom. Pressure on the pound was eased, partly by import and other restrictions in Britain, but mainly by the major fall in world prices. In November 1951 bank rate was raised (for the first time since September 1939 and only for the second time since 1932) from 2 to 2½ per cent, but apparently more to show the new government's ideological differences from its predecessor than for any effect on the economy. The fall in world prices in 1952 enabled the new government's restrictions to be quickly eased; and so Britain was able to take off with the marked world upswing from 1952 to a near-boom in 1955.

Unemployment, which had risen from 1.2 per cent in 1951 to 2 per cent in 1952, fell to 1.3 per cent in 1954 and 1.1 per cent in 1955. In 1954 prices were again rising, national output expanding, the balance of payments still in surplus, and the currency reserve still growing. These were indeed years when not just Britain but most of the non-Communist world, having largely recovered from war devastation and practising the new post-war policies of demand management, freer world trade, and fixed but adjustable exchange rates backed by the IMF and World Bank, were enjoying an unprecedented expansion of world production and trade. Butler spoke of doubling the standard of living in twenty-five years. But already in 1955 Britain was overdoing the pace possible in a de-controlled economy, and demand had to be restrained. Just at the wrong moment (economically), in April 1955, Butler stoked up demand by major budget cuts in taxation, and was accused of doing so in order to influence the general election which was held in May. Whether that was true or not, demand certainly overflowed in the summer and autumn, as the Chancellor himself had to admit by increasing taxation again in an autumn budget. The rise in retail prices was stepped up to 5.9 per cent in 1955, and in wage rates to 7.0 per cent; unemployment fell to 1.1 per cent; the balance of payments again swung into moderate deficit; and reserves were lost.

At this moment the phrase 'Stop–Go' was understandably coined to describe the Chancellor's record; not, however, really a very intelligent comment, if the other options were either permanent stop or the violent uncontrolled swings up and down of the 1918–33 period. In the event, after the 1955 boom British policy – as ever seeking to avoid last time's mistake – became too disinflationary, and so from this moment for the first time since 1945 British economic growth began to lag materially behind that of other Western industrial countries.[5] Disinflation, carried on right through from 1955 to 1958, involving a rise in bank rate in September 1957, restored the reserve and protected the pound at $2.80; but unemployment rose and industrial output actually fell in 1958. Yet output was still rising in the European industrial countries competing with Britain. By the spring of 1959, for the first time since 1940, unemployment in Britain was rising towards the million mark, and the atmosphere of the thirties emerged in the most vulnerable industrial areas. Mildly reflationary measures, introduced by the easy-going, empirical Chancellor, Derek Heathcoat-Amory, that spring – there was another election impending – and reinforced by a strong world upswing throughout 1959, generated a remarkably rapid recovery in demand and production in Britain. Industrial production actually rose 6 per cent that year. But the price was a growth of imports which again threw the balance of payments into deficit.

In August of this year, the Radcliffe Committee (whose members included Lord Radcliffe, Lord Franks, Sir Alec Cairncross and Professor R.S. Sayers) issued their *Report on the Working of the Monetary System*, containing some very illuminating reflections on the successful experiments of the forties and fifties. The committee examined the question whether the quantity, or stock, of money was the crucial element in the economy and most important instrument of policy. They concluded[6] that the quantity of money is

'only part of the wider structure of liquidity in the economy. It is the whole liquidity position that is relevant to spending decisions. . . . The decision to spend thus depends upon liquidity in the broad sense, not upon immediate access to the money. The spending is not limited by the amount of money in existence, [but by] the amount people think they can get hold of. . . . '

The committee also thought that the so-called velocity of circulation – the relation between the money stock and money spending – was capable of unlimited variation; in other words that the money stock was not the sole determinant of what happened.

It was in this period, however, 1958–9, that the first two really serious mistakes were made in post-war British economic policy, which progressively weakened the pound, the balance of payments, and the British economy generally. First, convertibility for sterling held by non-residents, already partly restored in 1954, was fully established in December 1958; and secondly, the quota restrictions on imports of manufactures, which had safeguarded the trade balance since 1939, but had already been relaxed, were finally abandoned. Convertibility was introduced as quietly as possible by Heathcoat-Amory, who implied that it was now largely a technical change since so many other currencies had become convertible. But in fact by allowing large sterling balances to be converted at will into other currencies the Chancellor had let loose a new adverse pressure on the $2.80 exchange rate. 'It was certainly a more significant step than the Chancellor made out,' J.C.R. Dow has commented.[7] Even more damaging was the removal of virtually all quota restraint on manufactured imports. This was all the more insidious because its effects would be gradual and could always later be attributed to something else. The damage was also lasting, because as a matter of basic policy Britain cannot remain economically viable without an export surplus in manufactured goods. Without such a surplus nothing but invisible exports are left (apart from temporary oil earnings) with which to pay for the inevitably heavy imports of food and materials required. If the pound was to stay strong, therefore, after the 1950s it should have remained a prime object of national policy to maintain the export surplus in manufactures. But in practice the exact opposite has happened as a result of a series of over-optimistic decisions to remove import restraints.

The figures are remarkable and little recognized. Manufactured goods represented only 18 per cent of British imports in 1950, but had reached 51 per cent by 1970, 61 per cent in 1978, and nearly 70 per cent in the 1980s. This extravagance in importing was a reversal of not merely the post-war, but also the pre-war, experience. For in 1928 manufactures comprised only 23 per cent of total UK imports and in 1938 only 19 per cent.[8] In any case 1959 was a bad moment at which to take this improvident plunge, since a general relaxation in other economic policies that year was calculated to generate a boom and a large increase of imports in 1960. The damage to the trade balance was immediate. Total British imports, which had been no higher in 1958 than in 1957, jumped from £3,386 million in 1958 to £4,141 million in 1960. As a result the current balance of payments, which had been in surplus in 1956, 1957, 1958, and 1959, swung into a £258 million deficit in 1960. In the words of the Brookings Report:[9]

'In 1956–58 there was a rough balance in the trade accounts; in 1961–63 an average trade deficit of about £100 m. appeared; and in 1964 the trade deficit increased to over £500 m. and produced a crisis. Thus there was improvement through 1958, some deterioration from 1958 to 1963, and then sharp deterioration.'

The Report, speaking of the trade balance, rightly rejects the view that 'British crises have been getting progressively worse since the early 1950s', and adds 'Indeed, until 1958–59, an improvement in the underlying trend appears.'[9] Some may argue that the imbalance after 1960 did not matter because the future lies with services rather than with manufactures. That would be comforting if imports of manufactures had lagged as well as exports – but they increased. And exports of services did not grow fast enough to cover the gap.

Nor is it any defence of those whose wishfully inspired decisions invited this relapse to say that they were well-meant, that it was all in the cause of freer trade, and that others were liberalizing too. These were worthy long-term aims; but the practical application was too hasty and rash.[10] If Britain, as in the mid-nineteenth century, had been a strong exporter, if the British public's propensity to consume manufactured imports had been low, these aims would have been relevant. But one notable and manifest feature of the British economy is its extremely high propensity to consume imported manufactured consumer goods – motor cars in particular. Those who took the decisions of 1958 and 1959 never ascertained, let alone demonstrated, that the economy did *not* possess such a propensity. They just, one fears, hoped that it would not, because they felt that it *ought* not to – a state of mind all too common among British policy makers in recent times. The doctrine, of which Montagu Norman was the great apostle, that because certain policies had favoured Britain in the nineteenth century, they *ought* to do so in the twentieth, still lived on. Some may argue that the increase in manufactured imports after 1959 was largely due to Britain's lack of competitiveness, not to the removal of restraint. But if British industry was not sufficiently competitive, this was all the more reason for not encouraging imports until competitiveness had been improved. If of course the liberalization had been part of a package deliberately allowing for the $2.80 rate to slide and take the strain, the other relaxation might have been more defensible. But the package excluded this also. Interestingly enough it was only after 1960, when these liberalization measures neccessitated repeated deflationary packages, that UK living standards began to fall behind those of some continental competitors.

It had been in a similar incautious and over-optimistic spirit that Britain, with the usual best intentions, undertook in the mid-fifties the lasting obligation to maintain substantial armed forces in Germany without making it an absolute condition that Germany should bear the foreign exchange (though not the sterling) cost. The balance of payments cost to Britain of military forces overseas rose as a result from £152 million a year in 1955 to £281 million in 1966–7: a subsidy in balance of payments terms from the British to the German economy.[11] Costs per serviceman have since continued to rise rapidly. The remedy for this should have been, not to refuse the military contribution, but to insist that the exchange cost was fairly borne (which it still is not).

And so the pound entered the 1960s with at least three major new burdens gratuitously laid upon it. The visible trade balance, which had more or less broken even in 1956, 1957, and 1958, fell into deficit in every year from 1959 to 1969 inclusive; and the current balance of payments, after a long run of surpluses in the 1950s, showed a deficit in 1960, 1964, 1965, 1967, and 1968. The story of the pound in the 1960s is largely a record of the struggle by governments to resist the consequences of the imprudent liberalization of 1958–9, which led remorselessly to the further devaluation of 1967. The relaxation in 1959 of both import restraints and internal policy, taken together, generated a balance of payments deficit of £258 million in 1960 (the highest since 1951) which led to new curbs on internal demand in that year and in 1961. From this moment onwards it became increasingly difficult, at the $2.80 rate for the pound, to maintain the level of demand needed for full employment without provoking an uprush of manufactured imports and so a new sterling crisis. Restrictions on demand in 1962–3 brought the payments balance into surplus in those two years. But as soon as restraints were relaxed it swung back in 1964 to a huge current deficit running at nearly £400 million a year when the new government came to power in October.[12]

Since after 1964 a whole new series of forces began to beset the pound sterling, it is useful at this point in the story to extract two pertinent morals which emerge from the record of 1945 to 1960. First, despite all difficulties, all internal and external shocks, changes of governments and unpopular 'stops' and 'go's', the remarkably and unprecedentedly low level of 1.5 or 2 per cent unemployment was maintained throughout the period, and indeed on into the sixties and seventies. And in spite of this the annual rise in the retail price index seldom exceeded 5.0 per cent. In the six years 1955 to 1960 inclusive, unemployment was below 2.0 per cent in four of them, and the highest annual rate touched, in 1959, was 2.2 per cent. The retail price index rose about 5.0 per cent in only one year, 1955, and was as low as 1.5 per cent in 1958. These figures are worth quoting, not just to look back with regret on what now seem almost golden years, but to reaffirm what many people in the 1980s seem already to have forgotten: that very low unemployment without runaway general price increases was in fact maintained in Britain for over twenty years after 1945. Nor was there any tendency, even in the late 1950s, for the rise in pay rates or prices to accelerate. Once again, it follows that if it *was* done, it *can* be done. This reminder also rightly concentrates attention on the relevant practical question: precisely what were the difficulties or failures which prevented this record being maintained in the 1970s and 1980s? It cannot be argued that it was Britain alone which, by some sort of luck, achieved these comparative successes up to the late 1960s. To give one contrary example, drawn from the precise years in question: the United States economy in the years 1960–5 maintained a high level of employment and, with the help of an incomes policy, almost no rise at all in the price level. Consumer prices in the USA rose only 1.3 per cent a year from 1961 to 1965.[13]

In the case of Britain, it may naturally be said that though employment remained high, and increasing, from 1945 to 1970, nevertheless productivity was low and real growth diappointing. A full discussion of that major issue is beyond the scope of this book, which is not intended to be an economic history of Britain. But two brief comments are worth making. First, it is of course true that, for any given level of employment, higher productivity will mean higher real output and growth. But it is equally true – and less often stated – that for any given level of productivity, higher employment will mean higher output and growth. And it may well at times be true – perhaps more often than not – that governments can influence the level of employment much more easily than the level of productivity. Nor is there any reason why they should not sometimes be able to do both. Secondly, though the real growth of the British economy certainly lagged behind that of many of her industrial competitors in the sixties and seventies, it did not start to do so until the late fifties. In the first five to ten years after the war the British economy grew comparatively rapidly. Real gross domestic product rose from 1947 to 1954 by nearly 4 per cent a year.[14] It was from the late 1950s onwards that British growth fell noticeably behind that of her industrial competitors. Thus growth in Britain remained high as long as a strong pressure of demand was combined with selected, direct physical controls, but began to slow down when more *laissez-faire* policies were adopted later.[15]

Notes

[1] A name reputedly derived from Leslie Rowan of the Treasury, George Bolton of the Bank of England, and R.W.B. (Otto) Clarke also, of the Treasury, who allegedly supported the plan.

[2] J.C.R. Dow *The Management of the British Economy 1945–60*, p. 84.

[3] *Hansard*, 26 July 1955, col. 1027.

[4] See W.W. Rostow, *The World Economy*, Chapter 24.

[5] *The Management of the British Economy 1945–60*, pp. 91–2.

[6] *Report on the Working of the Monetary System*, paragraphs 389–90.

[7] *The Management of the British Economy 1945–60*, p. 107.

[8] Alec Cairncross and Barry Eichengreen, *Sterling in Decline*, p. 15.

[9] p. 199.

[10] Sir Roy Harrod took this view (see *The British Economy*, p. 205); as did G.D.N. Worswick for an earlier period (see *The British Economy in the 1950s*, p. 69, Oxford, 1962).

[11] Brookings Report: *Britain's Economic Prospects*, p. 169.

[12] The statisticians at this time temporarily adopted a 'basic' balance of payments definition as including 'long-term capital' and so made it nearly £800 million. But the current balance was only half this.

[13] *The World Economy*, p. 350.

[14] *The Management of the British Economy 1945–60*, pp. 39 and 74.

[15] This and the later record are examined more generally in Chapter 25.

17

The Coming of Cost Inflation

For reasons described in Chapter 16 the new Labour government of October 1964 found itself faced, within hours, not merely with an economy weakened by improvident de-control of imports but with an immediately looming payments crisis. Current overseas payments were running at an annual rate of deficit of nearly £400 million, and with long-term capital outflow included, nearly £800 million. Four remedies could have been adopted: devaluation from the $2.80 rate; the floating of the rate according to market forces; restraint of manufactured imports by a surcharge or levy; or, finally, similar restraint of imports by quotas as in the twenty years up to 1959. In almost any circumstances devaluation will improve a country's balance of payments in money terms, but if governments devalue simply for this reason, without any proof of economic necessity, they will wreck any sort of international stability in exchange rates. In 1964 a convincing case for devaluation on the ground of comparative prices did not exist as it had in 1949. Also (at least in my judgement) it is morally difficult for a democratic party to go through an election giving the impression, as it must, that it will defend the currency, and then devalue next day. The case for floating the pound in 1964 was much stronger, though there is little evidence that anyone advanced it at this time very explicitly. It would have given quick relief, and economic forces would have borne responsibility for the new exchange rate which emerged. But such a decision is easier in practice for a Conservative than a Labour government. And it would have been contrary to IMF rules.

The third option – an import surcharge of 15 per cent on manufactured imports – was the one actually adopted. It immediately and impressively solved the trade balance problem –

for a time. But as it was indisputably illegal under the European Free Trade Area (EFTA) Stockholm Treaty of 1960, it had to be abandoned after eighteen months. The mistake here, on the part of senior officials as well as most ministers, was the surprising one of not realizing that in international as well as internal affairs legality is usually the best policy. In this case legality would have meant the fourth option: the restraint of manufactured imports by quota controls which had been explicitly affirmed in the Stockholm Treaty, at British insistence, to be legal. Such quotas would have enabled the curb on imports to be tightened or loosened from time to time in both quantity and range; could have been convincingly defended internationally; and would almost certainly have got the payments balance under control for the rest of the 1964 government's life.

That is supposition. In fact, while the surcharge was in force, the whole situation at first markedly improved. The balance of trade deficit was cut from £520 million in 1964 to only £237 million in 1965 and the current payments deficit from £362 million to £43 million. A major increase in exports was achieved (in volume from 111 per cent to 117 per cent in 1965 of the 1961 level) without any material rise in the volume of imports: some evidence that import restraints need not always provoke retaliation against one's exports. At the same time, thanks to a successful incomes policy, unemployment was held consistently under 2 per cent, indeed so low that some further restraints on excess demand were applied in the summer of 1965. The very high level of employment maintained in 1964–6 is yet another standing refutation of those who believe that some long-term, remorseless tide of technological advance is sweeping away all possibility of full employment. Unemployment was still below 2 per cent, not just in the 1940s, but in the 1960s, despite the mistakes in import policy already made. In 1966, with unemployment at about 1.5 per cent, the trade deficit fell further to £70 million, and current overseas payments showed a surplus of £113 million. Indeed it is some evidence of the success of the 1964 government's other policies that over the whole period from the start of 1965 till the third quarter of 1967 a rough balance was achieved on the current payments account, despite the very high level of employment[1] and a seamens' strike in 1966.

But the misjudgement of the import surcharge caught up with its authors after 1966. Because of vehement and justified attacks on its illegality from EFTA members,[2] the British government was compelled first to cut the rate from 15 to 10 per cent, and then to abolish the charge altogether in November 1966. Almost immediately, the surge of unwelcome manufactured imports re-emerged and began to threaten the $2.80 rate of the pound; and another disruptive force, added to this, made devaluation inevitable in 1967. This was the public announcement in May by Harold Wilson, the Prime Minister, that Britain was applying to join the European Economic Community. Sir Alec Cairncross speaks of

'a change of sentiment after the announcement by the Prime Minister on 2 May that the UK would apply formally to join the Common Market. . . . Although no official estimate of the balance of payments cost of joining the Community had been issued, it was known that it was likely to be substantial, and there was also a natural suspicion that, in view of this, Britain's entry might be made the occasion for a devaluation of the pound.'[3]

Financial opinion on the continent, and particularly in France, thus understood very well, even if many in London did not, that British membership of the EEC would be so heavy a blow to the British trade and payments balance that further devaluation of sterling would be probable. The visit of the French Prime Minister, M. Pompidou, in July 1966 had been heralded by persistent rumours to this effect. All these influences inclined foreign holders of sterling to convert their holdings into other currencies.[4] Indeed, as the Governor of the Bank of England himself also believed that EEC membership might involve devaluation,[5] it is not surprising that in the autumn of 1967 expectation of this (intensified by a dock strike) became so general in the exchange markets that the $2.80 rate could no longer be held. M. Couve de Murville, a senior French minister, also at the crucial moment made a speech to this effect which helped to weaken the pound.

So devaluation to $2.40 followed in November, not so carefully planned or skilfully executed as that of 1949, but also, ironically, occurring just eighteen years after that upheaval, as 1949 did after the devaluation of 1931. Even more ironically, within a few months General de Gaulle had vetoed Britain's EEC application, which had been one major contributor to the weakness of sterling. But the other basic cause of the 1967 devaluation was the excess of manufactured imports which followed the removal of quotas in 1959. This had made it impossible simultaneously to maintain for very long both full employment and the $2.80 rate, and in 1967 the government chose rightly to let the rate go. Some experts have since expressed surprise that devaluation did not prevent an immediate further increase in manufactured imports in 1968 and 1969. It seems tolerably clear to me that this increase was the effect of the de-control of manufactured imports in 1958–9, held back by the surcharge in 1964–6, despite devaluation. The Kennedy Round of tariff cuts organized internationally through the General Agreement on Tariffs and Trade, GATT (though this was at least reciprocal) naturally tended to strengthen this effect. Nevertheless in its overall and longer-term working the 1967 devaluation, though it needed time, achieved a remarkable, almost spectacular, effect on the sterling balance of payments and the pound. The current payments balance was back to a substantial surplus of £470 million in 1969, £733 million in 1970, and over £1,000 million in 1971. Overseas debts were repaid. The delay in recovery had been caused by the persistent upsurge in manufactured imports.

But while Britain's external balance was thus improving, in the years 1967–70, a new economic tide began to affect not just Britain and the pound sterling, but the whole Western industrial world: a sudden acceleration in the rate of rise in both pay rates and prices. This transformed the whole economic scene and before long the policies required to manage it, as compared with those of the previous twenty-five years. Three characteristics of this strange new economic world are now reasonably clear. First, though the rise in pay and prices did not begin in the late sixties, since both had been edging upwards since 1945, it did nevertheless accelerate markedly. Secondly, the change was international, and embraced virtually all the main industrial countries, though to a greater or less degree. Thirdly, it began several years *before* the oil price explosion ignited by OPEC at the end of 1973.

The timing, international range, and sharpness of the acceleration are well illustrated by figures given in *The World Economy* by W. W. Rostow,[7] for instance:

% Average Annual Increase in Consumer Prices

	US	UK	Japan	France	Germany
1955–65	1.5	3.1	3.8	4.9	2.3
1965–72	4.1	5.6	5.5	4.7	3.4
1972–4	8.6	11.7	16.9	10.4	6.8

Since these figures are slightly distorted by the inclusion of 1974, the year of the oil price explosion, it is worth also examining the comparison between 1963–9 and 1969–71, before oil prices shot up. The *UN Statistical Bulletin* figures for these years give the following picture:

% Average Annual Consumer Price Increase

	US	UK	Japan	France	Germany
1963–9	3.0	4.1	5.0	3.7	2.5
1969–71	5.2	7.8	7.1	5.6	4.3

What was the cause of this simultaneous, worldwide upward jerk in the rate of price increase?[8] The most usual explanation is that the Vietnam War, which intensified militarily and economically in the late 1960s, put a strain on the US economy which in turn influenced the rest of the world – rather like the more short-lived Korean boom of 1951. Certainly the Vietnam War was one factor at work in 1965–70; but it does not look like the whole explanation, at least not outside the United States. If that war had been the only operating cause, the upward pressure on prices and so on pay rates would have come from the side of demand, as it clearly did in 1951. But for several reasons the actual economic evidence from this period does not suggest that this was all that was happening. First, 1970 for instance was a 'recession' year in terms of the post-1945 short-run cycle. Production was stagnating and unemployment rising at this time in Britain and most countries outside the United States. Yet the price rise was accelerating. Secondly, these were years, notably in Britain, of low or falling profits. Net company profits as a percentage of fixed assets showed a persistent falling trend in Britain in the 1970s: from about 9.0 per cent in 1970–2 to 5.1 per cent in 1979 and 3.5 per cent in 1980.[9] A similar fall is shown overleaf in an estimate by the Institute of Fiscal Studies, published in the *Financial Times*,[10] of the pre-tax current cost accounting rate of return on capital of industrial and commercial companies:

	%
1973	9.1
1974	6.0
1979	5.2
1980	3.6
1981	2.7

Or to take another measure, Samuel Brittan,[11] quoting from *Economic Trends*, shows 'net trading profits and rent of companies' falling from 12.2 per cent of 'net domestic product at factor cost' in 1959–69 to 5.1 per cent in 1980. Yet a demand inflation almost always means high profits, because demand normally raises prices before pay and other costs are affected. The only circumstances which can explain rising prices and low profits occurring simultaneously is a cost inflation: that is, producers being compelled to raise prices not by demand but because their money costs are rising. Aubrey Jones,[12] chairman of the Prices and Incomes Board from 1965 to 1970, records that in nearly all the seventy applications for higher prices coming before the Board the reason was higher pay. Thirdly, the evidence, though it can seldom be conclusive on this point, suggests that levels of pay, if they were not rising before prices, were certainly not lagging behind. The sharpness of the rise in pay in the same years is also clear from the UN figures:

% Annual Increase in Hourly or Weekly Earnings

	US	UK	Japan	France	Germany
1963–9	4.5	6.7	13.4	8.0	7.1
1969–71	6.1	12.0	15.6	10.9	12.8

On the issue of timing, if one looks more closely at the rise in retail prices and pay rates respectively in these years, it does not seem that the initial pressure came from demand on selling prices:[13]

	UK Weekly Wage Rates	UK Retail Prices
1963	100	100
1966	114.4	112.5
1967	118.5	115.3
1968	126.3	120.7
1969	132.9	127.2
1970	145.7	135.3

The big jump in wage rates came between 1967 and 1968, and in retail prices after 1968.

These figures and the other statistics quoted in this chapter do not in themselves establish that the price rise of the late sixties was due to cost push; but they do throw doubt on the assumption that it was a traditional demand-led inflation. W.W. Rostow's[14] provisional verdict (written in 1978) on these years is that in the US both demand pull and cost push inflation were at work after the mid-1960s, but that the abandonment of 'wage-price guide-posts' in 1969 caused a surge in unit labour costs; while in Britain 'demand-pull inflation, accompanied by some wage constraint, set off a subsequent phase of determined wage-push inflation'. And this may well stand as a provisional summing up.

Coming to power in mid-1970, the Heath government was presented through the 1967 devaluation and the actions of its predecessors with the priceless boon of a £1 billion balance of payments surplus accruing in 1971, but also with the pent-up pressure of cost inflation still gathering force. What was needed in the next five years was the curbing of the cost inflation by at least as firm an incomes policy and credit policy as had operated in the 1960s. What actually occurred was a series of vigorous upward pushes to the already mounting cost inflation. Three of these pushes were self-inflicted wounds. The first was the abolition of the Prices and Incomes Board and of all effective incomes policy in late 1970. The second was the steep and artificial forcing up of British food prices and the cost of living by the adoption of the Common Agricultural Policy (CAP) in 1973–6. The third was an unrestrained expansion of private bank credit in 1971–3 which led to unprecedented speculation in the City in property and property company shares, and at its worst came near to causing a serious banking crisis. The spectacle of the property boom with its speculative profits, though it had little direct effect on the real economy, certainly did not make pay restraint, voluntary or statutory, any easier at this time.

The National Board for Prices and Incomes had been set up in 1965 and operated an incomes policy right through to 1970. This policy functioned mainly by voluntary means, backed by some statutory powers, for instance powers of delay; and by 1970 its reports had gained in authority and influence. The rise in the retail price index between 1969 and 1970 was still only of the order of 6 per cent, even though the cost inflationary forces were strongly at work and the rate of increase in average earnings was over 10 per cent. Unemployment was still as low as 2.6 per cent. It would be fair to describe the Board's struggle to keep down inflationary forces at that time as a drawn battle. With more time, support from the government, and at least toleration from industry, it might have succeeded. For in the event incomes policy and the Board did not 'fail'. On the contrary, the Board was first abolished by the Heath government, and then hastily resurrected with a pay and price freeze in November 1972 and a Pay Board and Price Commission with Statutory Powers in 1973. The effect of the temporary hiatus in pay policy was that, after a slight drop in 1971, the rate of increase in earnings had rebounded to 12.9 per cent in 1972, despite a rise in unemployment to 3.8 per cent. A very large rise in miners' wages had been forced on the government in February 1972. This brief experiment in de-control of incomes had thus brought both accelerating pay rises and higher unemployment. By 1974 the pay spiral had speeded up to 17.2 per cent,[15] and retail prices were not far behind at 16.0 per cent.

Yet in 1973, of all moments, with the cost inflation in full swing (and with the oil price explosion to come, even though this could not have been known in early 1973) Britain adopted the high-protectionist dear-food regime of the Common Agricultural Policy (CAP), and bound itself to raise food prices every year from 1973 to 1977 substantially above world prices – the most unkindest self-inflicted cut of all in Britain's post-war history. The objection in principle to taxing food and to high agricultural protectionism might not have mattered so much if the compulsory levies and duties on staple foods had been (as in fact were those under the Corn Laws between 1815 and 1846) comparatively low – of the order of 5 or 10 per cent. But in fact from the mid-seventies onwards EEC grain (including feeding stuff) prices were from 50 to 150 per cent above world prices, meat prices about 100 per cent above, and dairy products frequently 200 per cent above. For instance the EEC Commission's own agricultural report for 1977 showed EEC grain prices 110 per cent above world prices, beef 96 per cent above, and butter 288 per cent above. By the 1980s, when world deflation brought lower food prices from which Britain could no longer benefit, the gap became even wider. This steep rise in UK food prices affected all food of this type bought by the British consumer, not just food bought from the

EEC. Retail prices were for various reasons not raised by the full percentages quoted above; but since the CAP was adopted, retail prices of food generally have probably stood at an average 20 or 30 per cent above where they would have been otherwise. This is not temporary, but lasts as long as EEC membership lasts, and is not a purely nominal change such as a rise in both prices and consumers' money incomes; it is a real national loss which must show itself afterwards in either lower living standards or higher money pay, and therefore higher sterling export costs – or both. As a result of the oil price explosion and the adoption of the CAP together, the UK's terms of trade actually worsened by over 20 per cent in the two years between 1972 and 1974 – a severe blow at the real living standards of the whole nation.

In an article by Lawrence B. Krause the American Brookings Report of 1968 summed up the probable effects of the CAP on the British economy and the pound as follows:[16]

'The integration of British agriculture under the CAP of the EEC, however, would have deleterious effects on the British trade balance. The trade balance would suffer directly though net contributions to the agricultural funds and indirectly in trade through a deterioration of the British competitive position because of increased costs. Prices paid to farmers would be, on the average, higher under the CAP than under the existing deficiency payments arrangement, and prices to consumers would be sharply higher.'

The Report then concluded that the British balance of payments 'would have to absorb an adverse factor' of about £600 million a year from the third year after entry onwards.[17] This Report perceived that it was the CAP and artificially dear food which were the real threat to the British economy, and not mainly the EEC budget as many in Britain, including some in high places, have supposed.

Not content, however, with this body blow at a pound already falling in real value, the Heath government embarked in the same years, 1971–3, on the greatest bank-credit inflation in British peacetime history. In September 1971 the government introduced its new banking policy by publishing a White Paper called *Competition and Credit Control*. The effects of this experiment were notably different from what was ostensibly intended. It resulted in far more competition than credit control. The basic idea seems to have emanated from the Bank of England[18] and been foisted on a government, of which the amiable Anthony Barber was Chancellor, which can have had little or no idea what the consequences would be. Ever since the war up to this time governments, through the Treasury, had maintained 'ceilings' on the size of loans to private borrowers which the commercial banks could make; by this means they had held in check the natural urge of profit-making banks to expand their lending as far as their resources and official regulations permitted. These ceilings were now to be largely abandoned in favour of 'competition', market forces, and so on; and the main restraint was to be the price mechanism: that is, the rate of interest. 'What we have in mind', the Governor of the Bank (Lord O'Brien) explained,[19] 'is a system under which the allocation of credit is primarily determined by its cost.' But it was also part of the scheme that the reserve asset ratio of the whole banking system in future should be only 12.5 per cent (as then defined), whereas the main clearing banks had hitherto observed (though on a slightly different definition) a 28 per cent liquidity ratio.

Even an amateur student of banking affairs would have suspected that this would lead to a major credit expansion; almost certainly some Treasury officials did so. They were also not pleased that the Bank had worked the whole thing out in private without consulting them, and then planted it on bewildered ministers. The scheme was first sold to Chancellor Barber at a private dinner in January 1971.[20] Ministers, however, were persuaded to accept it for motives among which two seem to have predominated, one of which was sensible and the other less so. The first was a desire for a general expansionist strategy which, given overall and selective credit restraint and an incomes policy, would have been wholly desirable. The second, unhappily, was an ideological hunch that competition, free enterprise and market forces etc. must somehow be good things in themselves. The results[21] were spectacular. Between December 1971 and December 1974 the total assets of British banks[22] rose from £36,865 million to £85,204 million – a rise of £48,339 million or 131 per cent. Advances rose even more: by £46,747 million or 160 per cent. The banks' advances, their most profitable item, which had comprised 40 per cent of total assets in 1948–50, were nearly 80 per cent by the end of 1974. Even if deposits held by overseas residents are excluded, advances made to UK residents had increased by about £20,000 million, and both advances and deposits had doubled in three years. More pounds sterling were created in these three years than in the whole twelve hundred years' history of the pound since King Offa.

Who absorbed this huge new volume of loans and advances which created the massive increase in deposits? Not the government. Since a spate of propaganda has been disseminated in recent years, designed to suggest that credit inflation is usually, if not always, generated by government borrowing, the story of 1971–4 is particularly instructive. In the past the classic method for governments to inflate credit has been to finance budget deficits by direct new borrowing from banks, central or otherwise; this is admittedly the procedure normally followed in South America. But what happened to the pound sterling in 1971–4 was quite different. As compared with the total increase of over £46,000 million in advances, or the £20,000 million increase in advances to UK residents, the rise in lending to public utilities, national and local government from the end of 1971 till February 1975 was only about £1,800 million; while £6,000 million went to manufacturing industry, £2,300 million direct to property companies, another £2,000 million to 'other financial' and £2,000 million again to 'personal' other than house purchase. It may well be, of course, that the extra bank deposits created by all this private lending may have helped the government to borrow from the public other than the banks. But the rise in the government's borrowings in this period was in no way commensurate with the credit expansion; for which uncontrolled private borrowing of new money must bear the main responsibility.[23] The *Private* Sector Borrowing Requirement was the trouble.

The extra £6,000 million lent to manufacturing industry between 1971 and 1975 was no doubt partly needed to finance rising material prices and rising pay rates. It would be rash, however, to infer from this that the credit boom was the cause of the rise in pay rates. Figures already given in this chapter show that pay rates were already rising fast in 1969 and 1970 before *Competition and Credit Control* had ever been heard of. Some may argue that without the credit expansion the rise in pay rates could not have continued, and there is probably truth in this. But to have checked the pay rise at this stage by credit contraction alone would have meant a sharp wrench into deflation and unemployment (much as happened after 1979). One must also, when a credit expansion and a pay-and-price spiral are both moving upwards, be cautious in assuming that one or the other is the cause. For not surprisingly they normally move up together. However what is clear beyond serious dispute from this episode is that if you simultaneously remove all effective restraint, by way of either incomes policy or credit control, commercially minded banks will soon land you in a rapid credit expansion and probably an accelerated rise in both pay rates and prices. And the economic effects are precisely the same whether the borrowed money is spent on public or private account.

The consequences of the credit boom of 1971–4 were particularly damaging because so much of the new bank credit was used, not to create new productive capital, but to finance speculation in the true sense, in other words buying of assets – in this case property – not because the purchaser wished to use them, but in the hope of capital profits through rising prices. This type of operation, already described[24] as erupting in the 1929 Wall Street share and previous Florida land booms, seldom ends peacefully or happily. It was inflamed in the City of London in 1971–4 by the simultaneous emergence – presumably at first a coincidence – of an epidemic of new-fangled financial enterprises engaged in what was known as 'secondary' or 'wholesale' banking. These concerns,[25] which took various forms, accepted deposits, including the Euro-dollar deposits now rapidly expanding, and used them for purposes not normal in British banking, such as buying equity shares and real property. In 1972 and 1973 the shares of property companies, bought 'for a rise' with borrowed money, were the favourite, but by no means the only, speculative counters. Since the total increase in bank advances to property companies, 'other financial' and 'other personal' together rose by £6,300 million between the end of 1971 and February 1975, it is not surprising that real property values rose fast and far. As always in such cases, all sorts of enthusiasts, individual and corporate, joined in the scramble. Companies with well-known names such as Slater Walker Securities, First National Finance Corporation, and London and County Securities, not to mention the Crown Agents, were far from being alone.

But, as is usual in such cases and notably in Wall Street in 1929, a point was reached in the later months of 1973 when property values had risen so far in sterling terms that not enough people believed they would rise further. So those who had bought for a rise began to sell, and some of those who sold at a loss could not repay the money they had borrowed. In July 1973 the Bank of England's minimum lending rate (as bank rate was then called) had been raised to the crisis level of 11.5 per cent in a rather desperate effort to check speculation – a strange end to a dash for growth. This naturally tended to lower property values and make borrowing more difficult. And so at 9 a.m. on 19 December 1973 a series of secret crisis meetings started at the Bank of England, presided over by the Governor, and lasted till 3 a.m. the following day.[26] The immediate casualty was Cedar Holdings, an obscure secondary bank which had borrowed not wisely but too well, and could not repay because its depositors were hastily withdrawing their funds. Essentially, however, the Bank was confronted with the makings of a good old-fashioned nineteenth-century banking crisis, in which everyone rushes for cash which may then be found not to exist in the required quantities. Much in accordance with nineteenth-century precedents, in the course of seventeen hours on 19–20 December the Bank persuaded a group of clearing banks and pension funds to contribute £72 million for Cedar Holdings to be rescued, and to join in issuing a tranquillizing announcement before the markets opened the next day (20 December).

This proved quite insufficient, however, to prevent a collapse of secondary bank shares on the morning of the twentieth. On Friday 21 December the Governor was forced to call an equally secret but even more ambitious meeting of all the main City banks in order to mount a rescue operation of the unprecedented order of £1,000 million to avert what was seriously feared: a panic run on the High Street clearing banks themselves. The Bank succeeded; and by the afternoon of that Friday the celebrated 'Lifeboat' was launched with facilities on the scale of £1,000 million and a special bankers' committee to carry out the individual rescues over what turned out to be a period of several years. All this was almost unknown at the time except in vague outline to the general public or even the political world – perhaps even to the cabinet. In the best British – or Threadneedle Street – tradition, a soporific press statement was made of which only two sentences need be quoted here:

'In recent weeks a number of so-called "fringe banks" have experienced a withdrawal of deposits obtained through the money market. . . . In response to these developments, the Bank of England have established in conjunction with the clearing banks machinery whereby such cases can be promptly considered and the situation as a whole kept under continuous review.'

This time the tranquillizer worked, helped possibly by the fact that Friday 21 December was the last working day before the Christmas holiday.

Such was the melodrama, almost entirely hidden from view, of December 1973. And such was the demise of that dash for freedom: *Competition and Credit Control.* The affable Barber faded quietly out of politics and became, appropriately, a bank chairman. In the eventual outcome some £1,300 million was lent through the Lifeboat machinery to enable threatened companies to avoid default and collapse; and the loans were only repaid – so far as they were repaid – by a gradual sale over two or three years of such assets, mainly real property, as the companies still possessed. These sales led to a long fall in property values and Stock Exchange prices generally throughout 1974. The fall in equity share prices on the London Stock Exchange was the greatest since 1929–33. At the end of 1975 Lifeboat loans totalling £914 million were still outstanding, and a year later these had only declined to £783 million.[27] The total of exceptional finance provided has been put by some City authorities to be as high as £3,000 million.[28] Since many of the loans could never be repaid, the loss had to fall on somebody: the Bank of England is estimated to have borne about £100 million of this, and the big clearing banks another £50 million. (As the rise in both advances and interest rates had presented the clearing banks with a huge rise in profits, this £50 million sweetener seems fully justified.)

But since the Bank of England pays to the Treasury that part of its operating profits not put to reserve, some measure of public revenue was lost by the Bank's rescue operation, and to this extent the insolvent secondary bankers were saved from the consequences of their imprudent gambling by the taxpayer. Was the Bank of England justified in using its semi-public resources in this way? On the one hand it can be argued that this puts a private City speculator (if nominally a 'banker') in a very privileged position, since if he wins he keeps his profits, and if he loses he is rescued by the Bank, ultimately at the taxpayers' expense. Heads I win. . . . This is not exactly the traditional picture of the dynamic entrepreneur who earns high profits if he is skilful or lucky, but whose animal spirits are restrained by the knowledge that if he loses, it is he who will suffer.

As against this, the amounts of money at risk in December 1973 were so large that there was a real fear of a competitive rush for cash by depositors, which might soon have led, as happened in the United States in March 1933, to the ultimate bankers' nightmare of a revelation to the public that the available cash represented only a fraction of total deposits. Closure of the clearing banks would have brought much of the country's economic life to a standstill, if only temporarily. In addition, it would not have helped London's reputation as a world banking centre, particularly when by another strange coincidence (not them known to the actors in the melodrama) the OPEC cartel were just about to amass huge oil earnings which would seek investment somewhere. On balance, I would judge that the Bank was right to save the general banking system from possible collapse; and if it was right, it certainly acted with great speed and success. The pound sterling had a narrow shave this time, and a number of undeserving persons were distinctly lucky to have been rescued from the consequences of their own misjudgements. For the Lifeboat bailed out the just and unjust alike.

While the internal banking system was enduring the convulsions following this singularly ill-judged dash for freedom, externally the pound faced a new world. The Bretton Woods regime of fixed, but periodically movable, exchange rates broke down in 1971–2. In August 1971 President Nixon suspended the formal gold convertibility of the dollar and freed it to float down on the exchange markets nearer to its presumed real economic level. For years past the United States, as indeed it had often been advised to do, had been pumping dollars into the outside world, and the dollar had almost certainly become overvalued at the old parity. The new arrangement was converted in December 1971 into the Smithsonian Agreement with the Group of Ten developed countries, by which new parities were established. Currencies were to be allowed to fluctuate 2¼ per cent on either side of their parity, so that the rate between any two could vary by 4½ per cent from their cross-parity.

This was an attempt at medium-term stability, but it did not work for very long. The immediate effect was a devaluation of the dollar; and the dollar price of gold was formally raised for the first time since 1934 from $35 to $38 an ounce.[29]

Sterling, which after the August dollar devaluation had risen from $2.40 to $2.53 by 17 December 1971, was given a new 'middle rate' of $2.60. On 20 December it was valued in the market at $2.55. During the mid-1970s the dollar continued to depreciate against strong currencies such as the German mark and the Japanese yen. Its value against other currencies generally fell about 20 per cent between 1971 and 1978. Partly as a result of this fall in the dollar and the floating of other currencies, in June 1972 the Heath government decided to abandon the fixed rate for the pound and allow it to find its own level. Only one month before Britain had joined the EEC 'currency snake'; our honeymoon with this cold-blooded reptile was therefore mercifully brief. At the same time the British government, by removing the last preference for sterling area countries in the export of capital from Britain, effectively brought the sterling area to an end – presumably as part of the price of joining the EEC.

The main decision to float the pound was thus taken when Britain was just about to suffer the CAP and the other economic burdens of the EEC (from January 1973), and when the credit expansion described in this chapter was already under way. Fairly evidently the Heath government, though professing to regard EEC membership as an economic blessing for Britain, really understood that the result of both these policies would be a further fall in the exchange value of sterling – and decided on floating for that reason. And so it turned out. Between 1971 and 1977 the pound, after temporarily rising to $2.58 in March 1973, dropped on the exchange market by about 25 per cent against the dollar and at least 35 per cent in terms of the Bank of England's trade-weighted index of major currencies.[30] Thus in the first five years of Britain's EEC membership, though partly due of course to other factors, the pound fell by at least one third in exchange value. Before the float began, on 22 June 1972, the rate against the dollar stood at $2.57. The low point touched in 1976 (on 28 October) was $1.56. On that day, in terms of the trade-weighted index, the fall in sterling since the Smithsonian Agreement of 18 December 1971 was actually 48.8

per cent. Not till 1977 did the prospect of North Sea oil earnings begin to reverse the fall. The floating of the pound was in the circumstances a wise move; and a flexible rate, with sharp jerks smoothed out, is in the long term probably the best alternative system for the UK (as is argued later, in Chapter 25), since so much economic loss and political conflict have been caused in the past by prolonged and unsuccessful struggles to maintain an artificially high rate. But the policies actually being followed or impending in the years 1971–3 – an incomes free-for-all up to 1972, an artificial rise in food prices and living costs due in 1973, and a three-year credit spree – made the fall in the 1970s much sharper than it need have been.

Perhaps if the British government had known that at the end of 1973 OPEC would deal the whole world economy its heaviest blow since 1945 they might have desisted from imposing the other burdens. The world price of oil was nearly quadrupled between 1973 and 1974. And so the British public and the pound, already suffering from an internal cost inflation well before 1972, had all these loads – self-inflicted and OPEC-inflicted – thrust upon them at almost the same moment. As a result, between 1972 and 1975 the annual rise in the retail price index jumped from 7.1 per cent to 24.2 per cent; the rate of increase in average earnings rose from 12.9 per cent in 1972 to 26.1 per cent in 1975.[31] The trade balance on oil account worsened from a deficit of £660 million in 1972 to £3,970 million in 1976;[32] a huge deficit in manufactured trade with the EEC emerged;[33] and the current balance of payments, which had been in surplus for four years, fell into deficit in every year from 1973 to 1976. The exchange value of the pound fell to the low point in 1976 already mentioned.

How much of the damage was caused by the original spontaneous pay inflation, how much by joining the EEC, and how much by the oil price explosion, cannot of course be at all closely estimated. But clearly everything cannot be blamed on OPEC. For the rise in the retail price index had moved up from 6.4 per cent in 1970 to 9.2 per cent in 1973, *before* the oil explosion. And the fact that food prices in Britain rose faster than other prices from 1972 to 1976 (the years in which Britain swallowed the CAP), and that British prices generally rose faster than those of other OECD (Organization for Economic Co-operation and Development) countries in these years, suggests strongly that the CAP played a major part in the cost inflation. The unprecedented 26.1 per cent rise in average earnings in 1975 argues the same way. Dearer food pushed up living costs, which in turn pushed up pay rates.

The central truth about these years was that the already operating cost inflation was abruptly accelerated, but not originated, in Britain by two new factors: the oil price explosion and the CAP. From this evidence, and from the figures of pre-OPEC pay and price increases given at the beginning of this chapter, the real nature and origin of the worldwide cost inflation of the late 1960s and after becomes easier to understand. If it were true that throughout the full-employment period of the fifties and sixties the organized pay groups (including professional bodies and trade unions) in the Western industrial world had gradually come to realize their power in these conditions to enforce ever higher rises in money rates of pay, then the story of the fifties and sixties would have been something very like what actually occurred: a slowly gathering pace of pay and price increases in the early sixties, accelerating in the late sixties and seventies to a mounting spiral.

Sir Henry Phelps Brown has, very fairly I think, described what happened in these words:[34]

'At the end of the 1960s workers in much of the Western world began to display a deep-going change in their outlook – a heightening of expectations, an intensification of militancy, an increased capacity for independent action. This now appears not to have been a wave that would fall again in a number of years, but a generational shift that is persistent.'

In his *Origins of Trade Union Power*[35] Sir Henry further describes this turning point, which he calls 'The Hinge':

'This was the time when the attitudes formed in younger employees by the experience of recent years attained a critical mass with the whole body of employees, and this attitude was sparked into action by the example of student revolt beginning with the struggle in Paris in 1968. . . . The young people who were entering employment for the first time alongside [the previous generation] would be forming attitudes in settings of much greater security. . . . As their relative numbers grew, there came a time when . . . the new attitudes must predominate.'

I believe this to be a substantially sound diagnosis of what happened in the late 1960s. It would explain why an acute problem existed in the seventies which was not apparent in the fifties; why this change was common to almost all the main industrial countries; why it no longer answered to the successful demand management of the fifties; why the price inflation, low profits and higher unemployment ('stagflation') were all simultaneous and persistent in the seventies and eighties; and above all why it became so hard to check the rise in prices without creating unemployment. An old-fashioned demand inflation would have produced low unemployment and high profits, as it did in the early post-war years. Nobody talked about 'stagflation' in the 1950s. Of course in the nature of the case a diagnosis of this kind cannot be proved to be sound. But it is at least consistent with the facts; and other explanations, notably the traditional demand inflation, are not. No doubt other intervening forces, such as the Vietnam War, the oil explosion and (in the UK) the CAP, aggravated the upward pressure on money costs. But these can hardly be the main explanation, both because the upward movement began some years before two of them occurred – the oil explosion and the adoption of the CAP by Britain – and because countries not directly affected by these two also experienced the inflationary pressure. Britain and the Western world in the seventies had in fact – so the evidence suggests – stumbled into a new dilemma, generally misinterpreted then and since, which demand management alone could not resolve.

Notes

[1] Alec Cairncross and Barry Eichengreen, *Sterling in Decline*, p.175.
[2] I have described this in greater detail in *Change and Fortune*, Chapter 12.
[3] *Sterling in Decline*, p.187.
[4] Harold Wilson, *The Labour Government 1964–1970*, p.250.
[5] *The Labour Government 1964–1970*, p.252. See also T.F. Blackaby, *British Economic Policy 1960–74*, p.40.
[6] See *Sterling in Decline*, pp.202–3.
[7] pp.351–2.
[8] Similar figures are given, together with a discussion of the causes of the change, in Henry Phelps Brown, *The Origins of Trade Union Power*, pp.155–61.
[9] John Black, *The Economics of Modern Britain*, p.83.
[10] 3 February 1984.
[11] Samuel Brittan, *How to End the Monetarist Controversy*, pp.124–5.

[12] *The New Inflation: The Politics of Prices and Incomes*, p.26.

[13] As set out in *National Institute Economic Review*, August 1971, pp.90 and 91.

[14] *The World Economy*, pp.354–5.

[15] The relevant figures for this period are well summarized in the Second Brookings Report: *Britain's Economic Performance*, pp.32 and 94.

[16] Brookings Report: *Britain's Economic Prospects*, p.228.

[17] This is almost precisely the same estimate as I gave of the damage in *After the Common Market*, p.62. It turned out to be a sad underestimate, particularly of the trade deficit in manufactured goods with the EEC. See note 33.

[18] Margaret Reid, *The Secondary Banking Crisis 1973-75*, p.30.

[19] *Bank of England Quarterly Bulletin*, June 1971, p.196.

[20] *The Secondary Banking Crisis*, p.31.

[21] As revealed in the official publication, *Financial Statistics*.

[22] Defined as deposit banks, Bank of England Banking Department, accepting houses etc.

[23] This period, though the most glaring, was by no means the only one when the Private Sector Borrowing Requirement was increasing faster than the Public Sector Borrowing Requirement. In 1982–3 it was increasing twice as fast. See *Guardian*, 28 November 1983.

[24] Chapter 11.

[25] The whole episode is excellently described in *The Secondary Banking Crisis*, Chapter 3.

[26] See *The Secondary Banking Crisis*, p.3.

[27] *The Secondary Banking Crisis*, p.137.

[28] *The Secondary Banking Crisis*, pp.191–2.

[29] By the summer of 1984 the dollar price of an ounce of gold in the commodity markets stood at about $370 and the sterling price at £274.

[30] The 'effective' exchange rate.

[31] Second Brookings Report: *Britain's Economic Performance*, p.62.

[32] Second Brookings Report: *Britain's Economic Performance*, p.40.

[33] This had reached £8 billion by 1983, by which time the UK's share of the EEC's market for manufactures had actually *declined* since entry to the EEC. See *Second Report of the Trade and Industry Committee of the House of Commons*, 22 May 1984, which found the results of membership 'disappointing'.

[34] *Incomes Policy: A Modest Proposal*, pp.44–5.

[35] p.160.

18

The Petro-Pound

The new British Labour government of February 1974 came to office with no clear majority in the House of Commons, with the coal industry on strike and the rest of industry working a three-day week for lack of fuel, with a pay and price inflation steadily gathering force, and with a huge balance of payments deficit threatened by the sudden, steep rise in oil import prices. As yet Britain's net oil surplus on the balance of payments was several years away. The period of the Heath–Barber boom of 1971–4 demonstrated that with an underlying cost inflation mounting against you, you cannot (as you could in the fifties) achieve real economic growth and reasonably stable prices by a credit expansion and low interest rates alone. The 1974 Labour government's first two years demonstrated that you cannot achieve this objective in these circumstances by any kind of demand management unless you have an incomes policy. It should not have been necessary to establish either of these truths over again (they were predicted in the Employment Policy White Paper of 1944). But at least they *were* established. The government of 1974 was no doubt faced with even greater difficulties than that of 1970 because the first oil price explosion coincided almost exactly with its arrival in office. A trebling and then a quadrupling of oil prices powerfully aggravated the cost inflation and for a few years pushed the balance of payments into hopeless deficit. The UK's overseas balance of payments on oil account worsened from 1972 to 1976. Only in 1977 did this deficit begin to be reduced by British oil and gas earnings from the North Sea. The overall current balance of payments was therefore over £3,000 million in deficit in 1974, and over £1,000 million in both 1975 and 1976. The pound, now floating, fell progressively, as already recorded, to the low point of $1.567 on 28 October 1976; when the government acted vigorously, though belatedly, to bring the slide under control.

From 1974 till well into 1975 the pound was falling fast in internal purchasing power as well as on the exchanges. The government, preoccupied at first with the three-day week and with ending the Heath government's bitter conflict with organized labour, simply did not realize – or at any rate appear to realize – that it was being swept along by a remorseless cost inflation. It began by in turn abolishing Heath's Pay Board – an example by both administrations of party government at its worst. In 1974 average earnings rose 17.2 per cent and retail prices 16.1 per cent; and in 1975 earnings by 26.1 per cent and retail prices by 24.2 per cent.[1] Profits were still low,[2] and unemployment rising at the same time – the latter from 2.6 per cent in 1974 to 5.3 per cent in 1976 and 5.7 per cent in 1977. Had the inflationary pressure come from the demand side, profits would have been rising and unemployment falling. This was a cost inflation if ever there was one.

Thus in 1975–6 the government came abruptly face to face with the basic dilemma, which this book will later examine as the major problem of Western countries in the last years of the twentieth century: how do you escape from a cost push inflation when it has taken firm hold on a modern economy? If you cut off demand, and let the cost inflation run on, you will very rapidly cause very serious unemployment and waste of resources. And prices will go on rising. If you expand demand, and let costs spiral on upwards, you will generate less unemployment, but prices will rise even faster. Broadly the only way out of this dilemma is to hold down both money costs and demand until the pay pressure has moderated. And this indeed the British government came so near to achieving in 1976–7, as did few other Western governments, that by 1978–9 the price inflation and unemployment were both falling and the exchange value of the pound was rising. But this was only achieved after a number of false starts in 1974–5, and in face of a deep world recession, which was caused after 1973 by the oil price rise and the transfer of billions of pounds and dollars in purchasing power from ordinary consumers to Arab governments who could not spend them at that rate. Britain had a particularly uncomfortable gap to cover until North Sea oil earnings came to the rescue from 1977–8 onwards and so pushed the sterling rate up again.

The turning point was reached in August 1975 when the government agreed with the TUC a plan based on a maximum pay rise of £6 a week for twelve months with a freeze on incomes over £8,500. This was universally observed, and as a result average earnings came down from the peak of 26.1 per cent in 1975 to 16.5 per cent in 1976, and retail prices from 24.2 to 16.5 per cent. After this experience there were not so many people who denied that pay rises had been one main factor in pushing up prices. But this recovery was not fully realized at the time, and the oil deficit was still weighing heavily on the balance of payments. Speculative pressure on sterling therefore continued, despite various budget economies and a further pay agreement in August 1976 for a 5 per cent norm up to a maximum. When in October the pound fell on the exchange markets to its lowest rate, the Bank of England's minimum lending rate was raised to 15 per cent, and major drawings were needed on a $5.3 billion credit arranged with the IMF in June. Monetary targets and further budget cuts were announced in December 1976 – probably greater than was really necessary – and full agreement was reached with the IMF, covering a 'safety net' to protect the Bank against sudden withdrawals of sterling balances. By the early months of 1977 the Bank's reserve was recovering, and the exchange rate had settled down near to $1.70.

It can now be seen that the fall in the pound between 1972 and 1977 from $2.60 to $1.70 was caused by the persistent cost inflation in the British economy, unluckily aggravated by two simultaneous additional burdens, the oil price explosion and the effect of EEC membership on food prices and manufactured imports. The first was temporary, since Britain was due to be a net oil exporter in a few years. With perfect wisdom, the government would probably have acted sooner to check the upsurge in pay and prices which it found in full spate in 1974. But the first effective pay norm was only established in August 1975. Borrowing from the IMF was also in this case fully justified, since the IMF's main purpose is to meet temporary borrowing needs; and an oil importer, shortly to become an oil exporter, is obviously a suitable client. In the event the credits were easily repaid later out of oil earnings. As early as 1977 Britain had moved into general balance of payments surplus. But the success of the rest of the policy is the most instructive part of the story, since extracting oneself from an inflationary spiral is one of the most difficult of all economic operations. The rise in the retail price index fell each year from the peak of 24.2 per cent in 1975 to only 8.2 per cent in 1978, and average earnings from 26.1 per cent to 14.1 per cent. Unemployment reached a maximum of 5.7 per cent in 1977, and then fell gradually but steadily till 1979.

The rise in unemployment from 1972 to 1977 is again evidence that cost inflation and not demand inflation was at work, and its subsequent fall is evidence that an agreed incomes policy, by restraining pay inflation, can increase employment and production. From August 1977 the pay norm was 10 per cent except for productivity agreements. Unemployment (for Great Britain) fell from a peak of 1,567,000 in August of 1977 to a low point of 1,238,000 in May 1979. As soon as pay rates were under control, the real output of the nation rose steadily. The index of industrial production, after falling from 1973 to 1975, rose from 100 that year to 113.1 in 1979. Fixed investment in manufacturing industry rose 6½ per cent in 1977 and 8 per cent in 1978. By 1978, the balance of payments, with some growing help from oil earnings, was over £1,000 million in surplus. The pound – now a petro-currency – recovered on the dollar exchange to over $1.90. And the Bank of England's minimum lending rate was reduced to 5 per cent in the autumn of 1977.

The years 1976–9 were thus a period of marked recovery for the pound and for the whole British economy – particularly for the real economy. This is one of the few examples of any Western government in the seventies reducing both inflationary pressures and unemployment at the same time. A major share of the credit should be given to the leadership of Jack Jones in the TUC and Transport and General Workers' Union, not merely for largely devising the 1976–9 pay policy but also for persuading organized labour to accept it. The omens for the economy, with oil revenues growing fast, were set fair at the end of 1978, provided only that pay restraint was maintained. In the event that restraint did not, as has been often asserted, break down of its own accord. It was undermined by a combination of recklessly aggressive pay bargaining by certain groups and by political attacks from the then opposition. The break came when the government proposal to withhold contracts from the Ford Motor Company was condemned in Parliament on a motion moved on 13 December 1978 by an opposition which basically wished to abandon not merely incomes policies, but full employment itself, in favour of outright old-fashioned deflation. The withholding of contracts had been intended to deter the Ford Company from granting pay increases far exceeding what the existing policy allowed. The parliamentary vote naturally set off a series of competitive pay increases. Thus it was political intervention which actually breached the barriers and provoked the winter of discontent in 1978–9. But the basic issue on which the break occurred – how to restrain a private firm from granting pay increases likely to provoke general cost inflation – remains the most difficult hurdle which future incomes policies will have to surmount.

Looking back dispassionately now, however, at the whole record of the sixties and seventies, we must conclude that full employment policies were disrupted by the coincidence of the oil price explosion and the action of the organized pay groups in exerting bargaining power which they had in fact possessed since 1945, but had until the late sixties, for whatever reason, refrained from pushing too far. These two pressures together forced governments into the dilemma of having to choose either accelerating price inflation or growing unemployment. Only vigorous cost and pay restraint could have surmounted this dilemma, and only the government of 1976–9 succeeded for a time in achieving this. Those who believe that nothing could have been done by any government to stop the dam breaking in the winter of 1978–9, with all that followed, will put the whole blame on unreasonable pay demands. A fairer verdict would be that the true believers in *laissez-faire* collective bargaining must share the responsibility with the deflationists, who are always with us, and who by this time had started to call themselves monetarists.

Notes

[1] Second Brookings Report: *Britain's Economic Performance*, p.62.
[2] *The Economist*, for instance, wrote on 3 December 1983 (p.86): 'Real rates of return on capital and the share of profits in GNP have fallen for a decade.'

19

Deflation Again: 1979–83

The pound and the British economy, which had both been edging upward in 1978–9, were taken over in the latter year by a government which proceeded to treat a cost inflation as if it were a demand inflation. In the spring of 1979, before the change of government and of economic policy, employment and the nation's output were both rising. The official index of industrial production had moved up sharply and unemployment had fallen between August 1977 and May 1979.[1] Real investment had also been expanding in 1977 and 1978. National oil earnings were rising rapidly; and for the first time since 1945 the balance of payments need no longer be a brake on the growth of the real economy. To maintain this progress two basic policies were needed: a restraint on money costs and a steady maintenance of money demand. The new government, however, starting with the budget of June 1979, proceeded to do the exact opposite on each front. It abandoned any effective attempt to curb pay and cost increases, and it cut back demand by a whole series of fiscal and monetary measures. In effect the government held back demand by cancelling out the operation of the built-in stabilizers in the budget, which would otherwise have sustained it through falling tax revenues and larger borrowing.[2] The sequel was just what the critics[3] predicted, though quantitatively even more damaging: the sharpest fall in output, employment, and real economic activity experienced in the British economy since 1929–32.

The budget of June 1979 took the maintenance of the internal value of the currency as the over-riding aim of future economic policy, and assumed that the inflationary forces threatening that value originated from pressure of demand rather than costs;

although the extremely low level of profits proved that this was not so. Policy was therefore to be based on a severe and progressive limitation of government spending and government borrowing, which would, ministers hoped, limit the quantity of money available and so hold back the public's spending on goods and services. The total borrowing of the government and other public agencies, really only one among other elements in the national economy, was erected into virtually the sole criterion by which almost all other aims were to be judged. This strategy, however, could only have worked, if it worked at all, by curbing effective demand without also inflating money costs.

But the actual measures chosen were bound in many cases to inflate money costs also. The large rise of VAT from 8 per cent to 15 per cent both sharply lifted retail prices and therefore pay claims, and cut general demand through higher prices. Mainly as a result of this, the rise in retail prices shot up from an annual rate of 8 per cent in early 1979 to 21 per cent in 1980.

Meanwhile bank credit was to be limited, not by the direct ceilings on advances and by the rationing of credit practised ever since the war except during the Heath–Barber boom, but almost wholly by high interest rates. In the effort to check credit expansion by this method, the Bank of England's minimum lending rate, which had been brought down to 5 per cent by the previous government in 1977, was raised to the record level of 17 per cent in 1980. The even more imprudent decision in 1979 to abandon all the remaining exchange controls on export of capital by British residents meant that British interest rates were from now on tied to American rates. As a result for the next five years even 'real' interest rates (after allowing for falling money values) stayed at levels which were punitive for British industry, house building, real investment, and industrial modernization generally. On top of all this, the exchange rate of the pound was allowed to rise in 1980 to levels which seriously hampered British exports and subsidized imports, and then to stay at or near these levels for many months. The dollar rate for the pound rose to $2.45 on 4 November 1980 under the influence of prospective oil earnings from the North Sea and high interest rates. At that moment the decline in the 'effective' exchange rate of sterling since as long ago as December 1971 was only 20 per cent. The outcome of this series of measures was that British industry found its labour costs raised by one third in two years, its interest costs doubled, its export earnings slashed, domestic demand cut, and import competition generously encouraged.

From the point of view of the British economy as a whole the package was about as subtle in conception, and salutary in effect, as if one had driven a bulldozer into a symphony orchestra.[4] Presumably the results were not what the Chancellor, Sir Geoffrey Howe, had intended, since he explained in his first budget speech that his chief aim was to convert Britain into a growth economy. In fact the official index of industrial production, which had risen over four years from 100 in 1975 to 113.1 in 1979, dropped back in three years to 100 in 1982.[5] The output of British manufacturing industry fell by 15 per cent in these three years (at the worst point nearly 20 per cent); and the output of production industries as a whole, including oil and gas, fell about 10 per cent in real terms. If oil and gas are excluded, the fall in these industries between 1978 and 1982 was close to 15 per cent.[6] These were steeper annual falls in real output than occurred either in the Victorian depression years of 1873–96, or in the case of manufactures in the Great Depression of 1929–33. If oil and gas are excluded, the level of total industrial production in 1973 (the year of the oil explosion and UK entry to the EEC) had not even been regained in 1982. As a result unemployment, which had fallen to 1,238,000 in May 1979, started to rise in the second half of that year; rose by 100,000 a month throughout 1980; reached 2 million in 1981, 3 million in 1982; and still stood at over 3,160,000 in the summer of 1984. In the twelve months ending January 1981 unemployment actually rose 65 per cent. In the same twelve months it rose 3.9 per cent in Italy, 13 per cent in France, and 26 per cent in West Germany. By September 1983 in percentage terms UK unemployment had increased from 5.3 per cent of the labour force in 1979 to 13.3 per cent. In the summer of 1984 UK unemployment was still rising, and total real output, apart from oil, was still lower than in 1979.

The sudden sharp rise in unemployment plainly cannot be attributed, as some people have tried to argue, to the forward march of industrial technology, automation, the micro-chip, and so forth. Technological progress in industry did not suddenly begin in May 1979. The abrupt change which occurred in that month was a change in economic policy: from moderate expansion to severe – almost violent – deflation. Company liquidations, for instance, suddenly shot up from 6,890 in 1980 to an annual rate of close on 13,000 in 1983; and even the most puritanical deflationist would hardly attribute this to technological progress. Nor can the 1979–82 collapse in output and explosion of unemployment in Britain be mainly attributed to the secondary depression of world demand which followed the further uprating of the price of oil by the OPEC cartel in 1979–80. It is true no doubt that a further contraction of world demand (and inflation of costs) was caused by this second drastic rise in the oil price, and that this was aggravated still further by deflationary policies in various parts of the world. But by following more prudent and moderate economic policies a number of other countries avoided anything like the collapse suffered in Britain. In 1982, for instance, unemployment was held to 1.9 per cent in Norway, 2.9 per cent in Sweden, and 4.1 per cent in Austria. In Austria, thanks to an effective incomes policy, it was held below 5 per cent up to mid-1984, with the rise in prices around only 6 per cent.[7] In Sweden real recovery was well under way in 1983–4, with unemployment at 3.5 per cent.[8] In 1983 and 1984 real output and employment in the USA were growing rapidly, thanks to a large budget deficit. In addition, since the British economy had become by 1980 a net gainer from a higher world oil price, it would be somewhat perverse to quote that higher price as the cause of the damage.

Alternatively, can it be maintained that the heavy loss of real income in these years was justified by increases in productivity in British industry? Output per person employed in the whole economy, which had risen from 100 in 1975 to 109.5 in 1979, actually fell back to 107.5 in 1980 and then recovered to 112 in 1982.[9] The rise from 1979 to 1982 was thus smaller than that from 1975 to 1979. In recent history there have been several other periods when productivity rose faster than between 1979 and 1982. For instance in manufacturing industry output per hour worked rose 16.6 per cent between the first quarter of 1971 and the second quarter of 1973, as against 13.3 per cent between the last quarter of 1980 and the first quarter of 1983.[9] In any case the true measure of national productivity is not the narrow one of 'output per person employed', but rather the total output achieved compared with the total of persons employable. In this true sense a rise in unemployment is a fall in national productivity. As W.H. Buiter and M.H. Miller rightly put it,[9] after the above analysis of recent productivity statistics, 'The current productivity record of much of British manufacturing industry is like the cricket team that improves its batting average by only playing its better batsmen! As long as the tail-enders score some runs, however, it would surely be better to play them even if it does lower the side's batting average.'

Some half-hearted attempt has also been made to argue that all the real economic loss and damage was worthwhile in order to maintain the value of the pound sterling at home and abroad; though this idea too comes oddly from those who claimed that their policy was partly designed to promote economic growth and higher production. The actual effect of the general post-1979 measures was first to lower the internal value of the pound sharply by raising retail prices by over 20 per cent, and externally to push up the pound's exchange value to an unsustainable level from which it then fell to a low point $1.05 in the exchange crisis of January 1985. But to advance this plea is to fall into the major delusion of thinking that the value of the currency is something so sacrosanct in itself as to justify destruction of real national wealth and impoverishment of a major section of the population.

For the most devastating effect of the 1979–83 deflation has been the huge loss of real production and real national income in these years. A figure of unemployed manpower rising to 13.0 per cent, and the reports from the Confederation of British Industry on idle capacity throughout the period, make it seem highly probable that from the end of 1981 the proportion of ostensibly usable national productive resources – labour and plant – left idle must have been very large. Since only about 2 per cent of Britain's labour force on average were unemployed in the first twenty years after the war, and 13 per cent in 1983–85, it does not seem unreasonable to assume that at least 10 per cent of productive capacity must have been unused in the later year. A more sophisticated estimate of the lost income can be found, for instance, in *The Economics of Modern Britain* by John Black.[10] Mr Black is assessing, not strictly what might have been produced in 1980 or 1983–85, but what would have been produced then if the rate of growth in the post-war years up to 1973 had been continued. He tentatively estimates on this basis that gross domestic product would have been 6 per cent higher in 1980. Since the percentage of manpower unemployed rose between 1980 and 1983 from 6.8 per cent to 13.5 per cent, an assumption of 10 per cent capacity unemployed and income lost in both 1983 and 1984 can on this evidence hardly be an overestimate.

In 1983, however, gross domestic product was running at an annual rate of about £300 billion in the prices of that year. The loss of income due to underemployment must therefore have been something approaching £30 billion a year. Of course such an estimate cannot be precise. But as an order of magnitude, £30 billion a year is a figure which greatly exceeds most of the estimates of budget economies, public sector borrowing, tax changes and so forth, which are given so much publicity (important as these are if seen in their true perspective). It is equal to the total cost of Defence and Health and Personal Social Services put together. And the loss of real income in a given year from unused productive resources is something that can never be regained. Whatever happens in the future, the houses that might have been built by unemployed labour in 1983 and 1984, the new plant that might have been installed, the naval equipment that might have been supplied from idle shipyards – are all lost for ever.

Worse still, as the process of deflation spreads through the system productive capital which has stood idle too long and can no longer be maintained is finally closed down and in effect destroyed. In Britain since 1979 one after another plant or productive enterprise, which would have been perfectly viable, well managed, and fully employed if demand had been generally maintained, has been destroyed through no fault of its own. Sadly the examples are too well known to the British public for there to be any need to enumerate them here. But destruction of future wealth-producing capacity – and defence capacity – has certainly occurred on an unprecedented scale in the British economy throughout the 1980s to date.

It is sometimes argued that all this carnage is necessary in order that new industries and enterprises should support the old. But this is a highly superficial and oversimplified assumption. Naturally it is most desirable that new forms of production should expand and older ones contract; and in a reasonably fully employed economy this will, and does, happen without unemployment being created. But the fact that old industries are dying does nothing in itself to ensure that new industries will be created or will grow. For governments simply to let old industries die,, and do nothing to stimulate demand for the products of the new, is a sure way to destroy a modern industrial economy; and it is not the method by which new, large-scale, technically advanced industries were created by countries such as Japan and even France, which have launched them successfully in recent years. The right way to encourage the smooth growth of new capacity is to ensure, so far as is humanly possible, that the new enterprises absorb manpower at the same time and place as labour is released from the old. Otherwise the whole operation may well on balance diminish, instead of enhance, the total income and wealth of the community.

Finally it is claimed that by the 1979–84 experiment in old-fashioned deflation the annual rise in prices generally had been reduced from about 10 per cent to 5 per cent. This itself is true. On the hard factual test of these years, therefore, the cost to the nation of this 5 per cent relief (perhaps temporary) has been the sacrifice of £30 billion or so a year of real national income, the destruction of 10 per cent or more of our industrial capacity other than oil, and the loss of employment by about 2 million persons. Unhappily the rise of the North Sea oil industry does not compensate for the loss of other capacity: the oil supplies may dwindle in the 1990s. The destruction of productive capacity in the 1980s has thus inflicted particularly serious, because lasting, damage on the future of the pound sterling and the British economy.

After thirty-five years of constraint on economic policy caused by chronic balance of payments difficulties, Britain was granted from 1980 the remarkable and unpredictable good fortune of home-produced oil likely to flow in large quantities for some fifteen years. This conferred on the country two enormous blessings: fifteen years' freedom from balance of payments worries; and very large revenues, public and private, which could be used for investment in new capacity to produce the exports which would pay for essential imports when the oil ran out. The balance of payments gain at the peak should amount to between £10 billion and £20 billion a year, and the budget revenues to £10 billion. At the time of the North Sea discoveries almost every responsible commentator agreed, and urged publicly, that a major share of these revenues must be used for investment in the future and not dissipated in current consumption or, still worse, in the mere waste of unemployment. The example often quoted as a warning was that of the Netherlands, who twenty years earlier had pioneered major oil and gas fields and allowed them at the peak to raise the value of the currency too high; thus damaging the other Dutch export industries, and threatening serious difficulties when oil and gas supplies began to decline. Yet in the first few years of the UK's brief period of oil riches we have done worse, not better, than the Dutch; and would today, if oil revenues were suddenly eliminated, be left with an unmanageable deficit on our overseas trade and payments.[12]

To take full advantage of the pound sterling as a petro-currency the wisest policy would have been not merely to build up currency reserves in the good years (as was in some degree done), but to use the oil revenue for creation of new productive capital, and to smooth out fluctuations on the exchange markets so that the pound neither rose so high as to damage exports, nor fell so low as to raise too far the price of imported food and materials. However since sterling became primarily a petro-currency, its exchange value has been allowed to fluctuate wildly with very little apparent plan, policy, or purpose. On the dollar exchange market the pound, after moving fairly narrowly between \$1.70 and \$2.0 in 1977 and 1978, and having as already mentioned[13] shot up to \$2.45 on 4 November 1980, when oil reserves seemed limitless, then fell back to \$1.78 in September 1981 and had sunk to \$1.05 in January 1985. The dollar rate admittedly exaggerates the fall of the pound in 1982 and 1984, since the dollar itself was rising persistently in terms of most other currencies. High interest rates in the USA and a check to US overseas lending in 1983 encouraged the rise in the dollar, and the absence of exchange control in Britain made it all the harder to resist the fall in the pound. In terms of the 'effective' exchange rate against other main currencies the depreciation of the pound was certainly less in 1982–4 than with the dollar alone. By the end of 1983 the 'effective' rate had dropped about 17 per cent as against the 1975 average rate. This fall in the exchange rate was evidently the main reason why production in the UK generally did not fall even further in 1984 and 1985, even though unemployment was still rising. Nevertheless by the end of 1984 the depreciation was approaching the point where an uncomfortable rise in import prices and so in living costs generally might be threatened. Though Britain has indeed suffered much from unduly rigid exchange rates in the past, this last chapter in the story shows clearly enough that it is possible to swing too far the other way. The wild fluctuations of sterling in the 1980s so far have certainly gone beyond what was desirable from the point of view of either long-term export promotion or pay restraint.

In any fair and final judgement, however, on the whole 1979–83 plunge into deflation, it must be counted a tribute to the recuperative powers of the British economy that the downswing showed some signs of flattening out by 1983–4 despite the treatment the economy had received in the previous four years. Perhaps this is what Adam Smith meant when he remarked that there is a 'lot of ruin in a nation'.

If one looks back meanwhile from the 1980s at only the nineteenth- and twentieth-century chapters of the story of the pound, one or two points emerge which are worth discussing at this stage. One basic condition which made the nineteenth-century gold standard system workable was the ability of employers actually to reduce pay rates in depression periods. During the downswing years of the regular nineteenth-century trade cycle it was not unusual for money wages to fall, if only slightly;[14] this fall and the resulting drop in industrial and other costs were probably one cause of the subsequent recovery. If money wages could not have been cut, an obstinate gap would have opened up between the gold value (and therefore commodity value) of sterling and the real wages which British labour was claiming. That gap could only have been bridged either by a change in the gold value of sterling (as after 1931) or by an extreme and probably intolerable level of unemployment.

The major difference between the pre-1914 and post-1918 world was that in the latter money pay rates could no longer actually be reduced without extreme difficulty. This produced a new ball game whose rules had not in Britain become familiar to the participants and therefore workable until at least the 1930s. The major change in the post-1945 world was that money pay rates not merely could no longer be reduced, but actually had to be raised every year by means of a new institution known as an 'annual pay round'. That revolution in turn required yet another set of new rules, in the absence of which the system was by the 1970s again becoming unworkable, and beginning to swing uncontrollably between severe price inflation and indefensibly high unemployment.

One other moral at least emerges with reasonable clarity from the long history of the pound. Little or no correlation can be found between periods when the value of the currency was fairly stable and periods when the real living standard of the people was high or rising. Real standards have risen both in periods when the value of the currency was stable or rising, and when it was falling. It is generally agreed that living standards and real wages in England in the fifteenth century[15] were unusually high. Yet two major devaluations of the silver value of the pound were carried out in 1411 and 1464. During the two hundred years' reign from 1717 (apart from the Napoleonic Wars) of Locke's fixed gold value of sterling, it was not until about 1860 that the real living standards of most of the British people began substantially to rise. On the other hand real standards rose between 1873 and 1896, when prices were falling and the value of the pound rising. If we turn to the years of greatest success in economic policy in this century and perhaps in any century – broadly 1945–60, when the standard of living and the total output of the nation were indisputably rising most of the time – we find that these were years during which the value of the pound, whether measured in gold, dollars, or commodities generally, was persistently falling. This in itself is one of the most illuminating lessons from the whole long history of the pound. If we then look at the bare price index figures in the Appendix to this book, we could assert for instance that the pound in 1954 was worth about one thirty-eighth of its commodity value in the fifteenth century; or alternatively that its value in 1983 was about one fiftieth of its value in 1750. This would tell us something about the history of the pound, and a little about the economic history of Britain, but very little about the comparative living standards of the people at these various dates.

Despite rising standards after 1945, however, in the 1980s Britain and most of the Western world have found their economic life still swaying uncertainly between excessive unemployment and excessive price inflation, without any clear method of resolving the deadlock being yet agreed or apparent. What escape is possible, it will naturally be asked, from this modern form of the old dilemma, and what new system of rules can be devised? The remaining chapters of this book are devoted to the search for an answer to those questions.

Notes

[1] See p.162.

[2] See Willem H. Buiter and Marcus H. Miller, 'The Macroeconomic Consequences of a Change in Regime: the UK under Mrs Thatcher', pp.24–8.

[3] See Chapter 23.

[4] The internal government discussions which led to this curious policy mixture are described in some detail by William Keegan in Mrs Thatcher's Economic Experiment, Chapters 4 and 5.

[5] Annual Abstract of Statistics and National Income White Paper.

[6] Annual Abstract of Statistics and National Income White Paper.

[7] The Economist, 2 April 1984, p.59.

[8] Financial Times, 26 April 1984, p.3.

[9] 'The Macroeconomic Consequences of a Change in Regime: the UK under Mrs Thatcher', p.76. If the productivity comparison is made between 1973–7 and 1979–83, it is more favourable to the latter period (see Samuel Brittan in Financial Times, 25 June 1984).

[10] Chapter 2.

[11] Samuel Brittan (in Financial Times, 5 July 1984) gives some ground for thinking that by this date so much capacity had been lost that reviving demand might soon run up against actual lack of capacity.

[12] See pp.271–2.

[13] See pp.168 and 243–4.

[14] See W.H. Beveridge, Unemployment: A Problem of Industry, pp.42–3. Most markedly, between 1874 and 1886 Beveridge's index of money wages (1900 = 100) fell from 91.7 to 83.1.

[15] See, for instance, Henry Phelps Brown and Sheila V. Hopkins, A Perspective of Wages and Prices, pp.28–9.

20

Three Crucial Flows

In attempting to answer the critical questions asked at the end of Chapter 19, this and succeeding chapters will try, not to devise any novel analysis, but rather to elucidate more concisely what many economists have already said. In so doing, for the sake of clarity and simplicity they will stick to certain main essentials, which will enable the argument to concentrate on those processes which are capable of control and are responsive to practical policy. In learning to use a car one is primarily interested in how to drive it rather than in every detail of its intricate mechanism, still less the method of its manufacture. The aim will be to examine, in the light of the historical record, the main forces which determine the level of a community's output, employment, living standards, and price level; the inter-relationship of the money economy and the real economy; and the extent to which rational, human control can steer these elements towards the desired end in the real world. Hypothetical worlds will also be disregarded. This simplification does not involve assuming that innumerable other complications, qualifications, and peculiarities do not surround and affect almost every economic process. On the contrary it is to assume that these do exist, and must be allowed for. Living standards, for instance, at a given moment partly depend on things such as national resources, inherited equipment, the weather, efficient use of capital and labour, and human intelligence. Of course there is danger in oversimplification. No doubt, as Oscar Wilde said, the truth is never simple. But there is also a risk of allowing the mass of qualifications to obscure the central realities, of not seeing the wood for the trees, or indeed the trees for the branches, or the facts for the algebra. Some recent economics has perhaps been in danger of burying central truths in a forest of complexity.

It will also be helpful to look first at the operation of these forces within a 'closed system', that is, an economy which does not indulge in transactions with other economies using a different currency. This does not mean that the UK – a notably 'open', perhaps too open, economy – does not engage in such transactions, or that these transactions are not highly important for her future, but only that the implications can be more clearly understood separately. For some aspects of the central problem are common to both closed and open economies. The pound sterling is not unique in trying to be a means of exchange and a measure of value at the same time. Thirdly, the special problems of the UK will be examined separately later, both because some of them *are* special, and because I believe there is a good deal of confusion between difficulties specific to the UK and others which are more general.

A brief note about use of words will also be useful . First, the reader may have noticed that 'inflation' has been very sparingly used in this book. The term's ambiguous use has probably caused as much confusion as anything else in contemporary economic discussion. Few if any economists before, say, 1950 would have talked of 'inflation' when they meant a rise in the general price level or just rising prices. Yet today even serious journals print the ridiculous phrase 'rate of inflation'. In such cases, what does 'inflation' mean? Does it just mean a rise in the general price level? If so, why not say so? If not, what does it mean? A general rise in prices can be caused by a fall in the supply of goods as compared with an unchanged volume of spending on those goods. Is this 'inflation'? If qualified in phrases such as 'cost inflation', 'demand inflation', and 'dividend inflation', a reasonably specific meaning is conveyed. I propose therefore to use the word 'inflation' on its own to mean solely a general rise in prices caused by an expansion of the currency beyond the point needed for full use of real resources. A briefer definition that is still clear is difficult to find. Also confusing to many is the overworked phrase 'money supply'. To non-economists the word 'supply' suggests a flow, not a stock of money existing at a given moment. So the hybrid 'money supply' will be banished from this book, and the animal will be called the money stock or quantity of money, which is what it is...

For much of the nineteenth century, as already mentioned,[1] classical economics was hampered in its attempt to explain unemployment, because of Say's Law. This rule taught that in a process of exchange the supply of goods and services constituted demand, and therefore a lack of total demand relative to total supply was impossible. This view prevailed, despite a famous passage of Malthus[2] in which he described the 'opinion of M. Say' as 'the most directly opposed to just theory and the most uniformly contradicted by experience' of all the informed opinions he knew. The great advance of twentieth-century economics was to realize that the demand which actually influences prices, output, and employment is effective demand – money in people's hands seeking to be spent. This recognition enables one to start from a simple basic truth: *The total of money spent in any period on all final goods and services must be equal to the total of money received in that period by those producing and distributing them, because it is the same thing.* What is paid by the purchasers is received by the sellers. One woman's spending is another woman's income. Only expenditure on *final* products is relevant here, since the cost of intermediate, semi-manufactured goods is covered in the final price; and it is the final consumer (or in the case of capital goods, the user), including public authorities, who pays for the goods. Not merely consumer-durable goods but capital goods too must be included in the definition, since these goods represent a major element in output and employment, and the user of them, however he raises the money, is the final purchaser.

Total Effective Demand therefore means here the total of final expenditure on both capital and consumer goods and services. It is the first of three crucial flows which interact with each other. Strictly speaking, it should be called total final expenditure, rather than total effective demand, since some consumers will be seeking to spend money, which constitutes effective demand, but will fail to spend it because they cannot find what they want to buy. But this un-spent margin is not a major item, and since most people interpret the word 'expenditure' as consumer spending rather than capital spending, it seems clearer to use the phrase 'total effective demand' for the money flow in question. (I say 'total' because the alternative of 'aggregate' demand, output etc. seems to have no purpose other than that of using three syllables instead of two.) In the argument that follows, therefore, the phrases 'total effective demand' or 'total demand' are used in an identical sense to describe this money flow. It corresponds, for instance, to what James Meade and David Viner in *Stagflation* Vols I and II call Money GDP.[3] In the UK in 1982 it was running at £275 billion a year.[4]

This first of the three crucial flows – total effective demand – is the key factor, indeed the prime mover, in the modern economy. It is itself determined in turn by a whole family of influences, the most important of which are the incomes of consumers, private and collective; the proportion of this which they choose to save; the government's spending on goods and services and the taxes it raises, together with the pay and benefits which it hands out; the decisions of businesses to buy equipment; the money they are able to raise in order to do so; the action of the banking system in creating a larger or smaller quantity of money available for lending; and the effect of the rate of interest in disposing consumers or investors to borrow more or less. All these may raise or lower the flow of total demand in any one period. However the most important characteristic of total demand, both for understanding and for practical policy, is that it is a *flow* and not (like the quantity of money) a static stock. The distinction is fundamental. A flow is something which only has meaning in terms of a given period of time: so much per week or per year. A stock exists at a certain instant in time. The profit and loss account records the flow and the balance sheet the static picture. The latter is a photograph, the former a film.

The second crucial factor is also a flow, though in this case not of money but of *real* goods and services. It consists of the total of all final goods and services, consumer and capital goods, available for the consumer or investor, public or private, to buy in the relevant period. It is, I think, best called Total Output,[5] if this is understood to include all services as well as physical goods. Unhappily this flow cannot, like money, be counted in one single unit, because you cannot add together pints of milk, tons of coal, and gallons of petrol. The total may therefore appear at first sight to be less, rather than more, real compared with its monetary opposite number. It is possible, however, to measure changes in the various flows of physical products, 'weight' them according to their share in the value of the total flow, and so establish an index of total real output. Alternatively for the same purpose the total value of output may be corrected by an average of the principal price increases or decreases which have occurred. Quite apart from the fact that total real output is the object of all economic activity, and the basis of the standard of living – you cannot consume something until it has been either produced or imported – anyone who has doubts about the reality of total real output should reflect that if it did not exist, there would be no such things as a value of money, inflation, deflation, a price level, or a cost of living. So we may reasonably assume that, though elusive in theory, total real output certainly exists in fact. It is broadly determined in any given period by two factors: first, the available resources of manpower, materials, land, equipment, savings, organization, efficiency, technical knowledge, skill, training, education and so on; and secondly, the flow of money spending already described, which is indispensable to activate these resources and ensure that they are used. Neither will achieve much without the other.

There is also a third crucial flow in the money economy which is just as indispensable as the first two but less often mentioned. This is the total flow of all money costs: all payments to all the factors of production of final goods and services – wages, salaries, rent, depreciation, profit and other interest on capital – which have to be covered if all the means of production are to be fully used. This total must include the cost of producing final capital goods as well as that of producing final consumer goods, if it is assumed that payment for capital goods, however financed, is included in total effective demand. This third flow – Total Costs – is thus not an actual flow but normally a hypothetical one: what would be covered and has to be covered if all resources are productively employed.[6] In a private-enterprise or mixed economy at least the minimum level of profit necessary for production and employment to continue must be included in total costs, because without such a return equity capital will not be forthcoming, and without profit an enterprise must in time close down. Naturally, total costs is a money flow.

In the acute deflationary conditions imposed in the UK in 1979–84, total costs, which are not of course estimated as such in the official statistics, must have exceeded total demand by at least 10 or 15 per cent. At any given time in any community the actual figure of total costs will itself depend on pay rates established by collective bargaining or otherwise; rents and interest fixed by legal contracts; the price of materials and equipment; customs and excise duties and levies and local rates; the profit needed for the enterprise to survive; and, more indirectly, the whole current structure and organization of business and commerce. (Taxes on profits would normally be counted as a levy on income rather than a cost of production.) Few of these costs except profits can be varied in the short term by a firm's management, and only a limited range of them even in the longer term. But if receipts do not cover them, the enterprise cannot long survive.

Such in outline are the three crucial flows which constitute the essential dynamics of the modern money economy. If one examines their interaction, the first salient fact which emerges is this. The value of money – of the pound sterling or whatever – that is, the price level, is the ratio of the first to the second flow: of total demand to total output. The total value in money units of output sold, which is equal to the total spent on it, must also be equal to the total volume of units of output multiplied by the average price of these units. As an example, if all output consisted only of 1 billion gallons of petrol a year, the price was £1 a gallon, and all output was sold; then the total expenditure of the community, the total value of sales, the total costs (including profit) of the producers, and the total income of the community would all be £1 billion *a year*. If output of petrol was doubled next year to 2 billion gallons, and money incomes and expenditure remained the same, the price would fall[7] to 50p a gallon, and everyone's real consumption and living standard would be doubled. If on the other hand the community's money income and expenditure were doubled, and the supply of petrol was unchanged, the price would rise to £2 a gallon, and real consumption and living standards would be unchanged. There are many other possibilities even at the level of this very crude arithmetic. The supply of petrol might by some chance be cut by one half to half a billion gallons, and the total money spending remain the same; in this case the price would double and real consumption would be halved. (Some bewildered persons might then complain that 'inflation' had occurred, and even that this was the 'cause' of the fall in living standards.) Alternatively again, the flow of money might be halved and the supply of petrol be unchanged; in which case the price would again fall to 50p a gallon, but the living standard of the community as a whole would be no better and no worse than before. For living standards, strangely enough, depend on the supply of real things, and not on juggling with money and prices, except in so far as the latter themselves affect the supply of real things.

The simple arithmetic above is the heart of the whole matter, lurking behind much mystification. For though the actual economy which we all know consists of millions of commodities, and not one, and millions of consumers and producers, the central truths survive and the laws of arithmetic still prevail. It was indeed this particular elementary truth which Irving Fisher was trying to express in 1911 by his famous equation $MV = PT$.[8] What he meant was that the volume of goods sold multiplied by the price level is equal to the flow of money spent on them: an arithmetical truism. But he blurred the exposition in two ways: first, by starting not with the *flow* of spending, which in fact impinges on the flow of goods, but with M (the static stock of money) he was forced to perform an intellectual (or algebraical) sleight of hand by slipping in V (the 'velocity' of circulation) in order to transform the irrelevant M into the actual operative flow (MV). But V tended to cause obscurity in the debate because it meant little more than 'what converts the stock into the flow' – a purely statistical device. Its use is rather as if one were to define death as 'what converts a live person into a dead one', and then imply that one had explained what happens. The 1959 Radcliffe Committee on the Working of the Monetary System said very fairly that the velocity of circulation 'is a statistical concept that tells us nothing directly of the motivation that influences the level of total demand'. In addition the Fisher equation left quite unclear whether V might not change frequently, unpredictably, or otherwise; in other words whether total effective demand bore any special relation to the quantity of money. If it did not, then changes in M did not throw much light on P (the price level).

The second confusion arose from the final symbol T (transactions – though some disciples interpreted it as 'trade'). But what transactions? Taken literally, the word would include all the buying and selling of 'intermediate' goods through all stages of manufacture and distribution, and indeed exchanges of property claims and all manner of other wheeling and dealing. It can naturally be argued that the more exchanges of this kind occur, the more work would the money stock have to do. But it would perhaps have been more illuminating if Fisher had focused on the flow of final goods to the consumer or user, which are what the public generally regard as determining their living standards, the price level, and the value of money – the goods and services which are now accepted in most countries as rightly included in indices of consumer prices, retail prices, or the cost of living. It has always seemed to me that for these reasons Irving Fisher's V and T have tended to obscure rather than illumine the truths he had in mind, and that it is therefore worth restating these truths more simply. Possibly the historical and understandable obsession in economics with the 'quantity of money' was what induced Fisher to insert the not strictly relevant M into his equation. But however that may be, why should it be necessary now, somebody may well ask, to drag this moribund equation into the argument at all? Because, unhappily, M has in recent years raised its venerable head again, and the confusion over its significance has still to be resolved.

The general proposition that the price level depends on the flow of effective demand and the flow of output gives rise to one seductive false inference that must be avoided. It is true that the forces involved must so settle down that the volume of output multiplied by the price must equal the total value of the money spent. It is also true that if the flow of output changes and all else, including demand, remains the same, or if demand changes and all else remains the same, the price level must change accordingly. But it is not true that the flow of output and the flow of demand are the *sole causes* of the price level being what it is; or that human agencies can manipulate that level simply by varying the magnitude of one or the other of these flows. To say that would be to confuse identity with causation. For there are additional forces involved, working either through these two or in some other way. For instance an upward pressure on the level of money costs, not caused by or connected with any change in demand or output, may push up prices and so compel the other forces to adjust themselves to the new situation.

The reason for this is that most enterprises, if their money costs rise beyond a certain point, cannot long remain in business unless they also raise prices. That possibility, which may look like a special case, has in fact become crucially important in the actual world of the 1970s and 1980s. It fully deserves the name 'cost inflation' which it has been given earlier in this book, and the main argument will return to it later. The essential point at this stage is that a general rise in prices may have more than one type of cause. Much muddle has been inflicted on recent economic debate by the fallacy of supposing that because an event X *can* be caused by Y, it can therefore only be thus caused.

So much for the interaction of the first two flows, total demand and total output, and for the way in which the price level is determined. But the relation between total demand and the third flow, total costs, is equally important. It is a relation between two *money* flows. And it is basically this which in any reasonably short period determines how far the existing physical and human resources of production are actually used. In such periods, therefore, this relationship largely determines the level of output and total real income achieved. Potential real output depends on the resources of materials, labour, equipment, capital, and land available. But the *use* of these depends on the flow of total effective demand being at least equal over the whole economy to the flow of total costs (as defined here, including profit).

If total demand is equal to total costs the resources of the economy as a whole will be reasonably fully employed, and labour and other resources released from an occupation where demand is falling will have a reasonable chance of being re-employed elsewhere where it is rising.[9] There is then no need for prices generally to rise unless they are pushed up by the process of cost inflation already described. If, however, total demand falls short of total costs, some section of the economy and some labour *must* become unemployed, because the money will simply not be there to employ them. If, thirdly, total demand exceeds total costs, profits will in the first instance rise above the normal level allowed for in total costs; and if demand is pushed up again and faster than total output can rise, then a genuine and unnecessary price inflation led by money demand will set in.

The first vital objective, therefore, is to ensure that total costs and total demand should be, as near as possible, equal. But unfortunately there is no *a priori* reason why they should be, and no natural force, no hidden hand, which must somehow bring them together. No economic dynamic exists which automatically steers the two into equality. This is surely one of the over-riding truths about the modern money economy; yet it is rare to find it clearly expounded. At first sight it may appear that there ought to be a tendency for the two flows to coincide because the two are closely related to the national money income in question. But this is not so. For total costs are defined here, and rightly so, not as the actual costs – or total money incomes of the 'factors of production' – at a given moment, but as what these would have to be if the economy was fully employed. Total demand and *actual* costs of current output may very well settle down to an equality (but one which leaves, say, 25 per cent of capacity or 3 million people unemployed) and stay there until somebody, by spending more than their income on consumer or capital goods, begins to spur the idle resources into activity. Unless some intelligent, human agency takes conscious steps to bring these two flows into harmony, it will be a matter of mere luck – as it was for generations – whether it is the whole or a large part or a small part of the available resources that is actually employed.

Notes

[1] See p.69.

[2] *Principles of Political Economy*, p.363.

[3] In a closed economy total demand, as defined here, is strictly known as 'domestic expenditure at market prices' and the complication of imports and exports (visible or invisible) does not arise. Where it does arise, if one wishes to compute total expenditure on domestic products one must add the value of exports to total domestic expenditure, and deduct the value of imports; leaving one with the flow technically known as 'gross domestic product at market prices'. For the UK this corresponds with what is here called total effective demand.

[4] *Annual Abstract of Statistics* and *National Income and Expenditure Blue Book*.

[5] Strictly, for the purpose of this argument, it is the total of goods and services *sold* rather than the total of those produced, for these two may vary as stocks are increased or decreased; this may be regarded as short-term investment or disinvestment.

[6] It is akin to what traditional economics calls the 'supply price', and could be described as the supply price of total possible output.

[7] Assuming the petrol was sold and not hidden in a petrol 'lake' to hold up the price.

[8] M represented the stock of money, V the 'velocity of circulation', P the price level, and T the volume of transactions performed by the money stock.

[9] This does not of course alter the fact that each unit will only be employed if he, she, or it offers services considered worthwhile by the purchaser. Both conditions have to be satisfied.

21

The Central Dilemma

The simplified picture given in Chapter 20 does, I hope, make it easier to understand the normal, observed behaviour of the developed economies in the nineteenth and twentieth centuries. To fill out the picture, let us start by assuming such an economy is reasonably fully employed, with total costs and demand in balance, and a fair measure of spending on both consumption and capital formation (investment). Then let us assume that spending sharply falls off as a result either of a shock generated by the central bank or government, or by decisions of individuals to cut their expenditure. Demand will decline, profits will drop, and losses will appear over some sections of industry. The first casualties are likely to be the enterprises producing capital goods, because expectation of excess capacity will have been excited by the check to demand in the consumer trades. Employment will thus be curtailed and incomes fall again. As a result total demand will fall further below total costs, and unemployment will also grow further. It is no use, at this stage, encouraging those becoming unemployed to be more efficient and competitive, because if they are, they will necessarily make somebody else unemployed. It is falling demand, for which they have no responsibility, which has thrown them out of work, not their lack of efficiency. If total demand has fallen, say, 10 per cent below total costs, something approaching 10 per cent of the labour force must be unemployed or on very short time, however efficient or inefficient they may be. In these circumstances the labour and capacity 'released' would not be reabsorbed, permitting expansion in another section of the economy, and so enabling total production to be maintained, because there would be no countervailing extra demand. They would simply be wasted. The contraction would then continue cumulatively as falling demand cut down incomes, and falling incomes cut down demand.

This is the process of 'deflation', or 'depression' as it used to be called, and 'recession' as it is now called by those who prefer not to explain it but to treat it as a natural disaster mysteriously descending upon us like a pestilence. But it is not a mysterious disaster. It is a failure of money demand to keep up with money costs. And this is essentially the malady from which the UK has been suffering from 1979 to 1984, with factories closing, firms failing, and unemployment increasing almost every month for nearly five years. A coal strike occurred in the UK in 1984 largely because lack of total demand had temporarily cut down the money demand for coal. The pound sterling has been prevented from carrying out its first priority function as a means of exchange. Similarly a 'world recession' is no more than a corresponding demand deficiency on a world scale, which incidentally makes it equally useless for any government to urge their citizens to be more efficient and outdo some other exporting nation, since they would then merely export the unemployment to some other country's economy.

The question why any deflation or downswing need ever stop will be asked in a later chapter;[1] first, however, it is worth tracing the dynamics of the upswing too. Suppose, amid a deepening or stagnant deflation, some section of the community begins to spend or invest in capital goods well above their existing incomes, perhaps as a result of war, a major new technical discovery such as steam power or the motor car, or a fall in interest rates. Demand will first pick up at least to the level of covering costs at the existing level of output, which will stop the decline; and at this point expectation of recovering demand will probably induce postponed investment. So, given the initial stimulus, a cumulative upswing will normally develop, with output of capital goods expanding fastest to restore capacity, until available resources are near to being fully employed. Up till this point, as output, pay levels, profits, and living standards rise, there is no reason why prices generally should do more than recover, since, though some less efficient units may in some cases be used, the fuller employment of most plants will also mean lower unit costs. But if money demand is allowed to rise further after all resources are being fully used, then an unnecessary rise in prices will naturally occur; for expenditure will be rising faster than output. If those responsible for banking and budget policy in these circumstances allow total demand to go on rising, the price rise will naturally continue, and may perhaps accelerate. Employment will be high and profits probably rising.

This is the basic nature of a normal demand inflation: too much money chasing too few goods. For a demand inflation, like a cost deflation, is a perfectly possible phenomenon. Demand may be too high as well as too low. And if largely or wholly uncontrolled, it is likely to be first one and then the other. Most of the notorious historical inflations have been demand-led: the *assignats* of the French Revolution; the 1914–20 uprush of prices in the UK and elsewhere; the notorious German hyper-inflation of 1922–3; the pressure on prices in the UK and elsewhere in the Second World War and for a few years afterwards; and the more or less continuous inflations in South America, notably Brazil and Argentina, since 1945.

But these very sobering experiences have themselves led to a flock of misconceptions. First, it is not true that a government which has started a demand inflation by forcing or allowing demand to rise above the point needed for full use of resources is compelled to go on so raising it. If the government recklessly increases money demand by letting the banks create money without limit, perhaps by lending to the government, as did the German government in the early 1920s and South American governments since, then certainly the price inflation will accelerate. But a government does not have to do this. If it holds demand at the level then reached by money costs, prices need only rise further at the rate at which money costs per unit are rising. And if that becomes the cause of further pressure on prices, the process changes, and becomes a quite different animal – a cost inflation.

Though certainly high pressure of demand, at the point of full employment, may convert a mild demand inflation into hyper-inflation, it need not do. The resources of civilization are not exhausted at this point. It is therefore *not* necessarily true that inflation must cause unemployment. This facile assumption, though frequently and vehemently repeated, remains false. For a mild demand inflation does not itself lead to unemployment. It leads to high employment, high production, and high profits. It is only a reckless hyper-inflation which leads to breakdown and unemployment; and as this is demonstrably not the inevitable result of every incipient demand inflation, it is not true that the latter *must* lead to unemployment. Indeed the South American price inflations, running at rates varying from 100 to 200 per cent or more a year for many years, undesirable and unnecessary as that is, have shown that even this need not lead to ever-accelerating hyper-inflation. What does often lead to unemployment in these circumstances is a too vociferous demand from the public for the government to stop the inflation, which panics some governments into taking too drastic deflationary measures, overdoing it, and so starting the downward spiral once again.

Certainly at this stage of the process it is far from easy for a government to judge its pressure on the brake exactly right. The risk is that those in industry responsible for investment will take fright at the very whisper of restraint, heavily reduce their orders for capital goods, and so start the downward spiral before the government and banking authorities have grasped what is happening. The aim must therefore be to act judiciously enough to prevent this occurring, and if it does occur, to ensure that increased consumer demand makes up for the drop in investment demand. This is admittedly not easy. But there is no reason to believe it impossible, since a number of countries have succeeded in achieving it, including the UK and USA for most of the years from 1945 to 1970. Indeed in the UK in the years 1945–60 inflationary pressure from the demand side was strong and persistent. But price inflation was held within the 4–5 per cent range and unemployment was minimal, because the then governments had at least a general idea of what they were trying to do.

Unfortunately, however, if the threatened price inflation is cost-led instead of demand-led, the whole scenario and problem are different. In this instance a genuine, new, and so far unsolved – and often unrecognized – difficulty does confront us. Suppose the total of money costs (which normally consists of 70 or 75 per cent of salaries and wages) is rising at 5 per cent a year, and the volume of physical output is also rising at 5 per cent a year, no great snag need arise. Total demand can also be allowed to rise at 5 per cent, and average pay rates, incomes, spending, and real output can rise together without any need for higher prices. Suppose, however, that, for whatever reason, real output cannot rise more than negligibly, and money costs continue to rise at 5 per cent; a dilemma arises. If demand is also raised at the same pace as costs, by 5 per cent, then demand must by definition be raised to that extent faster than output. And so prices must on average also rise 5 per cent. But if demand is not raised, demand will fall below total costs to the same extent, and unemployment of that order must result. The difficulty is in principle the same if output rises by, for example, 5 per cent and costs by 10 per cent.

This is an inescapable dilemma, because it proceeds from simple logic. If the rise in money costs is greater than the rise in real output, then if demand rises with costs, it *must* exceed output and so raise prices; and if it does not rise with costs, unemployment *must* result because demand is below costs. In practical terms, if the managers of the economy are confronted with a rise in money costs greater than that in output, they are forced to choose between a rising price level or rising unemployment (or a little of each). By the obstinate laws of arithmetic, they cannot avoid both. This is what I call the Central Dilemma. It is, I believe, the trap into which the pound sterling, the UK economy and most of the Western world blundered uncomprehendingly in the 1970s; and it is this which, for the time, ended the era of full employment and rising standards. It should be noted, however, first hopefully, that this central dilemma arises only if money costs are rising faster than output; and secondly, less hopefully, that it is only the beginning of the difficulty.

The dilemma itself may develop into a vicious upward spiral. Suppose that physical resources only permit a rise of 2 or 3 per cent at most in real output, and that money costs rise 10 per cent, then if demand is raised by 10 per cent, prices will rise 7 or 8 per cent. The public will then feel cheated. If, however – and here is the rub – all those with the power to do so (right across the board from the solicitors to the doctors and the journalists) demand in the next round 8 per cent to compensate them for their supposed losses, and another 10 per cent to give them a real gain, then the price level will rise 15 per cent or so. This means that a cost inflation in these circumstances really will escalate into an accelerating price inflation, and the process will then indeed be very difficult, though not impossible, to check without transitional unemployment. This was almost certainly the point reached in the UK in 1975 when the then government was forced, rightly, to call a halt, and did so successfully. Though it is not true that 'inflation' as such *must* lead to unemployment, it *is* true that cost inflation *can* do so.

This analysis also explains why in these circumstances a novel situation develops, almost unknown in the nineteenth and early twentieth centuries, in which unemployment and prices are both rising at the same time and profits are low or falling: in other words, 'stagflation'. The predicament itself, and the name, both emerged in the 1970s. It is only a cost inflation which can generate stagflation; and this is the clearest proof that it was cost inflation, not demand inflation, which caused the trouble in the 1970s and 1980s. Expanding demand causes rising prices, high profits, high output, and high employment. Conventional demand deflation produces low profits, falling prices, falling employment, and falling output. In the nineteenth-century trade cycle demand, output, prices, profits, and employment normally rose and fell together. It is only cost inflation that can lead to low profits and rising prices and unemployment at the same time. And profits were exceptionally low, in the UK and elsewhere, in the 1970s, until high unemployment enabled them to rise in 1984–5.[1]

This account of the matter will also throw light on the supposed trade-off between unemployment and 'inflation' which was at one time believed to exist. According to this view, if employment rose, it had to be paid for in higher prices; and if prices were kept down, higher unemployment would have to be suffered. This hypothesis came to be associated with the famous 'Phillips curve' devised in 1958 by Professor A. W. Phillips,[2] who used wage rates as his indicator of 'inflation' and unemployment as his indicator of demand. Now in the circumstances of demand pressure in the 1950s this hypothesis was well founded, because the pressure of demand which pushed up prices would be needed to keep up employment. But in the cost inflation scene of the 1970s this would no longer be true, since if prices were being pushed up by rising *costs* this need no longer involve a pressure of demand which also ensured high employment and profits. And so the apparent trade-off would disappear in the years after 1970 – which is what has in general actually happened. Too much of the money demand in these circumstances came to be absorbed in higher costs rather than higher employment: in other words, stagflation emerged. Before 1970, as John Black puts it, the Phillips formula 'gave a tolerable, though not very good fit', but during the 1970s it 'clearly does not fit the facts'.[3] The Phillips curve thus ceased to 'fit the facts' in the sense that a rise in prices no longer more or less ensured a fall in unemployment; though the dilemma between the long-run objectives of high employment or price stability still remained.

Cost inflation can of course be started or aggravated by other forces than pay rates. A rise in import prices, due perhaps to a falling exchange rate, or to price movements or cartels overseas, or to the adoption of some grotesque apparatus such as the Common Agricultural Policy, may all start a cost inflation. But since salaries and wages normally account for 70 or 75 per cent of total costs, a substantial rise in pay rates is almost bound to exert a major effect on the total costs both of individual enterprises and the whole economy. If, for instance, with pay amounting to 70 per cent of total costs, pay rates rise 20 per cent, it would need a nearly 50 per cent fall in other costs to prevent a rise in total costs. And even a steep rise in the exchange rate could hardly ever achieve this in the real world; and if it did, it could not go on. It therefore seems beyond serious question – quite apart from the statistics – that rising pay rates were a major element in the cost inflation of the 1970s, and are likely potentially to remain so in the future. Of course nobody disputes that, in addition, the huge oil price increases made by the OPEC cartel twice sharply aggravated the cost inflation in 1974 and 1979–80. As already related in Chapter 17, it was a remarkable historical coincidence that OPEC – what the economists now call an 'exogenous' factor – should have intensified an already operating upward spiral. But since the spiral had begun some years earlier, in 1968–72, OPEC cannot be regarded as the sole culprit. Economists often insist that it is real wages, not money wages, which influence movements in the rest of the economy, and nothing said here is inconsistent with this. But wage earners must normally defend or improve their real wages by pressing for higher money rates, and this in turn, unless accompanied by higher productivity, forces employers to raise prices.

All the evidence, therefore, as well as more recent history, points to the conclusion that cost-push, based partly or mainly on pay pressures, has generated the central dilemma described in this chapter, and that that dilemma remains the major economic enigma confronting the Western world. It means, in short, that with restraint of money costs, you can have full employment without damaging price inflation. But without restraint of costs, you can only have full employment with price inflation, or unemployment without price inflation; or unemployment and price inflation at the same time.

Notes

[1] See Chapter 23.
[2] See, for instance, Frank Hahn, *Money and Inflation*, p.71, and John Black, *The Economics of Modern Britain*, pp.188–93.
[3] *The Economics of Modern Britain*, p.189.

22

Saving and Investment

In Chapters 20 and 21 I argued that the three flows of total demand, total costs, and total output, the first two of which are generally regarded as at any rate partly under human control, are crucial to the working of the economy, in the sense that their interaction mainly determines levels of prices and employment. Do the dynamics of saving and investment in any way invalidate this conclusion? A prolonged and complex debate on the significance of saving, investment, and the rate of interest, particularly since Keynes' *General Theory of Employment Interest and Money* was published in 1936, has not yet reached a clear consensus. But certain propositions can be advanced with some confidence. Saving is defined for this purpose as income less spending, and investment as the formation or acquisition of new real capital, whether fixed assets, working capital, or stocks. As a mere matter of definition we can therefore compile the following simple equations:

$$\text{consumption} + \text{saving} = \text{income}$$
$$\text{consumption} + \text{investment} = \text{income}$$
$$\textit{therefore} \text{ investment} = \text{saving}$$

But this does not mean that by some heavenly harmony one group of people's intention to save miraculously coincides with another group's decision to invest; even though investment certainly must involve saving, because it takes time – sometimes a long time – both to construct and to use capital goods. It would, however, be substantially true to say that while planned investment and planned saving can diverge at one stage, *realized* saving and investment must later coincide. The system adjusts itself to the various pressures in such a way that these two (as defined above) become equal, though some individuals' intentions are frustrated in the process.

Some other aspects of the behaviour of saving and investment are tolerably plain. It is well known and not surprising, for instance, that in an economic upswing the rise in output of capital goods should be sharper than in that of consumer goods, and that in the downswing the decline should be sharper. A rise of, say, 15 per cent in the demand for energy might raise the demand for new power stations, oil refineries, and tankers by 50 per cent or more. For this reason the steel and shipbuilding industries are always acutely vulnerable to recession. It is also evident that a rise both in investment and in output of consumer goods will stimulate a further rise in general demand, as the producers of the one or the other spend some of their higher incomes. But investment also displays some special peculiarities. One is that a rise in consumer demand will at some stage also be the main (though not the only) influence in generating demand for capital goods. A shift of demand from one type of consumer goods to another – for instance from cars to television sets – will normally lead to a contraction in one sector and an expansion in the other, and no net change in the total demand or employment in the economy. However a rise in demand for consumer goods will normally increase, not decrease, the demand for capital goods, as the producers seek to extend their capacity. A rise in output of capital goods will also increase incomes and so increase demand for consumer goods, for there is no automatic rise in saving to offset the extra spending on capital goods. So demand for capital and consumer goods, instead of each rising when the other is falling, tend both to rise and fall together; and this can hardly fail to be a destabilizing force in the economy.

Much has been written within and without the government machine in the past thirty or forty years in an attempt to determine what mainly induces business enterprises to invest: whether it is the rate of interest, technical development, competition, tax allowances, or something else. In the UK all inquiries (for example the Wilson Committee Report of 1980) have shown that inability to raise finance is seldom the obstacle to investment, as compared with doubts about future demand for the final product. The overwhelming empirical evidence suggests that the existence of a rising demand for the product, and the expectation that this will continue, are by far the most potent single incentives to invest. So far as that is true, two types of demand – that for consumer goods and that for capital goods – will naturally rise together.

Another peculiarity of saving and investment, and one more subtle in its working, is the influence exerted on them on the one hand by the rate of interest, which can itself be controlled within limits by central banks and governments, and on the other hand by the actual stock of money balances in existence at a given moment, which in this sense does have real significance. The recipient of an income may spend it, hold it, or lend it. His or her decision to hold money rather than spend it may sometimes be influenced by interest rates but more often by a desire to keep some money handy ('liquid'). The further decision to lend rather than to hoard is no doubt materially affected by the rate of interest, but also by the desire to possess income-yielding savings or property in the long term. The interest rate is likely to be most powerful in its influence on the borrower: on the industrial investor, for whom it will be the next potent influence after expanding demand, on the holder of business stocks, and also on the house purchaser, for whom it may be a major determinant of living standards. The decline in interest rate to 2 or 3 per cent in 1932 almost certainly started the housing boom of the 1930s, and the outrageously high interest rates of 1979–82 caused the greatest collapse in new house building in peacetime since before 1932.

In recent years the spread of automatic saving by individuals through pension funds and the decline of 'voluntary' individual saving must have diminished even further the influence of interest rates in calling forth saving. It must also have strengthened the conclusion that it is the effect on the borrower that matters, both on the business borrower for real investment and on the house builder and house purchaser, and also to an increasing extent on the purchaser of consumer durables through hire purchase and so on. Low interest rates will encourage these activities and so stimulate employment and incomes generally; and such rates will be a vehicle for expanding the total quantity of money if this is desired. High interest rates will similarly be restrictive. The banking system can normally expand both the volume of borrowing and the volume of investment by buying securities and offering to lend at lower rates; this is clearly one instrument for the control of total demand in the economy. The authorities in control (assuming there are some) will thus have to ensure that enough money, and not more than enough, is in existence both to enable those who want to hold cash balances to do so, and for total demand to be maintained as near the required level as possible. But this does not alter the fact that the maintenance of demand must be the prime objective if resources are to be fully used and the whole economy kept in balance.

It has often been argued that 'over-investment' is in some way the underlying cause of booms and inflationary pressures, and that stability cannot be restored without a period of relapse which allows the 'excessive' real capital to be dismantled, whatever is happening to total demand. This picture may naturally often appear plausible because high investment does coincide with booms, and some capital tends to be left unused afterwards. But this is not enough in itself to establish that over-investment has somehow been the culprit, because historic booms have usually been brought to an abrupt end, not so much by capital being proved to be surplus, as by the banking authorities or governments imposing controls or restrictions. Much more sophisticated versions of the view that saving and investment are at the root of the problem were put forward by Hayek as long ago as 1931 and later, as already mentioned,[1] by R.F. Harrod and Sir John Hicks in their respective books on the trade cycle. They raise the basic question: can there be, and if so in what sense, such a thing as 'over-investment'?

In his earlier writings (*Prices and Production*, 1931, and *Monetary Theory and the Trade Cycle*, 1933) Hayek argued at the time of the Great Depression that excessive lending by profit-seeking banks at artificially low rates of interest induced investment by industry which was excessive apparently in the sense that too little genuine saving was available even to cover depreciation on the new capital. (This is incidentally quite a different explanation from the much later ones of Milton Friedman, who tends to put the blame on an excessive quantity of money rather than on excessive investment. Deflationists' arguments alter greatly over time, though always reaching the same conclusion – that the depression is caused 'inevitably' by the previous boom, and that to avoid the depression we must check the boom even if this means unemployment.) Interestingly enough, the Hayek type of theory implies that if banks were not profit-seeking institutions, and new money did not have to be created by way of private loans, the periodic wobbles of the system, with their attendant unemployment, might not occur. It is certainly an oddity of the modern monetary system that the new money needed has to be largely created by loans from profit-making firms.[2] Hayek's 1931 account also, however, ignored the fact that a large section of bank lending is nowadays for consumers' spending and not for investment at all; and his picture of private banks' persistently hankering after *too low* interest rates never seemed realistic. In any case he later abandoned this explanation.

On the other hand a genuine theoretical possibility exists that real investment might run so far ahead of the proportion of income which the public wanted to save that inadequate funds would be forthcoming even to cover depreciation (and that new money created to offset this would result in excessive total demand). However, though theoretically possible this also seems unrealistic in the light of the empirical evidence. High incomes and full employment would themselves markedly increase saving; and actual business experience suggests that what makes capital equipment excessive is not the difficulty of covering depreciation, but the difficulty of selling the product. The theoretical possibility remains that rising depreciation charges might force up money costs and so consumer prices to a level where they could not be covered by non-inflationary demand; but it seems unlikely that, except in rare instances, depreciation charges would be large enough to upset the balance of the whole economy in this way. Indeed the experience of 1945–70, during which, by influencing demand, governments largely smoothed out the previous sharp upswings and downswings of the cycle, greatly discredits any theory which assumes that a total deficiency of saving compared with investment requires the boom to be expiated by a slump. If of course the source of the trouble is too much investment in one type of productive equipment rather than another, this is naturally not an issue affecting total demand, output, or employment. It is a matter of establishing more capacity in the one case and less in the other. If, alternatively, there is supposed to be too much productive capital in total for the products in total to be sold, the remedy is not to dismantle the capital, but rather to increase total demand, so that those products can be sold.

This possibility is not excluded by the version of events favoured by Sir John Hicks and R.F. Harrod,[3] who see the source of cyclical instability in the interaction of investment and incomes generally, each stimulating or depressing the other. Their analysis seeks to show with much subtlety *how* the economy, if unmanaged and left largely to itself in the nineteenth-century manner, may be expected to get itself into the regular lurches and wobbles which history records. They do not agree that the mere fact of expansion to near the limit of physical capacity, though it admittedly must involve a check (which may be an energy ceiling as well as a labour ceiling),[4] must also necessarily involve a disastrous relapse. For appropriate use of the controls might avoid sharp plunges into unemployment, as they in fact did avoid them from 1945 to 1970. For instance, at the end of his *Trade Cycle*[5] Sir John Hicks advocates measures to establish 'monetary security, combined with a moderate use of public investment and fiscal controls, designed to quieten, but hardly to eliminate the real cycle'.

Keynes himself seems to me to have at first fallen into error on one point; though his concentration on the flow of demand, and the inability of the system automatically to stabilize itself without unemployment, were of course immense and permanent steps forward. The error was to suppose that if depression and unemployment are threatened because planned investment is too low to equal planned saving, the only remedy must be somehow to increase the investment. But this simply does not follow. From the point of view of maintaining output and employment, it is just as useful to increase consumer spending. For the increase in consumer spending extinguishes the excessive saving, which is nothing other than the shortfall of spending compared with income – though it is true that if the unemployment is largely in the industries producing capital goods, a growth in consumer spending will take longer to absorb it. Would it be rash to suppose that Keynes fell into this misconception because it seemed on the face of it that if planned investment was too low, only higher investment could put this right? At one point[6] in the *General Theory* he certainly implied this: 'We established in Ch. 8 that employment can only increase *pari passu* with investment.' But this is not true. It can also increase *pari passu* with consumption (which extinguishes the 'excess saving'). It is total *spending* which must increase. To give one concrete example: in 1982–4 the US government of President Reagan achieved a massive upswing in US total output and employment by means of a huge budget deficit resulting largely, not from investment, but from tax cuts and spending on defence. Whether you call the defence spending 'consumption' or 'investment' makes no difference at all to the number of jobs created by this vigorous reflation. By either name the jobs will smell as sweet.

Keynes had of course recognized this at a later stage. Also in the *General Theory*[7] he wrote: 'If it is impracticable materially to increase investment, obviously there is no means of securing a higher level of employment except by increasing consumption.' Perhaps his earlier reluctance to accept this truth was the result of his natural wish for all the obvious reasons to see a greater growth of real capital, or even his own personal fascination with the whole spectacle of investment, financial and real, and the rate of interest. But to advocate investment as desirable or virtuous in itself is one thing. To advocate it as the only way to ensure employment is another. The fact that something is virtuous does not necessarily make it essential for the purpose in hand. And unfortunately some of Keynes' followers were for a time misled by the earlier passages into believing that, according to Keynes, only investment could yield the required extra employment, when the truth was that either capital or consumer spending could do so. Though investment is often the best way, it is not the only way.

So the argument leads us back once again to the conclusion that total output and employment depend on total demand, whether on consumer goods or capital goods. If this total expenditure covers total costs of all producers, then though some individually will be enjoying more demand than before, and others less, the total resources of the economy will be as near full activity as is humanly possible.

Notes

[1] p.70.
[2] See Chapter 26.
[3] See p.70.
[4] John Hicks, *Are There Economic Cycles?*, p.13.
[5] p.168.
[6] p.113.
[7] p.325.

23

Out of Step

The history of money has been dogged by the fact that the flow of total demand (money spending) and the flow of total costs needing to be covered have been perpetually fluctuating independently of each other, and that until the twentieth century few if any governments have consciously tried to steer them into equilibrium. So the two were more often out of step than in it. The level of prices has mainly depended on the relation between the flow of money demand and the output of goods and services, and the standard of living has depended on the resources available and the extent to which the flow of money demand enabled them to be used. Earlier chapters have outlined the factual record, and Chapter 23 now seeks to elucidate it further in terms of the three flows of demand, costs, and output.

In the case of the pound sterling the story is largely the record of these three flows getting into and out of step with one another; in the earlier period, particularly, money demand and output, and later in the modern economy more often demand and costs. In the fourteenth century, immediately after the Black Death, since food output and the number of workers had probably been sharply cut, while the money stock remained intact, prices rose steeply. Later, in the fifteenth century, as food output rose faster than population, and labour was scarce, prices were somewhat lower and real wages unusually high. Later again, after 1500, with both population and the money stock rising, prices rose substantially and employment probably did also, though real wages fell. At the end of the seventeenth century the combination of war, and the discovery of bank money with which to finance it, led to a mild demand inflation in the 1690s. This later resulted in the first major deflation of available money supplies and thereby of demand, enforced under the influence of Locke and Newton, in order to re-establish the pre-war silver value of the pound.

The comparative absence of monetary upheavals in Britain in the eighteenth century, apart from parliamentary intervention to regulate the issue of notes, looks on the evidence as if it was caused by the lucky coincidence of rising supplies of gold and a steady growth of banking and bank-created money. Together these kept up a sufficiently rapidly growing flow of demand to serve the increasing population and finance the far-reaching industrial developments in the latter part of the century. By 1793, when war came, sterling prices were already nearly 50 per cent above the level of 1713. From 1793 till 1813 the country experienced a straightforward demand-led price inflation, caused by expanded bank credit borrowed by the government. Exactly as one would expect, prices rose; the exchange rate fell; bank deposits and the Bank of England's note issue grew rapidly; and the war was won. After this episode nobody need doubt the possibility of a demand-led inflation. But after the experience which immediately followed, in 1819–23, neither need they doubt the possibility of a demand-led deflation. Again the volume of money and so demand were deliberately curtailed in order to restore the previous gold value of the pound; and as a result demand clearly fell sharply below costs, prices came rapidly down, and production and employment must have fallen heavily also. The country suffered the worst depression for more than a century, and demand recovered only very slowly.

The late nineteenth-century trade cycle, and some of the theories advanced to account for it, have been described in Chapter 9; and the date of the cycle's emergence in history would suggest a close connection with the growth of both bank credit and industrial investment. On this basis, and on the evidence, it would seem that the cycle can fairly be regarded as a sequence in which total demand and total costs, as defined here, were not merely successively, but rhythmically and regularly, getting out of step with one another. Excess of demand over costs would clearly lead to the upswing, and deficiency of demand to the downswing. Each process would be cumulative and would reinforce itself: for consumption stimulates investment, and investment stimulates consumer spending. However the question which remains to be answered is this: why should either the upswing or the downswing stop, as they did, and then reverse themselves? At least there is no dispute that the *real* upswing – of output and employment – cannot continue beyond the point of full use of resources, and that if total effective demand is increased still further beyond what is required for this purpose, the rise in prices will accelerate. Historically it is also clear that from 1850 to 1914 – and to some extent between 1918 and 1939 – the Bank of England in fact brought the upswing to an end by raising interest rates to whatever level was necessary to stop the outflow of gold. Whether or not the end of the upswing was connected with complex ratios of saving and investment, the action of the Bank of England – and other central banks elsewhere – would in themselves explain the end of the upswing as it actually occurred.

Why, however, since the deflationary forces, once started, also reinforce themselves, should the downswing ever come to an end? This has always seemed harder to answer. And it must not be forgotten that in the USA in 1933 it did not come to an end – but plunged into a collapse of the banking system as well as of industry, which only massive government intervention was able to overcome. This at least shows that the downswing need not necessarily come to a stop by some automatic process of its own accord. In order for it to end it is necessary that total demand should somehow cease falling below money costs and should then begin to rise. One way in which such a floor would be put under falling demand might be that expenditure out of depreciation funds on maintenance of the existing stock of capital could not fall beyond a certain point. This may have some force; but if capital was actually dismantled on any major scale, then even depreciation spending would fall also. Similarly again,[1] it may be argued that where industrial plant actually wears out, it must be replaced. But even this does not follow if total demand is falling fast enough. A more conventional and on the whole more plausible explanation is that the fall in money wage rates – an essential element in the Victorian trade cycle – would lower money costs and so obliterate the gap between them and demand. But unfortunately the fall in wage rates, if total money expenditure on labour remained the same, would not itself have increased total demand in the economy. It would have left it unchanged unless demand itself was being stimulated by the fall in rates or some other factor. Probably it helped; but the fall was seldom substantial and it is far from certain that it would normally have been enough in itself to achieve the turnround.

The one force which would have reversed the downswing would have been a recovery of effective demand which did not also involve a rise in costs. This would have been generated by the sharp falls in interest rates to very low levels which did actually occur in the Victorian cycle. These must have stimulated some investment not otherwise thought to be economic and some borrowing from the banks – if mainly for house building and replenishment of stocks – which would not otherwise have occurred. That was perhaps the greatest single factor which in these years restored demand before catastrophes like that of 1933 were encountered. But there may well have been others. It is worth remembering that in Victorian depressions widespread starvation would have occurred had it not been for increased spending from the Poor Law, from trade union unemployment insurance, from individuals drawing on savings if they had any, from loans and credit to those in need, and from private and institutional charity. In other words, as incomes fell, saving as a proportion of incomes would have fallen also. All these influences together would have restored demand relative to costs, and all in sum would have been more than negligible in helping low interest rates to reflate demand. Such an explanation is at least consistent with the evidence, since after the 1840s starvation was avoided; though the comparative weight of all the various reflationary forces at work cannot be precisely determined. In addition, if the nineteenth-century cycle did consist of a rhythmic imbalance of this kind between money demand and costs, one would have expected it to be greatly smoothed out, if not entirely eliminated, by a deliberate attempt to get the two into balance; and this is essentially what actually happened from 1945 to 1970.

In the First World War the UK experienced a straightforward old-fashioned demand-pull inflation, unmodified at first by controls, in which demand was set by the government's needs, and financed by expanding bank deposits and the note issue to whatever level was required to carry on the war. This experience was a lesson in the mechanics of an only partly controlled demand inflation. Employment, prices, profits, and government borrowing all rose steeply. Total demand in the later stages rose well beyond the level of total costs or possible total output; and the public was in fact partly taxed through higher prices. But even this experiment proved yet again that a strong demand inflation *need not necessarily* lead to hyper-inflation. In the spring of 1920 the combination of cuts in government orders, very high interest rates (7 per cent bank rate), and the collapse of purely speculative buying drastically and suddenly cut total demand to below the high level of money costs prevailing; and as a result output and employment fell precipitately from 1920 till 1922.[2] This time – probably for the last time in British history – a fall in pay rates of about 25 per cent between the end of 1920 and the end of 1922 cut back total costs, and so, assisted by the belated cut in bank rate in 1922, enabled output and employment to flatten out after that date. But the years 1922–9 are another salutary lesson that no automatic recovery need necessarily occur after a sharp deflation, despite further cuts in wage rates, if a government holds down total demand, as did governments and the Bank of England in those years in a vain effort to restore the pound's old parity. It is perfectly possible for the economy to stagnate at a low level for a number of years. It did so between 1922 and 1929 with unemployment varying between 1 million and nearly 2 million: a huge waste of national resources at a time when other countries, notably the USA, were enjoying real economic growth.

Few would now dispute that the collapse starting in Wall Street in 1929, and spreading depression throughout the world, was a violent, cumulative deflation of money demand probably precipitated by the end of the unsustainable sheer speculation on Wall Street (buying for a rise) described in Chapter 12. Sheer speculation, in which people buy not for use but in the hope of capital profits, is the one form of boom which cannot be continued beyond a point. It is probable that consumer demand in the USA in the years before 1929 was being sustained by the spending of capital gains, and that the sudden conversion of these into losses caused the first sharp fall in consumer demand. This does not mean that the slump, and the whole 1929–33 plunge, were irresistible. But it does mean that the US government and Federal Reserve authorities would have had to step in very rapidly and massively to expand demand sufficiently in other ways to make up for the losses spreading from Wall Street. This they did not do in time, and an avalanche of cumulative deflation carried the system downhill, with no automatic recovery, culminating in the memorable total collapse of March 1933. Demand fell calamitously below cost levels; indeed demand must have fallen faster than even rapidly falling output, since prices generally were also falling. The exceptional depth and force of this downswing could well have been caused by the extent to which in 1928–9 total demand in the USA was being sustained by speculative paper profits. If so, it was indeed a monetary phenomenon.

The measures which the Roosevelt government had to take, after some false starts, to rescue the US economy further strengthen the argument that only positive action to restore demand can achieve recovery from a deflation of this depth. After the first crucial freeing of the dollar from gold in March 1933, Roosevelt made the early mistake of seeking to raise prices by restrictive devices under the so-called National Recovery Administration (NRA). But raising prices without raising demand achieved nothing; and it was only when the government launched a general reflation of demand on all fronts – by raising the gold price of the dollar, by the budget, by public investment, and by interest rates – that the corner was decisively turned. So basically in Britain in 1932–7 a respectable upswing was achieved by three measures which all stimulated demand: the fall in the sterling exchange rate, the low interest rates which promoted a housing boom, and the tariff on manufactured goods which preserved and increased home employment.

The immense success of British economic policy in the 1939–45 wartime years is a standing answer to those who maintain that total demand and cost levels cannot be controlled or brought into, or near to, balance by conscious effort. They were controlled in just this way after 1939. Both the demand-led inflation of 1914–18, and the twenty years of wasteful unemployment between the wars, were after 1939 likewise avoided. Demand and costs were at last kept tolerably in step. This was done by allowing money demand to operate up to the point, but not beyond it, where labour and capacity existed, and by moderating the rise in labour costs by holding down the prices of necessities. The success of this policy, some will no doubt claim, rested on a battery of physical controls which would not be justifiable or tolerable in peacetime. However those people who readily advance this comment do not always see the implication of what they are saying. As pointed out in Chapter 14, they are no longer arguing that these policies are impracticable.

They are contending instead that such methods are both morally justifiable and practicable in order to win a war, but not to avoid unemployment of 2 or 3 million in peacetime. This may or may not be valid as a moral judgement; and there is a genuine moral dilemma in deciding how much loss of individual economic freedom is justifiable for the sake of the general welfare. But that is very different from saying that these measures are economically unworkable.

Similarly, in the twenty-five successful years after 1945 a much better balance than before the war was by and large achieved in the UK between the flow of demand and flow of costs, despite acute balance of payments difficulties, for the simple reason that peacetime governments were for the first time trying to achieve it. Some have argued that this whole success was the result of investment demand held over from the war. But in that case why did it not happen after 1918? Why the collapse of 1920–2? Others who wish to belittle the 1945–70 performance find it difficult to say that it is impossible, because it actually happened. So they tend to maintain instead that for some obscure reason this success carried the seeds of its destruction within it, or was gradually though invisibly disintegrating from the start. But in one crucial particular at least it was visibly not disintegrating for a long time. Take for instance a year as late as 1966. In that year unemployment in the UK still stood at 1.6 per cent and the cost of living rose only 3.9 per cent. Some twenty-one years, that is to say, after demand management policies had first been introduced in peacetime – not immediately after the war – unemployment still stood at a minimum level, and prices were rising at barely 4 per cent a year. The picture of a steady worsening of the employment or price indicators is one which ignores some of the plain facts. Certainly the exchange rate had to be lowered in 1967; but as in 1931, 1949, and 1972, if changes in the exchange rate are necessary to maintain the full working of the economy, they must be accepted as justifiable.

In one respect, however, it is perfectly true that a damaging and disruptive force began to make itself felt in the late 1960s and 1970s. This was the emergent cost inflation described in Chapter 17 which, though no doubt latent since 1945, became more aggressive after the mid-sixties and so transformed the problem of the demand–cost ratio into what I have called the central dilemma (Chapter 21). As soon as pay rates rose substantially faster than physical output could rise, governments were ineluctably forced to choose between unemployment and accelerating price inflation. Samuel Brittan, in his otherwise judicious booklet *How to End the Monetarist Controversy*, rather hastily dismisses cost inflation as the main cause of the breakdown in the 1970s, suggesting that this assumes a 'mysterious outbreak of union militancy all over the world'. But something much deeper, more persistent and steadily developing than a fit of 'union militancy' is being assumed by those who put forward this sort of explanation. What appears to me to have happened is that all or most of the organized pay groups, in many of the advanced countries, had gradually come to realize after twenty years of the full-employment society that their power to exert pressure in demanding pay rises was much greater than it previously had been. This change would have taken a period of years to emerge (just as did the impracticability of *reducing* pay rates after 1918); and would very naturally have emerged in more than one country in roughly the same period. The very international character of the cost pressure supports this general interpretation.

This is a hypothesis of a type not statistically demonstrable, but distinguished by being the only one which seems consistent with the relevant facts: the timing of the start of the pay explosion (before the first oil shock); the fact that rising prices coincided with rising unemployment and falling profits (which proves that the trouble was not a demand inflation); and the complete disaster which followed the attempt after 1979 to cure it by deflating demand. The further fact that the cost inflation of the 1970s was predicted by few, and unrecognized by many, is also some evidence of its unfamiliar character. Most people had learnt, as they thought, from history that all inflations were demand inflations. Interestingly enough, Keynes himself (though not explicitly in the *General Theory*) came near to predicting what actually happened.[3] He wrote in a Treasury memorandum as early as 1944:[4] 'I do not doubt that a serious problem will arise when we have a combination of collective bargaining and full employment.' That this was Keynes' clear view, and not just a casual comment, is shown by the inclusion in the Employment Policy White Paper (also in 1944), which he influenced, of this prophetic sentence: 'Action taken by the Government to maintain expenditure will be fruitless unless wages and prices are kept reasonably stable.' Keynes' 'serious problem' did not 'arise' as soon as one might have expected – probably for the reason given above, that the pay groups took time to appreciate fully the new power which full employment had given them. But its prediction by Keynes so far in advance is both a tribute to his foresight and evidence that, if he had lived, he would have seen it clearly for what it was: a cost inflation.

Unfortunately the new government of 1979 did not. What was needed then was restraint on costs and maintenance of demand. The policies adopted amounted to exactly the reverse:[5] curtailment of demand and no curb on costs. The result was precisely what the foregoing analysis would forecast – a yawning gap between total demand and total costs. For several years the two were not so much out of step as marching in different directions. The inevitable and predictable result was a rise in unemployment in under three years from below 1½ million to over 3 million. Admittedly the havoc was made worse by a reckless uprating of VAT and a rise in the sterling exchange rate. But essentially this was an old-fashioned demand deflation enforced in the face of an all-too modern cost inflation. In his persuasive 1982 booklet, already quoted, Samuel Brittan says rather oddly that 'no-one did predict that unemployment would rise to anything like its present heights'.[6] But he is wrong here. It was foreseen by those who understood the need for management of both demand and costs. Lord Kaldor, in his evidence in the *Report to the House of Commons Treasury and Civil Service Select Committee*, published on 17 July 1980,[7] said that for the then government's strategy to succeed, unemployment 'would need to be more like 3 million'. Professor Minford, however, a high priest of monetarism, said in 1979,[8] 'Any temporary loss of output is likely to be of modest significance.' In his evidence to the 1980 Select Committee,[9] Professor Minford repeated that: 'The simulations of our model suggest that on the assumption that policies are properly understood when they are announced and implemented, the disturbance to output and employment from reduction in the money supply and in the PSBR [Public Sector Borrowing Requirement] would be minimal.' Professor Friedman, the ayatollah of the movement, is recorded as saying in the *Report to the Select Committee*[10] in 1980: 'I conclude that . . . only a modest reduction in output and employment will be a side-effect of reducing inflation to single figures by 1982.' The extreme monetarists evidently had little or no idea of the sensitivity of the modern industrial economy to shocks of this kind. Yet in some sciences the ability to predict events correctly is regarded as an argument in favour of any theory.

Notes

[1] See J.M. Keynes, *The General Theory of Employment, Interest and Money*, p.253.

[2] See pp.84–6.

[3] So did Beveridge (*Full Employment in a Free Society*, pp.199–200), who wrote: 'How real is this possibility [i.e. cost inflation] cannot be decided on theoretical grounds.'

[4] Quoted by D.E. Moggridge, *Keynes*, pp.30 and 137.

[5] As already recorded in Chapter 18.

[6] *How to End the Monetarist Controversy*, p.22.

[7] p.97, note 1.

[8] *A Return to Sound Money*, p.31.

[9] *Report to the House of Commons Treasury and Civil Service Select Committee*, 17 July 1980, p.142.

[10] p.61. Indeed in this competition in prophecy the amateurs seem to have scored rather more highly than the professionals. Unemployment rose in 1979–83 three times as high as the London Business School predicted (*Financial Times*, 27 February 1984, p.15). In case I am accused of being wise after the event, I did make the forecast (writing in 1979 in *Change and Fortune*, p.501) that the 1979 government's policies would 'mean prolonged deflation, high unemployment, no growth and a very low level of investment'. And I said in the House of Commons budget debate of 16 June 1979 (*Hansard*, col.980): 'We shall have rising pay claims and rising unemployment, higher interest rates and falling production and investment.'

24

Illusions and Fallacies

Certain illusions and fallacies have in recent years gained enough popular currency to be worth sweeping away before asking what policies now hold the best hope for the future. The misleading inference from Keynes' *General Theory* that investment was somehow a more assured way of expanding employment than consumer spending has been mentioned in Chapter 22. Investment must be justified on its own normally very great merits, not by spurious arguments.

Perhaps the most widespread popular misconception in the early 1980s has been what may be called the technocratic fallacy, after the so-called technocrats who propagated it widely in the Great Depression of the early 1930s. This is the belief that with the rapid spread of automation, information technology, computers and so forth, less and less labour will be needed for productive work, and all the wants of the human race will be satisfied while only a proportion of them are employed. This view has always looked, and always does look, plausible in a depression, because total effective demand is below total costs, so that 'surplus capacity' (surplus not to needs, but to money demand) emerges in many industries, and in some of these rapid technical advance will be actually and visibly releasing labour. Where is the employment to come from, people naturally ask?[1] The fallacy is not to see that if total effective demand were maintained at the level needed for full use of capacity, the labour released from one form of output would be balanced by the labour re-employed in another. Difficulties, time-lags, and bottlenecks would naturally occur; and large switches of manpower will often be necessary.[2] But any loss of total employment would be small and temporary. The 'technocrats' also often forget that technical advance makes it possible not merely to produce as much with less labour, but also more with as much labour. If you give people enough money, they will spend it on what they choose, whether that choice is some of a new product or more of an old. *Their* choice will determine where the employment comes from. If the flow of demand is still too short, the remedy is to increase it.

If it is still further contended by the technocrats (against all the evidence of our eyes) that all the inhabitants of say the USA and the UK now have all they will ever want, there remain several thousand million people in the Third World who certainly have not, because we have not yet found an effective enough way of bringing them into the system of exchange by supplying the necessary money to them, whether as useful producers themselves or otherwise. If the demand of those thousands of millions were made effective, for generations to come there would be no talk in the advanced countries about lack of markets. And the most hopeful way of bridging the gap, vast as it may be, is to supply poorer countries with the finance which will enable them to develop their own productive resources and so build up their purchases from the developed nations: a task which many governments and organizations like the World Bank have already successfully begun. The implication of this is that poorer countries must be enabled to sell their products to the developed world in exchange for what they buy. In the long view progress in this field is as fully in the interests of the developed economies as of the less developed ones. The only limit on human demand is a monetary limit; and that is under human control.

Such are the basic weaknesses in the technocratic argument. But the historical evidence confirms its falsity even more conclusively. In every depression since at least 1800 the technocratic cry has been raised; and a few years later demand, employment, and production have again risen higher. In each depression it is of course claimed that *this* time the End of the World is Nigh. But wait; and the Second Coming is again postponed! However plausible these lamentations sounded in 1932, by the late 1940s and 1950s they had again proved false. And to those who think that the dread day really did arrive in 1979–84, the answer must be given that technical advance in industry did not suddenly break out in May 1979. Why, on the technocrat argument, was unemployment falling in the UK from 1978 to 1979? And did the great technological thunderclap really arrive by coincidence simultaneously with a general election in May of the latter year? More fatal still to this argument is the contemporary experience of the USA, the land of microchips, information technology, and computers galore. Total employment in the vast US economy actually rose 17 per cent in the ten years 1973 to 1983;[3] and real gross national product rose by 6 per cent or more in 1983–4[4] as a result of President Reagan's unintended, but high and effective, deficit spending. The truth is that, though living standards partly depend on technology and productivity, employment depends on demand.

Another but quite different group of fallacies cluster around what in the 1980s is crudely known as 'monetarism'. Such labels as 'monetarism', 'Keynesianism' and so on, though beloved by some, have been little used in these pages, since they are liable to generate more fog than illumination. The phrase 'monetarism' in particular covers, if not a multitude, at least a variety, of doctrines. Samuel Brittan has helpfully distinguished between 'narrow' and (presumably) broad monetarists.[5] With some of the latter's tenets there need be no quarrel. In so far, for instance, as broad monetarists are merely saying that if a government or central bank creates paper money without limit (for bank deposits are not 'printed'), then people will in time spend most of it, and that when all or nearly all productive resources are employed, prices must rise; this is surely something that nobody will dispute. But this has been very well known and repeated *ad nauseam* at least since the *assignats* at the time of the French Revolution. The process thus described may also properly be called 'inflation', and it is what Keynes meant by saying that 'inflation is nature's remedy'. It is also disputed by scarcely anyone that if the process of money creation is continued beyond a certain point, the rise in prices will accelerate, and that correcting it will be a painful, though not impracticable, operation. But it should also be noted that both these propositions necessarily imply that the pressure on prices in the relevant case came from the *demand* side. People got hold of the new money and spent it.

Nor need anyone dissent from the broad monetarists when they maintain that this process *can* be set going by governments borrowing newly created money from central or other banks. Of course it *can*. A Brazilian Finance Minister once told me that he had to borrow from his central bank in this way because rich men bribed his tax collectors to under-assess them, and he could not find enough unbribable characters to run his direct tax system. This is no doubt a possible, though hardly a universal, predicament. Nor need it be disputed that historically a number of demand-led inflations have actually occurred, notably in the First World War in the UK and elsewhere, though to different degrees; or that in Germany in the early twenties the process was intensified into hyper-inflation. Nor again should anyone deny that if a government, confronted by pay rises exceeding any practicable expansion in output, proceeds to increase money demand sufficiently to preserve full employment, prices generally must rise. And beyond this it is perfectly reasonable for monetarists, if they wish, to describe the minimum level of unemployment below which it cannot be materially lowered, and below which the only effect of rising demand would be to raise prices, as the 'natural level of unemployment'; as long as there is no implication that some natural process exists which automatically brings this level into existence. There is not. It would be a better use of English to call it the 'minimum'[6] rate of unemployment; and it is interesting to remember that the actual minimum in 1944 in the UK was under 100,000. But if broad monetarists wish to call it a 'natural' rate, and accept that it would be about 1.5 per cent in the UK in peacetime, as experience has shown, there need be no quarrel with that either.

It is when the monetary fundamentalists start to pontificate beyond these simple truths that the trouble begins and the fallacies multiply. The full fundamentalist creed may perhaps be briefly, and I hope fairly, summarized as follows. There is a great evil called 'inflation' which consists in ever-rising prices. It is caused solely by excessive increases in the quantity of money. Such excesses are generated by those (governments and banks) who control the quantity of money, and not by the demand for it. The pressure on prices comes wholly from the demand side, from those who spend the money. There is no such thing as a cost inflation, and pay groups and trade unions have no power to raise the general price level. Excessive increases in the quantity of money are usually caused by government borrowing, which for some reason is more 'inflationary' than private borrowing. A nation's total money income (my total effective demand) maintains a constant relation to the total stock of money, and increases in the size of both merely affect prices and have little or no effect on output or employment.

In this form the doctrine is simply riddled with fallacies, the major examples of which may conveniently be identified and scrutinized at this point. Error number one, which may be called the stock–flow fallacy, is the mistaken belief mentioned in earlier chapters that it is the *stock* of money, and not the *flow* of demand, which directly influences prices. This is manifestly not true. It is the total flow of money spent (not the static stock) to which the total volume of output, multiplied by the price level, must be equal. It is only by affecting the flow of money demand – not by some mysterious alchemy – that the stock of money can influence prices. Certainly the stock of money *may* itself affect the flow of demand and so indirectly affect also prices – and in historic demand inflations has done so; but it is only *one* of many influences affecting demand in this way. Other such influences are individuals' propensity to spend, save, or hoard; government's decisions to tax, spend, or borrow; and business decisions to expand, contract, or invest. All these can activate or sterilize the stock of money in existence (or, in Fisher's terminology, change 'the velocity of circulation'). To pretend that they cannot do this is sheer perversity, a sacrifice of common sense to holy writ. To point out, on the other hand, that the size of the money stock must be *one* material influence on the flow of demand is both true and relevant. The reason why the importance of the money stock has come to be greatly exaggerated in this way by those who write on economics seems to be largely past history: the history of money and theories about money, which were developed at a time when the idea of the stock was much easier to understand and (in the case of silver, gold, or notes) much easier to measure then the flow of demand or national income.

Milton Friedman in particular has made prolonged attempts to bolster up by statistical records his basic argument that it is the stock of money which determines price levels. Even if history did demonstrate coincidence or near coincidence in time between changes in the stock and changes in the price level, this would not establish which was the cause and which the effect. Expansions of the quantity of money in the modern world are largely carried out by banks making loans; and banks find it easier to lend if someone is willing to borrow. And people may become more anxious to borrow to finance higher pay or prices or for many other reasons.

However this may be, the statistical records simply do not endorse what Professor Friedman is seeking to prove. For instance, Lord Kaldor has shown in his evidence to the Treasury and Civil Service Committee of the House of Commons[7] that there was no clear or constant ratio in the 1960s or 1970s between the stock of money (M3) and the flow of demand (money GNP) in any but three of the following ten countries: the USA, the UK, Belgium, France, West Germany, Italy, Japan, the Netherlands, Sweden, and Switzerland. In West Germany M3 was 36 per cent of nominal GNP in 1958 and 67 per cent in 1978. In the case of countries where one version of the money stock shows a close relation with GNP, other versions often do not. Not merely does the record seldom show any constant ratio over time in one country, but also none between one country and another, as Lord Kaldor has also demonstrated[8] for a group of countries selected by Friedman (India, Israel, Greece, Japan, Korea, Chile, Brazil, the USA, and the UK). A further effort has been made by Friedman and Anna Schwartz[9] to show that a direct ratio existed in the UK from 1867 to 1975 between the money stock and national income. This was exhaustively examined by David Hendry and Neil Ericsson of Nuffield College,[10] who concluded that Friedman and Schwartz had 'not credibly established a significant number of the main empirical claims about monetary behaviour in the UK', and that 'one cannot take at face value many of the inferences conducted [by them] leaving their conclusions stranded as assertions devoid of empirical support'.

So the prosaic verdict on the static quantity of money must be that it is only one element in the whole economic process. Its erection in the 1970s into a sacred totem pole with learned acolytes dancing round it is a spectacle of surprising absurdity. The attendant ritual by which Wall Street and the London Stock Exchange await in awestruck tension monthly figures of the 'money supply', and guess from these what they think the monetary authorities will think and do next, is more akin to the incantations of the witches in *Macbeth* than to sober economics:

> *By the pricking of my thumbs,*
> *Something wicked this way comes.*

The next fallacy, to which the preceding argument has already pointed, may be called the push-or-pull fallacy: the belief that all inflations are demand-pull inflation and that cost-push inflation cannot exist. The truth is that either, or conceivably both at once, can emerge. The assumption that all inflations are demand-led is completely refuted in the case of the 1970s' inflation, as already pointed out in Chapter 17, by the fact that profits were low or falling throughout the period. It is also contrary to the experience of every business manager who has ever had to raise his prices because his labour costs had risen. Challenged on this point in a discussion recorded in the Institute of Economic Affairs publication *Unemployment versus Inflation*?,[11] Friedman replied that it 'looks to' the simple businessman as if the rise in labour costs has forced him to raise prices, but this was 'because somebody somewhere else in the system was increasing demand'. But this is not necessarily true at all. It *might* happen that way. But it also might happen that a successful pay claim forced a rise in salaries or wages, and that the employer in question, in order to stay in business, was compelled to increase his bank overdraft until he later recouped himself through higher prices or charges. In that case the demand from the employer for more money would induce the bank to increase its advances. The demand for money would thus be the cause of the increase in the stock of it (just as it is when the Bank of England's note issue grows before Christmas). So, far from a gratuitous – or 'exogenous' – increase in the stock of money causing the rise in prices and pay, the rise in pay in this case would have caused both the rise in prices and the credit expansion. It is again purely perverse to deny that this *can* happen. There is really no reason to do so, except an *a priori* unshakeable belief that this ought not to be true.

To that someone may perhaps reply that if the bank refused the overdraft, the rise in pay and prices could not occur. Certainly. But this is precisely the point at which the system approaches what I have called in Chapter 21 the central dilemma. If the rise in money costs is allowed to go ahead, and the money needed to finance it is refused, then you will definitely provoke unemployment, falling output, closures, and bankruptcy. In 1980–1, for instance, prices were rising at about 20 per cent and the quantity of money at about 10 per cent; no wonder the economy was bled white. This is indeed a strong reason why a correct diagnosis is particularly vital in this case. To diagnose a cost inflation as a demand inflation is no less damaging in practice than to diagnose appendicitis as pneumonia. But the fact that refusal of an overdraft can have this effect is no reason at all for supposing that upward pressure from costs cannot start the inflationary process. At root, therefore, the push-or-pull fallacy springs from the delusion that because demand can start an inflation, nothing else can do so. It is like arguing that because a cigarette end can start a forest fire, nothing else can. And in practice in the 1970s and 1980s it has led to the disastrous mistake of diagnosing a cost inflation as a demand inflation.

In very recent years some monetary arch-purists,[12] perplexed perhaps by the heavy unemployment unexpectedly resulting from their policies, have intellectually taken wing into what Shelley called 'the intense inane'. Some of them have been bold enough to maintain that, though unemployment appears to exist, it is really all voluntary. According to this argument, since there always exists a 'market-clearing' price for labour at which everybody would be employed, and since ordinary mortals must be assumed to know this and to foresee accurately the consequences of their own actions, the very fact of their being unemployed proves that they deliberately chose to be so. (This argument would also appear to establish that if someone is injured in a road accident, they must be presumed to have done it on purpose because they had failed to take the precautions necessary to prevent it. But let that pass.) The perfect foresight attributed by this school of monetarists to ordinary people is called 'rational expectation'; and the comforting conclusion is reached that there cannot really be people willing to work at existing pay rates but unable to find a job. I said in Chapter 20 that classical economics did not allow for mass unemployment because it had no clear conception of effective demand, and Keynes wanted to amend the theory accordingly. Now we are in effect told by these Mark II monetarists that what was wrong was not traditional economics, but the popular belief that involuntary unemployment exists.

The ordinary reader, despite his perfect foresight, may indeed ask whether this new doctrine is really meant to be taken seriously. Since Friedman himself has described the Bank of England as 'myopic', an image springs to mind of a myopic Governor of the Bank discussing the economic outlook with, say, a ticket collector of perfect foresight in the Bank tube station. But let us assume that this doctrine is not an intellectual leg-pull. Its most obvious weakness is precisely the same as the one involved, as already observed, in the belief that technological advance has caused the unemployment of the 1980s. If the doubling of UK unemployment in the eighteen months after May 1979 was all due to these millions of far-sighted individuals all coming to the conclusion at almost the same moment that they were unwilling to work for existing pay, why did it happen all at that moment? Can anyone really believe that all these persons, male and female, young and old, suddenly, and for no apparent reason, and contrary to their own interests, and at roughly the same moment, jumped to this conclusion? And was the massive and rapid rise in unemployment in 1929–33 also caused by such a sudden Gadarene rush? Such suppositions are simply not within the bounds of credibility. Suppose, however, that one attempts to restate the doctrine in a more positive form. If in deflationary conditions everyone were willing immediately to accept a pay cut, some reduction in unemployment would result. As a hypothesis this might in some circumstances be true. But at best it would have the same measure of truth as statements such as: if every woman in the world were as beautiful as Greta Garbo or Cleopatra, or if every journalist wrote like Shakespeare, the world would be a better place. These assertions are true, but not of this world.

If we return now to earth, we can see the modest kernel of fact which lurks behind these airborne hypotheses. Certainly it is true that if the total flow of money available to pay all salaries and wages were fixed, and pay rates rose by 10 per cent, and all other things were equal, then fewer people would be employed; and if pay rates fell by 10 per cent, more people would be employed. (Even so, employment would not fall or rise by exactly 10 per cent, because the change in real pay offered would affect some people's willingness to work.) But the fallacy here is to suppose that some fixed sum exists available to pay all wages and salaries. To suppose this is to return to something very like J.S. Mill's 'Wages-Fund' theory, which has been abandoned by economists of all schools for more than a century. In fact the money stream available to pay wages and salaries is not fixed, but is dependent on many things – primarily on the flow of total demand as defined earlier. Thus the argument leads back to the central truth that all available labour can be fully employed if, but only if, total costs are covered by total demand.

To put it another way, monetarists are fond of saying that there is a 'market-clearing' price for labour as for other things, and that if that price prevails, the market will then be 'cleared' and everyone employed. This proposition is not a falsehood. It is a half-truth. It ignores the more important half of the truth: that the price at which the market would be cleared is itself determined by demand. Raise demand, and you raise the market-clearing price. Lower demand, and you lower it. This is as true of real demand for labour as of money demand, since real demand cannot exert itself in the marketplace unless it is converted into money demand. Let us therefore examine this argument, assuming unrealistically for the moment that major pay cuts are possible. If, first, it is merely suggested that a cut in one type of pay balanced by a rise in another might effect a change in labour allocation, that is not in dispute; but it would not increase total demand or reduce unemployment. The issue here is whether unemployment as a whole would be reduced. It is therefore not applicable to a fully employed economy.

Suppose, however, in any economy with major unemployment a general cut of, say, 5 per cent in money pay rates is imposed. If it is assumed that the total money demand for labour remains the same, then employment should increase proportionately and the total money spending of the labour force should remain the same. Prices would fall and total output rise (with all sorts of frictions and time-lags). But exactly the same result, in real terms, would be produced by raising total demand correspondingly (and with far less friction). Employment and total output would rise; and the only difference would be the nominal one that prices would not fall. And if the rise in demand stopped short of full employment, there need be no inflationary rise in prices. If, alternatively, it is assumed that the cut in pay rates would increase the total money demand for labour, then it is admitted that the extra money has to be found, and can be found from somewhere: from a larger stock or more active use of the existing stock. In that case why not do the whole job by raising the flow of demand?

The pay-cut remedy thus only achieves the same real result by cutting pay rather than raising demand; in other words it proposes to do the same thing by an impracticable, rather than a practicable, method. It is one of the most startling contradictions of orthodox monetarism that, in proclaiming incomes policies to be unworkable, it maintains that efforts to restrain pay rises are impracticable. But at the same time it implicitly assumes that actual pay cuts *are* practicable. Yet whatever else is true, it *cannot be true that a policy of making actual pay cuts is more practicable than one of restraining increases*.

One further serious weakness, this time a contradiction, is deeply embedded in Mark II monetarism. It teaches that in practice reflation of money demand has little or no effect on real output or employment, but is wholly absorbed in rising prices. In that case why is inflation so great an evil that almost all other aims must be sacrificed to avoid it? It is a glaring contradiction to say that a certain policy has no effect on the things that matter, and at the same time that its effects matter so much as to make it the greatest of all economic evils. Nor is it clear whether monetarists are claiming that reflation has no effect on output and employment when labour is fully employed, or no effect at any time. If the former, nobody disagrees. If the latter, the whole experience of almost every major country in the last fifty years proves that this is not so.

The next delusion of the extreme monetarists is one harboured not so much by the theologians of the movement as by the lay preachers and politicians, the Scribes rather than the Pharisees. This may be called the household fallacy. It is the most pervasive, the most plausible, and the most damaging of the lot. It is the belief that because the individual or the single household benefits by saving out of income, or at least by not spending beyond his income, the same must always be true of a community or a government as a whole. It was classically expressed by Stanley Baldwin when he said: 'The national household is but the individual household writ large'; and it is a confusion into which Mrs Thatcher falls headlong, no doubt with the utmost sincerity. But it is a falsehood, for this reason. When an individual or family refrains from spending, it does not thereby cut down its own money income. And when it overspends, it does not increase it. But when a community or a government cuts its expenditure, it does automatically cut its own money income as a result.[13] And when idle capacity exists in the economy, it cuts its own real income. The point is very clearly put by E.V. Morgan: 'For a closed community, income and expenditure are identical, but for an individual they are not.'[14]

The household fallacy is plausible because there are two conditions under which it has genuine substance. First, while the analogy is false if applied to a closed system – that is, in so far as the internal workings of the economy are concerned – it is true of that economy's transactions with other currency areas. (The argument of this book so far has been concerned with a closed economy; and the other general implications of external dealing are set out in Chapter 25). If a nation exports more than it imports (earns abroad more than it spends), it is genuinely acquiring capital assets which will be of benefit in the future. If it imports more than it exports, it will lose such assets or incur debts. It is therefore normally prudent for a nation, like the individual, not to overspend outside its own currency area. But if the nation cuts its spending internally (whether capital or consumer spending), it simply reduces its own income. Internally the community's flow of money spending and money income are the same thing. The second condition which would give some substance to the household fallacy is the assumption that the economy is running with total demand above the point needed for full employment. In that case a cut in total spending, though it will reduce total money incomes, will not materially reduce real incomes, and will then do no harm.

If you remove these two conditions, however, and contemplate the now common case of an economy running well below the point of full employment, and a cut being made in its internal spending, the consequences will be wholly damaging. Total spending is cut, and total incomes in money terms are also cut automatically as a result. Then, owing to the widening gap between total money demand, which is being cut, and total money costs, which remain the same, total real output also goes down, and so real living standards fall. The authorities responsible for the economy delude themselves into thinking that something has been 'saved' – that somehow, somewhere, something 'invisible to mortal sight' has been achieved. But actually all that has happened is that the real income of the community as a whole has been diminished. The confusion arises from the fact that many people, realizing that if they saved individually something would be preserved, do not perceive that this is not true of the whole community. Indeed the very ambiguity of the word 'saving' encourages the illusion. To the economist saving normally means refraining from spending, but to the individual it has the additional meaning of preserving an asset. The individual's saving involves both; the community's saving involves only the first if its lower internal spending cuts its own income. In these circumstances no asset is created for the community; since though it may borrow less in money terms, it will reduce its future income as well as reducing its future interest obligations. But to refrain from consumption, and neither preserve nor acquire thereby any asset, is sheer loss. A nation cannot get richer by producing less.

And so it follows, to give one practical example, that the internal budget economy campaigns conducted from 1979 onwards in the UK by the Thatcher government have not merely achieved nothing, but have actually done economic harm. All these expenditure cuts were made at a time when the economy was substantially underemployed, so that the resulting cut in internal incomes and demand merely made the underemployment and waste of resources even greater. Cuts were made, for instance, in expenditure on health, education, housing, and naval ship building. As a result unemployment appeared and had to be financed in one section of the economy after another. Those forced to make cuts in, say, the Health Service were told (and some believed it) that though the service was damaged, some economic gain was achieved in compensation. But the hard truth was that a double injury was suffered by the nation: first the harm to health care, and secondly the resulting cut in the demand of health service workers for the services of others. And those others thus made unemployed were then told that nothing could be done for them because there was 'no demand' for their services! Again, the sufferers in the squeezed or starved national services were supposed to be comforted by the assurance that the money needed could not be 'afforded' (as though there were some limited pile of money in the Treasury and Bank of England). In truth a nation can afford – as the Second World War taught us – what it has the capacity to produce. Ordinary people instinctively feel that there must be some limit to what we can 'afford', and they are right. The limit is what we have the capacity to produce.

This fallacy shows itself perhaps most clearly in the case of the government's claims to have 'saved' manpower by releasing employees from the public service or elsewhere. If total demand were such that those released were re-employed on useful work elsewhere, their release might yield a genuine real gain to the nation. Here again the belief that there is a gain depends on the unconscious assumption that the economy is fully employed. If it were fully employed, there might be a gain. But if, as in the years in question, the release merely added to unemployment, all that really happened was that the nation paid people to do nothing instead of paying them to do some work. If you refrain from building houses when building labour is unemployed, or frigates when shipyards are idle, not merely have you not 'saved' anything – you have also lost the houses or ships the nation might have acquired at no real cost. In the latter case you may even have lost through closure a shipyard which otherwise might have been, genuinely, 'saved'. Thus the household fallacy has probably proved in practice the most deadly of the whole noxious brood, and to have been more responsible than any other single factor for the blunders of 1979–84. The high priests of monetarism themselves cannot perhaps be accused of openly preaching it, because its falsity is too obvious for that, but their reluctance to expose it is a reproach all the same to the intellectual consciences which they would claim to possess.

Another more specialized, though not more sophisticated, fallacy concerns public spending. I would not lay it at the door of the broad monetarists, but it is persistently propagated by the fundamentalists, and by their hangers on in politics and in the City of London. It takes two forms. The first is the belief that public borrowing from the banks is somehow more likely to generate excessive creation of money than private borrowing. This may be called the money-creation fallacy. The second, which proceeds from it, is the idea that something called the Public Sector Borrowing Requirement is the main, if not the only, engine of credit expansion and so of inflation. This is a myth rather than a fallacy, and may be called the myth of the PSBR. Both these beliefs are unfounded. Money creation occurs nowadays when the banking system as a whole increases its lending and thereby the total of its deposits. The economic effects of this, whether on prices, output, or employment, are substantially the same whether the money is borrowed by a government, an individual, or a private firm, provided that the money is spent by the borrower in each case (or indeed if it is hoarded in each case). There may well of course be different effects according to what the money is spent on; but this will not depend on whether the borrower is public or private. If 100 people receive £100 a week each, it is unlikely to make any difference to their spending or saving whether they are members of the armed forces paid by the government or employees of ICI. And if £100 million is borrowed and spent on the construction of a power station or the building of houses, the economic effects are precisely the same whether the borrowing and spending is done by a public or a private agency. The question whether this operation has any expansionary effect on the economy as a whole depends on whether it involves an increase in bank deposits and in total demand, not on whether the agency is private or public.

As a matter of historical fact in the UK, almost all the huge expansion of bank money since 1945 has resulted from private rather than public borrowing. The statistics of this for the great Heath–Barber credit boom of 1972–3 have already been recorded in Chapter 17. Lord Kaldor has set out the statistics for years extending from 1963 to 1979–80[15] which show that, in his words, the PSBR 'can have only played a minor role in the change in the money stock, whereas bank lending to the UK private sector played the major role'. Of course credit expansions *can* be based on borrowing by governments, and in Brazil and Argentina, for example, frequently have been. But they can equally be based on private borrowing, and in the UK in recent years (whether justified or not) have been almost wholly the result of private borrowing. Let all credit be given to Friedman,[16] who in a candid moment said: 'There is no necessary relation between the size of PSBR and monetary growth.' The notion that credit excesses are caused only by public borrowing springs either from the belief that we are still living in the days of Henry VIII, when kings tampered with the coinage, or else from the simple error of supposing once more that because something can be done in one way it cannot be done in any other.

Thus the presumed paramount desirability of squeezing the PSBR, which has been preached so vociferously since 1979, rests on the double mistake of imagining that the PSBR is a unique engine of credit expansion and that spending out of it is somehow particularly inflationary. But the mythology does not stop even there. It also involves a factual error about what the PSBR in the UK actually is. It is *not*, as so many have been led to believe, a budget deficit. Such a 'deficit' means to most people, and should mean, an excess of current spending over current revenue. And this is what under the British budget system a deficit did mean, from the chancellorships of Gladstone to Stafford Cripps, not notable spendthrifts. Capital expenditure, which could legitimately be met by borrowing, ranked until after 1945 as 'below the line' and did not count as part of a deficit. In many years between 1945 and the present the British budget on this definition has shown a *surplus*. Current revenue has exceeded current spending, and this surplus in recent years has contributed to financing part of the government's and other public authorities' capital expenditure. Public capital expenditure, that is to say, has *exceeded* public borrowing. Or to put it another way, the whole of public borrowing has been used for 'capital formation', and a current surplus has been used also to make that capital formation even larger.

In the budget year 1982–3,[17] for instance, current revenue exceeded current expenditure by £6.6 billion. Total capital expenditure by the public sector (including capital grants and loans from public authorities to the private sector) totalled £15.4 billion. The reality was that a current surplus – 'saving' in the ordinary sense – was contributing nearly £7 billion towards capital expenditure of £15.4 billion. The PSBR was £7.5 billion (the balance being capital receipts). Thus the PSBR simply consists of that part of public sector capital expenditure not covered by a current surplus and capital receipts; or to put in another way, the excess of all current and capital expenditure over all current and capital receipts. So the public sector as a whole has been in the same position as a private firm which financed part of its capital expenditure out of retained profits and part out of borrowing. Nobody would suggest that this was anything but a prudent and proper procedure. But very few people – very few MPs, I fear – know that this is how the British budget has in fact been operating in recent years. For the public have been led to believe, even by respectable journals, that the PSBR represents a 'deficit', with the implication that the public sector is in some sense 'overspending'.

Still more misleading and absurd is the further doctrine advanced by the more politically minded monetarists that by selling public assets, and so cutting the PSBR, a government is somehow restraining inflationary tendencies. 'Privatization', so the argument runs – the sale by the government of shares in BP or British Telecom

– reduces the PSBR, and since the PSBR is an engine of 'inflation', it therefore restrains inflation. But in fact the sale of these shares is simply an alternative to the sale of gilt-edged securities by the government; in other words, it is a swap of, say, £1 billion worth of one type of securities for £1 billion worth of another. The only material economic effect of this is that the government loses the future dividends from the securities sold and saves the interest payments on the gilt-edged which it would otherwise have had to issue; and there may thus be a minor financial gain or loss of future income. But a swap of securities of this kind has no material effect on total demand or on prices, output, or employment in the economy. The pretence that it somehow contributes to regulating the economy is little more than a hoax on the public.

Indeed it reveals itself as this in one further respect. Some monetarists used to argue that the public sector's sale of gilt-edged to finance public capital spending mopped up the savings available in the 'capital market' (the City), and so 'crowded out' unfortunate private industrial and commercial borrowers who might have expanded national investment and employment. But if the raising of £1 billion by the sale of government securities 'crowds out' the desirable private borrowers, the sale instead of £1 billion BP or British Telecom shares by the government must mop up a similar £1 billion from the pension funds and so on, and crowd out other borrowers in precisely the same way and to the same extent. It must also have a similar effect on interest rates.

The Economist,[18] commenting on the Treasury's apparent belief that higher public spending paid for by selling shares in British Telecom is all right, whereas higher public spending financed by selling gilt-edged stocks is not, remarks very fairly that 'the strain on financial markets and the resulting upward pressure on interest rates is the same in both cases'. The idea that you diminish 'crowding out', or ease the Treasury's financial problems, by 'privatization' is either a sincere delusion or a fraud. Though academic monetarists may be innocent of this imposture, it is hard to resist the conclusion that those who do perpetrate it are trying to dress up in the garb of reputable economic argument a programme which really springs from mere ideological prejudice.

The final major flaw in the monetarist system consists of two unanswered questions. When, as in the UK in the 1980s, a violent deflation has been imposed on a previous cost inflation, and the rise in prices has been reduced from, say, 10 to 5 per cent at the cost of over 3 million unemployed, what happens next? First, why should any recovery automatically occur, especially if the low interest rates of the old trade cycle are no longer operating? No convincing reason has yet been advanced why, unless active steps are taken to increase demand, the economy should not stagnate at a high level of unemployment for a very long time. Recovery may happen by luck; or it may not. In the summer of 1985, after six years of deflation, there was no sign of unemployment falling.

But an even more serious question remains unanswered. If for any cause, fortuitous (such as a fall in the exchange rate) or deliberate, a recovery did begin, what is to prevent the whole process starting all over again? The fact that even after the extreme deflation of 1979-84 pay settlements in the UK in 1984 and 1985 were still running as high as 7 per cent suggests the genuine recovery would start a new upsurge. With existing pay-bargaining conditions, a substantial recovery in demand must surely again stimulate higher pay claims; this will then stimulate higher prices; and by the time full employment is reached, or before, the economy will all too probably be forced back into the vicious spiral which compelled a halt in 1975-6. Huge sacrifices will have been made, and nothing will have been gained. The dilemma will be exactly the same, but faced by a poorer country with less productive capacity. What reason is there to suppose that something like this will not be the course of events even if recovery does occur? To this question no convincing answer has been given by any of the monetarist schools. Only in the USA, thanks to its huge productive capacity, is the dilemma likely to be long delayed.

Illusions and fallacies, however, are not the monopoly of monetarists. Many others abound, and two at least are worth looking at here. One is the belief that rising population is a major cause of unemployment. This may, no doubt, be true of an undeveloped country which as yet does not have the physical capacity to employ everyone able to work. But for a developed country to treat additional population as an embarrassment rather than an opportunity is simply a sign of incompetent organization or misguided policies. The suggestion is sometimes made that rising unemployment must be due to higher population, since the total number employed has not fallen. But this is like saying that one's children's shoes are too small because the children have grown, not because the shoes are the wrong size. The object of policy is to make use of the services of all those wishing to work, and the more of them there are, the greater the opportunity of higher output. The total costs which have to be covered by total demand are the sum of all payments needed for a fully employed population.

From this it also follows that the popular arguments for earlier retirement and shorter working hours, if they are urged as a means of reducing unemployment, simply rest on a mistake. If shorter working hours or a shorter working life are advocated because the individual prefers leisure to income, that is a perfectly rational preference. But where this is not so, failure to use available services or skills at a time when half the world's population has pitiably low living standards is a sign of a failure either to organize the physical resources needed – energy, transport, equipment and so on – or to convert real demand into effective demand. In advanced countries, where better health has already lengthened active life, the aim of an intelligent government should be to use, not to waste, the energies of all who prefer to work, whatever their age, to lengthen not to shorten working life, and so to build up all the real wealth and higher real standards that lie within our power. To condemn much of the world's population to abject poverty because we believe in a wholly imaginary absolute limit to the amount of work or amount of money available would be an extraordinary new human perversity.

The remaining delusion still persisting in the UK is the doctrine that 'free collective bargaining' is an over-riding economic priority, and that it cannot be regarded as a possible engine of cost inflation. This article of faith is an understandable residue of history, like the belief of the extreme sound-money men that a stable value of money is the supreme priority. It dates from a period when individual wage earners and salary earners were normally at a hopeless bargaining disadvantage compared with the employer. But in the eighties and nineties of the present century to deny that cost inflation may be, and has been, a major cause of price inflation and so of the abandonment of full-employment policies, is no more tenable for free-collective-bargaining fundamentalists than for monetary fundamentalists. For all the reasons given earlier in this book, and after full allowance has been made for the two 'oil shocks' of the

1970s, it cannot reasonably be denied that excessive and aggressive annual pay claims were a major contributory cause of the breakdown in that decade of previous successful policies. In the winter of 1978–9, for instance, it was the unthinking pressure of such claims, just as much as the activities of a factious opposition, which disrupted the encouraging success of the Callaghan government in reducing at the same time both unemployment and price inflation. Free collective bargaining, like sound money, must take its place as one among other objectives of economic policy, but not as the ark of the covenant.

Notes

[1] Samuel Brittan calls it the 'lump of labour fallacy' (*The Role and Limits of Government*, p.159).

[2] This is where 'regional' policy comes in, because the transfer is far easier if labour is released and reabsorbed in the same areas.

[3] *The Economist*, 10 December 1983, p.27.

[4] *The Economist*, 4 February 1984, p.80 and 28 July 1984, p.30.

[5] *How to End the Monetarist Controversy*, pp.16–17.

[6] But Friedman says it is not this (*Unemployment versus Inflation?*, p.24), meaning, it seems, that it is the existing, not the possible, minimum.

[7] *Report to the House of Commons Treasury and Civil Service Select Committee*, 17 July 1980, pp.109–116.

[8] *The Scourge of Monetarism*, pp.27, 35, and 36.

[9] *Monetary Trends in the US and UK: their Relation to Income, Prices, and Interest Rates 1867–1975*.

[10] *Assertion without Empirical Basis:* Report published by the Bank of England, December 1983, pp.1–2.

[11] *Unemployment versus Inflation* p.34.

[12] Known to some as Mark II monetarists.

[13] This fallacy also has a plausible appeal to bankers. Even such writers as John Cooper in his excellent book *The Management and Regulation of Banks* speaks (p.299) of the 'day-to-day "micro" experience of practising bankers' being 'directly applicable to the "macro" context of national economic policy'.

[14] *A History of Money*, p.95.

[15] *Report to the House of Commons Treasury and Civil Service Select Committee*, 17 July 1980, pp.116–17.

[16] *Report to the House of Commons Treasury and Civil Service Select Committee*, 17 July 1980, p.56.

[17] *Financial Statement and Budget Report 1982–83, March 1983*, p.36.

[18] 25 February 1984, p.29.

25

Trade and the Exchange Rate

The argument in the previous five chapters has been mainly concerned with a closed or single-currency economy, and with the interaction of demand, costs, output, employment, and prices in such a system. But, it will naturally be asked, how is this relevant to the pound sterling and the UK, a notably open economy selling to other currency areas over 30 per cent of the goods and services produced at home and buying over 30 per cent of what it consumes from elsewhere? The previous argument is, I believe, relevant in this sense that greater clarity can be achieved by elucidating first the inter-working of economic forces in a single-currency system, and then revising the picture to allow for the forces at work in an internationally trading economy like that of the UK.

Certain peculiarities of an open system are obvious enough. First, while a government can restrain imports into its own country, and can within limits control demand and create as much new money as it thinks right in its internal economy, it cannot control demand or create new money in somebody else's country. (It is true that by means of export credits, 'tied' loans, sales promotion campaigns and so on the authorities can influence foreign demand for its products – but only to a certain degree.) Beyond a point you cannot persuade others to buy more of your goods at a given price. Therefore, subject to these minor possibilities of influence, in the short run the demand for a country's exports has to be taken as 'given' by those attempting to control economic policy. A second clear condition which they have to accept is that if the home country's current and capital transactions show a deficit, that deficit cannot normally be paid off in their own currency. After a time it can only be settled by payment in gold or acceptable foreign currencies, by borrowing or by sale of other foreign assets. And the latter (as the UK found in both world wars) cannot continue indefinitely.

Thus there are special risks and uncertainties in international trading – but there are also gains. It is worth a country's while to indulge in international trade and so raise its living standards, if it sells what it can produce at lower real cost than others, and buys what in turn is produced more cheaply by others. Fundamental 'real' ratios are involved in this exchange. It will not occur unless the buyer thinks he is getting real value commensurate with the cost, and unless the seller thinks he is getting a real reward commensurate with the effort involved. These are hard facts which the government of one country cannot alter by juggling with exchange rates or prices, though it can prevent mishandling of the money symbols from obstructing a desirable exchange. In addition, the real gain to either country will be the greater, the more economically the output and marketing of its products are organized; in other words a higher reward will be earned by a given productive effort. And the living standard of either country will be affected by the number of units of its product which it has to sell in order to buy a given number of imported goods in exchange.

From even this rough sketch of an exceedingly complex process, the familiar moral can be drawn that it is crucially to the benefit of an internationally trading country to produce with the highest possible efficiency the goods which it wants to export. And on this truism rests much of the case for the whole galaxy of private and public policies, now known as 'microeconomic', which promote productivity and the economic use of resources in production and exporting. To catalogue these in detail is outside the scope of this book, but nothing said here should be regarded as denying or questioning their importance. Here are two examples. The UK, as a result of having the uneconomic Common Agricultural Policy forced upon it in the 1970s, has gratuitously raised the sterling retail price of food indefinitely and substantially above what it would otherwise have been. This in turn, by raising money pay rates, has pushed up UK labour costs in sterling right across the board of competition in both import and export markets. By contrast since 1945 Japan has created and expanded, under central government stimulus and control with government-regulated interest rates and capital markets, a whole series of new industries. By astonishingly skilful planning of resources that country has stimulated a worldwide demand for its goods which gives immense strength to the yen and major buying power over necessary imports.

Though all this is true, the argument for efficiency and competitiveness must not be pushed too far and become yet another article of faith. If every country became more competitive at the same time, the various surpluses and deficits between them need not alter, and there might be no net gain in employment throughout the system, though there might be a gain in the living standards of those already employed. Only a world expansion in total demand can expand employment throughout the world.

Since both gains and risks are involved in international trading, a wise individual country's policies will be based on an informed balance of both. They will not be based on sweeping ideological doctrines, whether in favour of private or public trading, protectionism, free trade or the like. There is a basic choice to be made here. The more 'open' a country's economy (free imports, low tariffs, and no exchange control), the more real gains are possibly – with luck – obtainable; but at the same time a greater risk of external shocks, crises and upheavals is – with ill luck – incurred. Conversely the more stability and security are assured, the more possible gains by international exchange are forfeited. The choice is essentially the same as paying an insurance premium and being rid of anxiety, or saving the premium and running the risk. The UK has suffered plenty of such disruptive external shocks since 1945: the 'convertibility' crisis of 1947 due to pressure from the USA, the Korean War boom of 1950–1, and of course the oil shocks of the 1970s. (The damaging high UK interest rates of 1980–4 cannot be blamed on external shocks, since they were mainly caused by the abandonment of exchange control in 1979.)

The choice between security and stability on the one hand, and higher incomes on the other, is all the more crucial in practice because so often the gains and losses fall on different people. For instance when the pound was overvalued in 1925 lower import prices probably secured lower living costs for all, but at the cost of imposing years of extreme hardship on the coal-mining labour force. Conversely in 1949 and 1967 by depreciating the pound the government rightly preferred to preserve full employment at the cost of rather higher import prices. In the other example already mentioned – the removal of all tariffs on cars imported from the continent after 1972 – buyers enjoyed the alleged pleasure of driving continental cars, but the West Midlands engineering industry (incidentally the core of UK defence production) was massacred and heavy unemployment caused. The moral of this particular mistake (the consequences of which were never foreseen by those who advocated it) is that an upheaval which gives small gains to many but very heavy losses to a large minority is most unlikely to be a national gain because of the gross inequality of the sacrifices imposed. This is a guiding principle which has wide implications for international trading policy.

This principle is particularly relevant for a government which needs to decide at what level total demand should be set in order to keep the economy fully active, but is faced with a persistent deficit in its balance of payments. Clearly in reaching such a decision a government must allow for a realistic estimate of probable exports and imports, and then aim at providing the balance of demand needed. To say, as has at times been argued, that demand cannot be too low merely because a lot of goods are being imported is simply to misunderstand the problem. What, however – and here is the rub – are the authorities to do if without an increase in internal demand unemployment will increase, but with an increase the external deficit will grow worse?

This familiar predicament is a sign that a country is asking too high a real price for what it sells – in other words offering too few goods or services in return for what it is importing. It is in the same quandary as a shop which is losing total revenue because it is charging too high prices. There are two ways in which a country can extricate itself from this difficulty. It can cut down demand in the home market in the hope that fewer imports will be bought and more goods will be released to be exported. This should at some point redress the balance by curtailing imports and increasing exports. The nation in question will thus buy less and sell more. But unemployment will also be increased by the cut in home demand; and the whole burden of the adjustment will fall on those losing their jobs. If of course before the adjustment total demand at home was running above the level needed for full employment, then a reduction to that level would be justified because no significant unemployment would result. But if demand were not above this level, the adjustment could be made in another way: by allowing the home currency's exchange value to fall.

This also will restrain imports by making them dearer at home, and encourage exports by making them cheaper elsewhere. It will achieve the objective, but in doing so will not cause unemployment. For home output will be encouraged by both the higher exports and lower imports. It was, for instance, very largely the long fall in sterling from $2.45 to the dollar in November 1980 to $1.20 in late 1984 which at last checked the violence of the deflationary downswing in the UK economy from 1979 to 1983, even though it failed actually to reduce unemployment. The correction of an external deficit by deflating demand imposes the cost of the change only on a minority; whereas the same correction achieved by a fall in the exchange rate, by holding prices higher than they would have been, imposes the cost on almost everybody. The latter is normally much fairer; which establishes a general presumption, though not a rigid rule, that this sort of adjustment is best made by changes in the exchange rate – to the 'market-clearing price' if you like.

So much for the uncomfortable posture of an economy in persistent deficit. Alternatively a country may be in international surplus but suffering substantial unemployment at home – a situation known in West Germany in recent years. Both in its own interest and that of others it should increase its internal demand, and so expand its own output and employment and buy more from less fortunate countries. If, yet again, a country is both in surplus and fully employed, its economic managers will legitimately feel not too unhappy. This is the normal good fortune of Japan. It gives the authorities of such a country the enviable choice of building up large currency reserves, investing more overseas, or allowing its own population to buy more imports. It is evidently in the interests of the outside world for that country to choose one of the latter two courses, and best of all if it imports more.

One clear conclusion emerges from even a brief glance at the impact of international trading and lending on demand and employment: exchange rates between currencies must either be allowed to change with market forces or be within the ability of governments to alter. Fixed exchange rates, even if you call them 'monetary stability', are a dead hand on economic policy. In an age when, unlike the nineteenth century, pay rates cannot be jerked quickly up and down, fixed exchange parities jam the machine. On the other hand violent changes in rates, like the upswing of the pound to $2.45 in 1980, and down again below $1.05 in 1985, inflict brutal wrenches on what should be a sensitive mechanism. Such changes provoke understandable demands for a return to fixity from those who have already forgotten the last experience of trying it. In periods of exchange rate swings during the past fifty years both theorists and practical men have called loudly for stability, and during periods of fixity have called equally loudly for flexibility.

But this is notably a case where, with a little wisdom and common sense, a compromise can be devised. Both short-term instability and long-term fixity are undesirable in exchange rate regimes. Short-term stability and long-term flexibility are desirable. The latter two cannot be secured by leaving everything to market forces, because in the very short term capital movements, often speculative, dominate the market, and left to themselves would generate excessive upswings and downswings which in turn are damaging to trade. Exchange rates are largely determined in the short run by capital movements ('hot money'), in the medium term by trade and payments balances, and in the long term by relative prices and costs in different countries. Market forces, therefore, left to themselves, would generate major and unpredictable instability in the short, medium, and long term.

The Bretton Woods Agreement of 1944 sought to combine short-term stability and long-term flexibility by a system of 'fixed but variable' rates. The parity was fixed at any one time, but could from time to time be altered. For twenty-five years this certainly helped to achieve the greatest international economic progress in modern history. But its practical defect was that the adjustments – usually 'devaluations' – could only be made after long political struggles, much damaging publicity, and equally damaging speculation; these in themselves caused upheavals and diverted energy from more constructive economic programmes. When the dollar took the plunge in 1971, the system, which really had been a dollar standard, was effectively at an end. The Common Market 'snake' and European Monetary System (EMS) are another attempt to combine short-run stability with longer-run movement; but they suffer from the same defect as Bretton Woods – periodic disruptive jerks when a currency can no longer be held within the permitted range.

Probably the best and most viable compromise would be something on the lines of what used to be called the 'crawling peg'. Under this regime the exchange rate would be so managed by the central bank (buying and selling its own or other currencies) that it was kept on any day within, say, 2 per cent either side of a peg fixed for that day. The peg itself would be fixed as equalling the average of the market price over the last, say, six months. This would mean that the rate could not vary by more than 4 per cent in one day, but over a period it would move with preponderant market forces, and over a year or two years would move substantially. If introduced, this system would effectively combine moderate short-term stability with longer-term response to persistent economic forces. It could also be tried by one or more countries at will without needing a probably unattainable international treaty; though it would need international understandings on its working.

Naturally many variants of the crawling peg idea are possible, but in the present state of human wisdom and foresight no such system looks likely to be adopted. The second-best but more practicable alternative strategy must be to allow medium-term and long-term market forces to operate on the exchange rate, but for central banks to smooth out the abrupt, short-term speculative swings. In the absence of an ideal solution governments responsible for managing the pound sterling would be best advised to maintain absolute freedom to influence the exchange rate, in order to avoid the agonizing struggles of the past – in 1925–31 for instance – to hang on to an uneconomic exchange rate at the cost of heavy unemployment and damage to the economy. All schemes for limiting the basic freedom to influence the exchange rate of one's own currency should be treated with the greatest scepticism. Indeed almost the only mistake in economic policy which British governments have not made since 1970 is to join the European Monetary System (EMS). The broad guiding principle should be to treat the exchange rate as a consequence of other desirable policies and not as an instrument for enforcing them, still less as an end in itself.

So much for trade and exchange rate policy in general. Application of this to the pound sterling must clearly take account of the special characteristics of the UK economy. In recent years various misconceptions have arisen here from confusion between the general problem of economic management and the special characteristics and experience of the UK. Most of Part IV of this book has been devoted to the general issue, but though a scrutiny of the entire UK economic problem is beyond its scope, certain specific confusions are worth resolving. Basically, since it is a physical necessity for the UK to import food and raw materials on a major scale, it must pay for these by exporting manufactured goods, services, or coal and oil when it has them. Its primary long-term strategy should, therefore, be to import the food and materials freely at the lowest possible price, and if necessary limit imports of less essential manufactured consumer goods. Whenever the UK has followed this policy, its economy has usually grown and living standards risen. When it has done otherwise, stagnation has set in.

The first plain misconception is to suppose that the UK could possibly have retained the percentage of world trade which it enjoyed in the second half of the nineteenth century or even the early part of the twentieth. A country which boasts barely 2 per cent of the world's population cannot hope for very long to carry 20 per cent or even 10 per cent of its trade. In particular after 1945 the recovery of West Germany and the rapid industrialization of the Soviet Union, China, Japan, and India were bound speedily to reduce UK trade as *a percentage* of world trade nearer to her percentage of world population. It need not, however, reduce UK trade in absolute terms, since these other countries' rising standards would raise their imports also. This fall in the percentage, combined with a rise in the absolute total, is not necessarily a disadvantage to the UK. And the actual performance of UK exports in volume terms since 1945 has been far more impressive than seems to be understood by those who, disregarding the statistics, lament parrot-wise a story of so-called 'decline'.

If UK visible export volume (not value) is taken as 100 in 1900, it stood, after two world wars and the shock of the Great Depression, at 98 in 1946, rose very rapidly up to 1951, and had risen (though more slowly) to over 500 by 1977 when oil became important. The annual growth of UK export volume in the 1970s was still over 5 per cent, not far different from other Western countries, even before oil was a serious contributor. At present UK exports of goods equal 25 per cent of gross national product, and exports of goods and services together over 35 per cent. Total UK exports are a higher percentage of GNP, and a higher total per head of population, than those of

Japan, and far higher than those of the USA – and also higher than ever before in UK history. The pressure on the UK balance of payments since 1945 has sprung mainly not from a failure to export but from a failure to restrain imports, and in particular from a disastrous rise in imports of manufactured goods from barely 10 per cent of total imports in 1950 to nearly 70 per cent in the 1980s. The mistake has been not so much exporting too little as importing far too much.

The second major misconception is the belief that the UK's real standard of living per head, before the mistakes of policy made from 1960 onwards and before the abandonment of free imports of food in 1972, was lower than that of most West European neighbours. It was not. This illusion springs from the error of converting the internal money values of one currency into another simply by means of existing exchange rates, and making no allowance for comparative cost-of-living levels and therefore the real purchasing power of currencies concerned. That method undervalues the real incomes of a country like the UK, whose cost-of-living levels, given existing exchange rates, were much lower until the adoption of the CAP. The only reliable true comparison was made in 1975 by the UN in an exhaustive report rather polysyllabically entitled *A System of International Comparisons of Gross Product and Purchasing Power by the Statistical Office of the UN, the World Bank and the Industrial Comparison Units of the University of Pennsylvania*. This report showed that there was little difference between real consumption per head in the UK, West Germany, Belgium or the Netherlands in 1970 or 1973.[1] This conclusion is also confirmed by figures of comparative consumption or ownership of, for instance, telephones, cars, television sets, housing, holidays and so on. Real living standards in the UK actually rose about 80 per cent in the twenty-five years up to 1972, probably faster than in any previous twenty-five years in our history. It was not until after the artificial raising of food prices via the CAP that UK real standards comparatively fell materially back, and not until this, together with the adoption of Value Added Tax, that the comparison of purely money incomes gave a truer picture. (The two oil shocks of the 1970s naturally affected everyone and do not influence the comparison.)

That much must be said to set the record in its true perspective, but not to suggest that many mistakes were not made in the later period, or that the performance might not have been even better. For it remains true that, at any rate from the late 1950s onwards, growth in GNP per head in the UK fell below that of most of our industrial competitors,[2] and that productivity in manufacturing – in the sense of output per man hour – was in many cases lower. Even allowing for the fact that West Germany, Italy, France, and Japan all started from very low levels in 1945, the annual rise in GNP in the UK was comparatively disappointing in these latter years (though the USA did little or no better until very recently). Investment as a percentage of GNP was also persistently lower in the UK than in most of her industrial competitors (again apart from the USA).[3] Part of the failure to achieve faster growth in the UK in the later post-war years was certainly due to repeated balance of payments difficulties, arising originally from the war, which forced governments to hold back demand so as to restrain imports. This would also have handicapped productivity by under-using capital and labour, and deterred investment by raising doubts about future demand. It is notable that these difficulties got worse after the 'liberalization' of manufactured imports in 1959–60, and worse again after the further removal of tariffs on imports from the continent after 1972.

Nevertheless since other countries, notably West Germany, fared so manifestly better in these liberalized surroundings, must there not have been something deeper and more persistently wrong with British industry over many years? When one turns to wider forces and long-term causation, judgement is much more difficult. Many explanations have been offered for an apparently deteriorating comparative performance by the British economy in the late nineteenth and twentieth centuries, varying from restrictive practices generally, to trade union militancy, the classical education of the professional classes, excessive taxation or government expenditure, and too many class barriers. It would be rash to say that there is nothing in any of these explanations, but there is one grave weakness in all of them. Why, if so deep-seated, did they only show themselves in fits and starts rather than persistently throughout the period?

British industry was the wonder of the world from about 1780 to 1860; but the professional classes were certainly no less disposed to a classical education then than now. From 1880 to 1914, though growth was slowing up, the UK economy was not doing too badly, with large and persistent export surpluses (as long as nobody had heard of the balance of payments, we were permanently in surplus). But surely no one is suggesting that the class system and the old-boy network were not operating in late Victorian and Edwardian times. More strikingly, there was marked growth and forward movement in British industry from 1932 to 1937, and indeed from 1946 till the 1960s; but nobody will suggest that trade unions were not reasonably active then. These long-term explanations do not seem to fit the short-run spurts and halts which actually occurred.

But there is one unique characteristic of British industry which might point to a more convincing explanation. It started first, and so in early times needed little protection against imports. It thus made the greatest relative progress when it had few competitors. But this left it vulnerable by the time when, from the mid-century onwards, its competitors – Germany, the USA, and France at first, and later Japan, Italy, and many others – all industrialized behind a strong protective wall, and maintained it in greater or lesser degree for long enough afterwards to preserve a reasonably secure home market. I have already quoted in Chapter 13 Professor Mathias' view that in the nineteenth century the British steel industry suffered seriously from the absence of a protected home market, as against Germany, France, and the USA. This would have been equally true of other manufacturing industries.

So far as it was generally true, the early start, combined with a free-trade dogma pushed too far, became a positive handicap to British industry as soon as the inevitable competition developed.[4] That would explain why Britain, while capable of brilliant innovation right through from the steam engine and the textile inventions of the late eighteenth century to the jet engine and nuclear power in the twentieth, first advanced rapidly when there was little competition up to the mid-nineteenth century. Then she fell back gradually as protected competition developed and so right on up till 1932; recovered markedly from 1932 to 1937 with moderate protection; performed excellently during the Second World War; and maintained a major export surplus in manufactures from 1946 until the dismantling of import controls initially in 1959 and 1960 and more drastically from 1973 onwards; after which the surplus disappeared for the first time since the eighteenth century. I would claim no more for this diagnosis than that, together with the factors mentioned earlier, it would at least explain the historical record; whereas so many of the other explanations offered simply do not account for the successive swings forwards and backwards which actually occurred. The UK's comparative loss of ground since 1960 must be mainly attributed to the policy mistakes made since then and analysed in these pages.

This does not mean, I must repeat, that all the microeconomic remedies normally prescribed for British industry – more technical education, for instance, and persistent pressure for efficiency – are not necessary. The case for them is indisputable. But it does carry two other warnings. First, though the traditional free trade doctrine, given secure full employment, an equal start, flexible exchange rates, fair competition, and world peace, remains one of the eternal verities, it becomes misleading and damaging if pushed to the point of believing that any import controls on any commodity at any time must be harmful to the country practising it.

Secondly, the doctrine reaches its most dangerous form when it maintains that unbridled import competition will *automatically* produce greater efficiency. Sometimes it will, but not always. If a pneumonia patient goes for a brisk walk in a cold wind when he has reached a certain point in his recovery, his return to health may possibly be fortified. But if he does so too soon, the experiment is just as likely to be fatal. A major fault in the treatment of Britain's industrial maladies in recent years has been the over-hasty and almost carefree assumption that the patient had reached the point where a cold wind would cure rather than kill. As a result of this miscalculation the UK finds itself in the 1980s with the first manufactured trade deficit for nearly two hundred years: not a very good omen for the future of the pound sterling. We should have been wiser to stick to the gradual GATT system.

Notes

[1] The figures were given in *Financial Times*, 2 December 1975, and quoted in my *Change and Fortune*, p.435.
[2] The earlier record is summarized in Chapter 16.
[3] Brookings Report: *Britain's Economic Prospects*, p.271.
[4] As suggested on pp.107-8.

26

A Plea for Moderation

My conclusion is a plea for moderation. We need to free ourselves from the extreme viewpoints of both monetarism and free collective bargaining and to be guided instead by the facts. Neither unemployment nor damaging price inflation is inevitable. But the Western world, misled by false if well-meaning prophets, has blundered into a morass of unnecessary poverty and grossly wasted resources because no natural mechanism exists which can bring the streams of money demand and money costs into stable balance with each other. Since the 1960s many bewildered governments – though not all – have given up even the attempt to achieve the required balance by rational policy. Much of the world, including the UK, has as a result lurched into what I have called in Chapter 21 the central dilemma: a predicament in which if you do not raise money demand sufficiently to cover money costs, you will have unemployment; and if you do, demand will rise faster than output and you will have rising prices.

In this sense unemployment *is* a monetary phenomenon. It springs from a mismanagement of the two crucial monetary flows. To get out of this deadlock we must first cease treating either the value of money or free collective bargaining as ultimate values to which all else should bow down. The primary function of money is to act as a medium of exchange, and the primary function of collective bargaining is to ensure that the weaker contributors to economic life are fairly rewarded. If either device is used in such a way that it clogs the machine, it is failing in the job for which it exists. I am not arguing here that the balancing of money costs and demand is the whole sum of economic policy: very many other policies, 'micro' and 'macro', are needed to expand UK productive capacity. But the balance between demand and costs is unique in this sense: that if it is *not* achieved, then all the other measures taken together cannot ensure that the system makes full use of that capacity.[1] Indeed they may make the waste of potential wealth ever greater. The demand–cost balance is therefore a *sine qua non*. Swift said that the man who made two blades of grass grow where one grew before would be worth the whole race of politicians together. In the twentieth and twenty-first centuries, the man who keeps the flow of demand and costs in balance will be worth the whole race of cosmonauts and econometricians together.

For what is the ultimate objective of all economic effort and the criterion of success? It is not to 'fight inflation' or even to preserve the value of money. It is to achieve the highest attainable output of all the goods and services needed for the welfare of mankind, including those serving unquantifiable needs such as health, environment, leisure, and education, and to achieve the minimum inequality in their distribution. In its function as a measure of value the pound sterling – or any currency – is in the last analysis only a symbol. If one midnight another nought were added to, or subtracted from, every money transaction from that day on (as indeed General de Gaulle did once ordain) no economic reality – food, drink, work, consumption, employment – need be altered. If you measured the distance between Chicago and Cambridge in kilometres instead of miles, the distance would stay the same.

Certainly changes in the value of money are inconvenient, disturbing, and beyond a point unjust. Other things being equal, they are to be avoided if possible. Indeed, if allowed to run too far, a fall – or a rise – in the money measuring-rod becomes a useless absurdity, and later on a dangerous menace, just because it disrupts real economic activity. That is where moderation comes in. The familiar South American phenomenon by which the price level rises 100–200 per cent or more every year, and all pay and prices and the exchange rate scramble to keep pace, is not impracticable, and may even continue for a considerable time. The objection is that it is pointless, that it almost certainly involves arbitrary injustice and inequality, and that for these reasons after a point it becomes itself an obstacle to real output.

It is therefore futile to carry an expansion of demand beyond the level needed for maximum real output. But it is also futile to cut it down below that level at the cost of unnecessarily lowering real output. These truths are in themselves a clear pointer to the right criterion of policy. Keeping changes in the value of money to the minimum is a sound policy objective up to the point after which actual real output is sacrificed as a result, but not beyond that point. For if you push it further, then money, which should be a means of exchange, becomes a bar to exchange. It is rather as if you emptied the car of petrol in order to lighten the load, or drained the body of blood in order to bring down the temperature. Indeed some fanatical believers in 'fighting inflation' at any cost fall precisely into this intellectual trap – and so into the very 'money illusion' which they often denounce. They point to the illusion that you would be richer if there were more money, but no more goods. But they then advocate deflationary policies which actually *reduce* the total supply of goods, while comforting themselves with the thought that as prices are lower and (as they assume) their money incomes constant, they must get richer. But if the total supply of real goods and services is lower, the community as a whole cannot get richer and some must get poorer. The fanatical fighters against inflation are therefore really assuming, probably unconsciously, that they themselves will get richer while others get very much poorer. For this is exactly what happens in a deflation. The total real income goes down, but those lucky enough to possess a secure money income actually gain because the newly unemployed get very much poorer. That may be one reason why so many sound-money men turn out to have secure incomes.

The practical moral is therefore that the maximum of real income or output should be the normal objective, and that changes in the value of money up or down should be avoided up to the point where they do not conflict with this criterion, but not beyond it. In applying this criterion it is sensible to allow for the fact that both the reflationary and deflationary processes are cumulative, and that the further they accelerate the more troublesome they are to stop. For instance, if in the course of restraining demand in order to check a rise in prices in the UK, the rate of unemployment rises about 2 or 3 per cent, that should be regarded as the danger signal. It probably means that total real output is being sacrificed, or will soon be sacrificed, to the secondary objective of preserving money values; and also that a dangerous and cumulative deflationary slide, difficult to check later, is gathering force. Conversely during the upswing, if the price level in the UK is rising by 7 per cent or more, that also is a red light, and a warning that a cumulative inflationary spiral may be threatened. Restraint at this point would be justified strictly on the suggested criterion of maximizing real output. For when, at any rate in the UK, the price rise reaches the 10–15 per cent rate, public opinion must be expected to demand a halt, and a halt at this point, as much experience shows, is likely to mean for a time an outright loss of output and employment.

The normal policy criterion can be expressed as follows. Wherever there is a clash between the objective of maximizing real output and stabilizing the value of money, the benefit of the doubt should be given to the former. Given this aim, whether the figures suggested above are the best guides to the range, within which one should seek to operate, is a matter of judgement not logic; I only offer them as such, and as applicable to conditions similar to those in the UK. So far, so good. What, however, is to be done if it proves impossible to stay within this range; in other words, if the restraint of demand needed to keep the rise in prices down to 7 per cent or so has to be so vigorous as to push unemployment above 2 or 3 per cent? The answer is, for all the reasons given in earlier chapters, that if that is true, the economy *must* be suffering from cost inflation rather than demand inflation. If curbs on demand cannot stop a cumulative rise in prices without causing major unemployment, then it must be mainly costs and not demand which are pushing up prices. In that case the argument is brought back once again to the central dilemma: how do you stop money costs rising faster than potential output?

Before pursuing this final hard core of the contemporary problem, it is worth setting out clearly the broad practical options open to those managing the modern economy, and the probable consequences of pursuing each of them. Totally to ignore the problem, and put one's faith in some invisible helping hand, is simply not possible, however much *laissez-faire* extremists may wish it was, because governments are in any case forced to take decisions on the control of bank money and on public expenditure and taxation. There are three practical options: first, to restrain demand and leave costs to look after themselves; secondly, to expand demand to the point needed for full output and leave costs and prices to the mercy of market pressures; and thirdly, both to keep demand at the level needed for full use of capacity, and to hold the rise in costs to the rate of possible rise in total real output.

Option one, restraint of demand but with no control of money costs, is the method that has been followed by the UK government since 1979. Its immediate effect is that total costs come to exceed total demand because demand is held back and costs are not. As a result unemployment starts to increase rapidly, as it did after June 1979. But pay rates continue to rise also. As consumer spending falls further because of the growing unemployment, the gap widens, and the fall in demand and rise in unemployment merge into the familiar cumulative deflation. As a result of the fall in consumer spending, real investment falls even faster. But the pay rise, though it may moderate slightly, will continue upwards, because there is little to stop it, and because those in employment can claim, rightly, that prices are still rising. At this point a widening budget deficit will emerge, as unemployment benefit payments mount higher and higher and tax revenues dwindle. But if an attempt is made to curb this deficit by heavier taxes, either industry's costs are raised still higher, or the public's spending is further reduced.

It may be that at some stage in the growth of unemployment the rise in prices and costs will slacken. But it is highly probable that only a small slackening of the price rise would be achieved by a huge rise in unemployment. Some monetarists are fond of arguing that increases in demand may raise prices without any effect in reducing unemployment. They forget that this might just as easily work the other way: that cutting demand might increase unemployment heavily with very little effect on prices. No exact trade-off can be calculated, as it depends on circumstances. But the objective sometimes advocated by naïve monetarists, an entirely stable price level, might well (with no incomes policy) require 30–50 per cent unemployment in modern conditions in the UK. The only sure result of such a deflationary blood-letting would be a huge loss of real income over a period of years, and before long of productive capital also; in fact a long-term loss by the purged country of wealth, influence, defence capacity, and political status in the world. There is no reason why the stagnation induced by such policies should automatically end unless the policies are changed; nor why the whole process should not begin over again if an upswing did fortuitously appear. The outcome will depend on the pure chance of some external change in the economic weather coming to the rescue at the right moment.

Option two is to expand demand as necessary to preserve or to attain full employment and leave pay rates to free collective bargaining. If the economy started, as now in the UK, with massive unused capacity almost everywhere, this policy need not generate excessive price inflation until unemployment is brought down to a low level. But as soon as the economy reached full capacity, the difficulties encountered in 1975–6 would reassert themselves. Since most modern economies, including certainly that of the UK, cannot when fully employed raise total real output by more than about 3 per cent a year at the best, it follows that unless the average annual pay rise is held to that figure prices generally must in these circumstances rise sharply. And anyone who believes that in full employment conditions and with no direct restraint on pay rates the average rise could be held to 3 per cent is not taking the contemporary problem seriously. What would most probably happen is that as the various groups tried to recoup themselves for the loss which they felt the higher prices had inflicted on them, the rise in pay would accelerate and the familiar upward spiral take over. In the case of the UK, as soon as oil earnings ceased to plug the overseas payments gap, the exchange rate would probably fall faster and threaten a further upward pressure on prices. All those who are above all anxious to end the hideous and unnecessary waste caused by mass unemployment would be wise to face the fact and, however reluctantly, reject this option. I fear that the chance of any future government carrying out as skilful and speedy a rescue operation as did the 1975–7 government are frankly slender.

And so we are left with option three: a concerted attempt to influence both total demand and total costs so as to keep them in reasonable balance not merely with each other, but also with the practicable rate of growth of the real output of the economy. If these three flows could be kept rising at something like the same annual rate, there is no insuperable reason why the rise in prices should not be kept below the 7 per cent danger level and the high employment and growth of the twenty-five years after 1945 resumed. At least this programme has the laws of arithmetic – quite a useful ally – on its side. The objection commonly raised against it is not that it would not achieve the desired result, but rather that it just cannot be done because it is all too difficult in practice.

Certainly it is difficult – that can be agreed straightaway. But as the Greeks said, everything worthwhile is difficult; and since in this case such immense issues for the future of mankind hang on the issue, one should surely not abandon the struggle in advance until it is shown to be not merely difficult, but impossible. After all, we should already have learnt something from experience; and that experience, I believe, enables us for a start to elucidate rather further the nature of the practical difficulty. First, macroeconomics is not an exact science, and the practical steering of an economy must be based on continuous judgement and not on precise instruction or infallible forecasts made in advance. This is not surprising because, though the forces with which one is confronted may be identifiable, and their magnitudes estimated, the exact result of their interaction at a given moment in the future cannot be forecast. A car driver does not extract from a computer a detailed advance schedule of the required pressures on the various controls at each moment in his journey. But he does normally know where he wants to get to and may also be guided by a reliable map; after this he keeps his eyes open and responds to the circumstances of the moment. This is at least a better analogy for economic management than that of the plane temporarily handed over to the automatic pilot on the assumption that the relevant circumstances will not change for a major period.

And though analogies must never be pressed too far, that of driving a car is relevant in one or two other respects. Those who aspire to demand management would be wise to start by understanding that you sometimes have to use the brake as well as the accelerator. Experience has shown that some learners become so enthusiastic about the accelerator that they regard any use of the brake as inadmissible if not immoral. Even with the best car in the world, these enthusiasts are not likely to stay long on the road. Indeed few things would discredit demand management more quickly than a moral taboo on any use of the brake. The skilled driver should also assume from the start that there is no final solution. What is called nowadays an 'exogenous factor' and used once to be called a *deux ex machina* – a devaluation, a strike, an EEC crisis, or an oil cartel – may at any time erupt, and knock you suddenly off course.

What then are the possibilities, and what are the instruments for keeping the vehicle under control? The aim is to hold, so far as humanly possible, both the rate of unemployment and the rate of rising prices within the range suggested above; and the principle means of achieving this will be to keep the flow of total demand as defined here in line with total costs of all the factors of production available. At any particular moment it will have to be decided whether or not an expansion, restraint or contraction of demand, or restraint on costs is or is not needed. (Deliberate boosting of money costs is hardly likely to be required!) The prime necessity will be to realize that total effective demand is the key element in the economy which has to be watched and influenced.[2] It is the beginning of wisdom in practical economic policy to recognize this, and to see the mere quantity or stock of money for what it is: a single factor among the many which influence the flow of demand. Few will at any rate deny that for governments and central banks working together influencing demand is in some measure less difficult than influencing costs. In deciding at a given moment whether demand needs curbing or stimulating or leaving alone, the best dial to watch will normally, though not exclusively, be the level of unemployment. As Sir Alec Cairncross – and nobody has more experience of the task – says in his memorandum to the Select Committee already mentioned:[3] 'Of all the indicators, those relating to the labour market seem to me the most significant since what goes on in the labour market is central to an understanding of the functioning of the economy.'

When the dials have been read, and a decision taken on the required treatment of demand, what levers are at hand to enforce it? Despite all complications and controversies there will, I think, be general agreement that two major instruments are available: the control of public expenditure, taxation and borrowing on the one hand, and the management of bank credit on the other. Since in the UK the current and capital expenditure together of governments and public agencies forms 40 or 50 per cent of total national spending, clearly changes in public spending must have a powerful effect one way or the other. Other things being equal, a rise in spending will tend to stimulate demand, and a fall to depress it. One other thing which will often not be equal is taxation. If the government claws back in extra taxation as much as it hands out in extra spending, then the effect on total demand must be expected to be neutral. But if it finances the extra spending by borrowing, then total demand will be expanded moderately if the money borrowed is saved by the public out of income, and less moderately if it is financed by newly created bank credit. The questions whether money ought to be borrowed, and how much, must depend on the level of total demand required.

If it were not true that governments can stimulate demand when they wish, then there would not have been a vigorous demand inflation in both the UK and the USA in both the world wars, and unemployment would not have been wiped out in each case. Though presumably nobody would deny this, it has become fashionable recently to repeat that in the present age for some unexplained reason you cannot overcome depression by reflating demand. This is true in the sense that if you allow a cost inflation to run away with you, you cannot stop *that* by simply spending more. But if it is suggested that government spending cannot stimulate an economy and employment when they are running far below capacity, this has been crushingly refuted by the Reagan administration. By means of a huge budget deficit of nearly $200 billion in 1983–4, it succeeded in massively reflating the US economy, raising real national output by 6 per cent a year or more, and rapidly increasing employment as already recorded (p. 212). The reality of this success is in no way altered by the fact that President Reagan did not mean to do it and did not admit he was doing it. His failure to balance the budget saved him, even though he professed not to know what he was doing. Nor is the success of the great Reagan reflation of 1983–4 made any less real in the USA because interest rates were pushed to high levels. The damage done by high interest rates is that they deter investment or spending. But if the money is being spent anyway, and interest rates rise as a result, the damage to the spending country is minor.

Certainly the high interest rates damaged some less developed countries. But it cannot fairly be argued that the Reagan reflation injured the rest of the outside world. On the contrary, by greatly increasing imports and incurring a huge visible trade deficit, the USA was so far exerting a stimulating effect on other economies, even though it would have been more stimulating if US interest rates had been lower. But it was not very reasonable for countries such as the UK to complain that US interest rates were forcing up UK rates when it was the removal of exchange control by the UK which effectively tied UK interest rates to Wall Street. This particular wound was self-inflicted. The sensible course for a western European nation during the years of the Reagan reflation would have been to take full advantage of the rising US demand for imports but keep its own interest rates down by exchange controls. The more successful countries had it both ways.

Nor, purely from the point of view of reflating or disinflating demand, does it normally matter what type of spending it is proposed to expand or contract. It may be that some forms of spending will impinge more completely on the home market or be more labour-intensive; and this is relevant. In general, however, the *quantity* of spending should depend on the needs of total demand, but the *type* on the merits of the particular spending programme. Many of us would like to see reflation by way of capital investment, both public and private. But that is because the country will need capital equipment in the future, not because it is necessarily more reflationary than spending on school meals or old age pensions. Many others would prefer to see the Reagan Administration spending their $200 billion deficit on social investment rather than defence. But the expansionist effects are not necessarily different. Pound notes and dollar bills do not trot around the economy with a label saying 'I am virtuous. I came from the Public Sector', or 'I am sinister. I came from the Arms Budget.' Nor do the recipients spend them differently according to their origin, or indeed know it. The Romans understood this when they said: 'Money does not smell.' What is relevant here, however, is the obvious truth that governments can and do, and indeed must – even if they do not wish to – influence total spending and so the whole course of economic life in the nation concerned.

The second important instrument of control is the power of governments and central banks together, as recorded in earlier chapters, to influence the total quantity of bank money (broadly notes and deposits) at any one time. There is no need to fall, as some narrow monetarists have seemed to fall, into the trap of believing that the Chancellor of the Exchequer or the Governor of the Bank have only to pull the right lever, and the quantity of money next week will somehow assume the precise total intended. Control of the money stock is not like switching on an electric light, with an instant and predictable result. The quantity of money is partly determined not by the government or central bank, but by the public, whether as individuals or groups, and their propensity to spend, save, hoard, or borrow. Changes in the total, therefore, cannot be exactly predicted, even if they can be measured. And measurement itself is not easy, since if certain types of 'money' are controlled, the public – at least the professionals – may devise other paper 'promises to pay' which people are willing to accept. To attempt to control output, employment, and the price level purely by manipulating the stock of money would be like trying to drive a car from the back seat with bits of string tied to the controls. You would have to go very slowly, and you would not get very far. A government exclusively concerned with the stock of money would be seeking guidance from something they could not easily measure or control, and whose effect on the operative flow of demand was highly uncertain.

On the other hand, there need be little doubt that if the authorities push long enough and hard enough on the monetary levers they will normally produce some effect. By swimming against the tide, or leaning on the wind, they will usually make some headway. For when all the complexities have been unravelled (and it is easy here to become blinded by a tangle of technicalities and statistics), at least two powerful levers remain in the authorities' hands. First they can, with reasonable competence, vary interest rates. A rise in interest rates, by raising overdraft rates, is itself a rise in the costs of most businesses and therefore of total costs in the economy; and a fall is a drop in total costs. In addition, however little interest rates may influence people to hoard or lend, there is not much question that they influence the potential borrower; notably the house-building industry, and to a less extent the industrial borrower over a large field. They can also exert a substantial, though short-term, reflationary or deflationary effect by encouraging or discouraging the holding of stocks. Both the outstanding success of low interest rates in the UK in 1932–7 in generating a housing boom and as a result a general expansion, and the lamentably low level of industrial and housing investment in face of the penally high interest rates of 1979–84, are further confirmation of this generally accepted fact.

But can the authorities in practice push interest rates the way they wish? Since the 1960s a new doctrine has sprung up which maintains that interest rates not merely are, but must be, determined by inhuman 'market forces'. But this myth is refuted by twentieth-century history. Of course if you leave interest rates to market forces, they will be determined by these forces. But, as already described in earlier chapters, bank rate in the UK was held at 2 per cent almost continuously from 1932 to the end of 1951; and during the Second World War and for many years afterwards the level and direction of bank lending were largely decided by government policy without very much regard to the rate of interest. Indeed it was largely the abandonment of this system after 1970 which led to the disasters of *Competition and Credit Control* and the Heath–Barber boom.[4] Naturally the system of control does not mean, any more than any other form of rationing, that you can have both low interest rates and no limit to borrowing. It means that there must be a limit, and that the limit is imposed by direct decision and not by market forces. But whether this system is considered good or bad, nobody can deny that it is a possible system because it did in fact operate for at least twenty years. The responsibility for high interest rates in the UK in the 1980s, therefore, whether they are welcome or not, rests not with market forces, but with the decision to leave rates to market forces; and notably with the ending of exchange control in 1979, which ensured that UK interest rates would be largely determined by market forces not in the UK but in the USA.

Secondly, a central bank, even if working in a partly or wholly de-controlled system, can, if all else fails, raise or lower interest rates and the quantity of money by buying or selling government securities in the market. If an expansion of the economy is wanted, and there are no other borrowers, by buying securities the central bank is in effect lending. New money is created by this means. The borrowers' strike would only be absolute if nobody was willing to sell securities to the central bank at any price; and history does not record such a calamity. Certainly it might be harder for the Bank to sell securities except at very high yields; but in these circumstances it would presumably be seeking credit restraint and higher rates would not matter. If on the other hand the general need were for expansion, some growth of credit would be permissible. The difficulty would be at its greatest if restraint were generally desirable, but the government insisted on borrowing on a huge scale. But this is merely to say that there is no monetary magic which enables a government or central bank to have it all ways; and that if in a fully employed economy a government seeks to borrow heavily, it is following too expansionary a budget policy. It should either reduce its borrowing or accept higher interest rates. But the pound sterling and the UK economy are a very long way from that particular dilemma in the 1980s. Indeed in the UK in 1984-5 the most effective single means to ensure recovery would have been, and still is, a drastic cut in interest rates, to achieve which a return to exchange control would be essential.

Nevertheless it remains a strange anomaly, seldom noticed, in our modern money system that the money required by the public can only be brought into existence in the form of loans from mainly private banks. There is no logical reason why this should be so. It just happened that from the eighteenth century onwards, when the world needed rapidly expanding means of payment, the banks discovered how to generate them in the form of bank deposits or notes which started life as promises to pay. And then it came to be taken for granted that this was the natural system. But if a bank or anyone else creates new money and lends it at interest, or buys securities, the interest it earns is what once used to be called a coiner's profit. For this reason, because it was thought right that this profit should accrue to the community, for many centuries only the king or government was allowed to issue new money. By the 1844 Bank Charter Act, already described, and by the 1928 Act the profit on the 'Fiduciary Issue' of notes had by law to be paid to the government;[5] and indeed today the income from the more than £13,000 million worth of securities held by the Bank of England's Issue Department against its note issue must accrue as part of the Bank's profits to the Exchequer. But purely as a result of historical evolution the greater part of the money stock in the UK consists of deposits in private banks. Yet there is no corresponding obligation on these banks to contribute to the Exchequer any part of the profits due to the creation of this new money. The anomaly becomes even more grotesque when the banks actually charge interest for lending to the government money which has been created not by the government but by the banks; and that in turn goes a long way to explaining why bank profits are consistently high in boom or slump.

This strange system, though paradoxical and not really socially defensible, is nevertheless not unworkable. It is better than having no machinery at all for steadily creating new money. For everyone agrees, even the purest monetarists, that the quantity of money ought to be steadily expanded if the national income is to grow. If one were starting from scratch, it would be more sensible to devise a system by which the new money which has to be created in such substantial amounts should either be used in the first instance to finance the state's expenditure; or at least by which the profit due to the creation of new money, made by private firms, should accrue to the Exchequer. In principle, the case is strong either for public ownership of banks (as in France over a wide area) or at least a special tax on their profits. In the twenty years of 2 or 3 per cent interest rates it could plausibly be argued that the system worked and the baby was a small one. Though still minor, when seen against the whole multifarious brood of macroeconomic policies, it is not quite so small today. This baby is growing up.

One other, though less direct, lever for influencing the flow of demand remains within the reach of the authorities: the exchange rate. A fall in the exchange rate will normally stimulate demand for home products by increasing exports and restraining imports; though higher prices of imports may force some consumers to cut their other purchases. Conversely a rise in the exchange rate will tend to depress demand. But wise governments refrain from using the exchange rate as a normal means of influencing demand, because its prime purpose must be to keep the external trade and payments account in balance without too violent jerks. It will not often be possible to use it for both purposes at once; and the effort of doing so, as the fiasco of the rising exchange rate in 1980 demonstrated, may end with the worst of both worlds. Despite the array of all too obvious difficulties, trip wires, and banana skins, therefore, it is clear that a modern government holds a far from negligible range of instruments in its hand for influencing demand if it wishes to use them. So long as it realizes that it is practising the art of the possible, that the weather will often change, that sometimes one must lean with the wind and sometimes against it, and that different pressures will be needed at different times, it would be absurd to regard the control of demand as beyond known capacity. Indeed experience confirms the argument, for the early post-war years of success were more numerous than the recent years of failure.

Notes

[1] The same point is put very fairly by an American economist, Richard N. Cooper of Yale University: 'Economic growth is concerned with the capacity of the economy to produce, whereas management of aggregate demand is concerned with the level of total demand relative to the capacity of the economy; it is this which determines the level of unemployment.' Brookings Report: *Britain's Economic Prospects*, p. 162.

[2] As both James Meade and Samuel Brittan have constantly urged. The latter (*The Role and Limits of Government*, p. 129) gives this flow the name of 'money GDP' and adds a useful list of labels for it.

[3] *Report to the House of Commons Treasury and Civil Service Select Committee*, 17 July 1980, p. 144.

[4] See Chapter 17.

[5] See Chapter 8.

27

Incomes Policy?

Demand, however, is only half the battle. As the argument of this book has shown, what we are faced with in the 1980s is a threat of cost inflation; if we merely expand demand, we are almost certain before long to be involved in accelerating price inflation also. On the other hand if control of costs can be achieved, the basic economic problem of the rest of the twentieth century is solved; there are immense gains to be secured and growth and full employment become possible. And that is the over-riding reason why the difficulties of applying a workable incomes policy, formidable as they are, have got to be faced, and why to abandon the effort would be a counsel of despair. For the objection commonly raised to incomes policies is not that they are invalid in principle, or contrary to the laws of economics or arithmetic, but that in practice they will not work. The question, however, whether a policy will work is one that cannot be decided by argument, but only by trying. If it is finally shown in practice that an incomes policy cannot work, and if we still want high employment without price inflation, we will have to resort to more drastic remedies in our industrial system, such as much wider co-operative employee share ownership and possibly other forms of ownership as well.

Meanwhile I have to declare an interest as one who opposed incomes policies throughout the fifties and sixties on the ground that they were unworkable, but was converted in the seventies by the demonstration that, however imperfectly, they could work, and that full employment was unattainable without them. The conventional propaganda wisdom, more often repeated than argued, is that such policies not only merely did not work in practice, but that after a time they 'collapsed'. But the record just does not bear this out. In fact, in the UK and elsewhere since 1945 the effort to maintain restraint policies of some kind has been a drawn, and not a lost, battle; and such policies have not so much 'collapsed' as been prematurely abandoned by governments either because they lacked the courage to continue them, or because they wanted to reverse what a government of another party had been doing.

In 1947–51 the pay restraint policy gave four years of very low unemployment, very rapid real growth, and only a moderate rise in prices. It was abandoned by the new government in 1951–2 because conditions appeared to have eased. The 1965–70 pay and prices policy also permitted substantial growth and rising employment, and restrained the rise in prices up to 1969, but was then weakened just when the upward pressure on pay rates was gathering force. Controls were abandoned in 1970, but had to be reimposed in a statutory from in 1972. Following another attempted dash for freedom in 1974, the pay rise accelerated to the crisis of 1975–6. In 1977–9, while a renewed restraint policy was in force, both unemployment and price inflation fell together for nearly two years until the winter of 1978–9; after which all forms of incomes policy were again abandoned by a new government in 1979, with the results we know.

Some considered judgements on the experience to date have been recorded by those who actually held responsibility. Aubrey Jones, who headed the Prices and Incomes Board for five years, reaches the clear conclusion in his survey,[1] published in 1973, that restraint policies for incomes and prices, given various improvements, are both workable and necessary. He has since proposed[2] a more positive pay reforming authority for the future. Sir Frank Figgures, Chairman of the 1973–4 Statutory Pay Board,[3] having frankly listed the major complexities involved, states that on the whole the policy favoured the low-paid; that the 'compliance and acquiescence of employers and employees was forthcoming in large measure, albeit under protest on occasions'; and that the Board 'rarely needed to use its legal powers'. A verdict on the economic effects of incomes policies was given by the National Institute of Economic and Social Research in their memorandum to the House of Commons Treasury Select Committee:[4] 'As far as incomes policy effects are concerned, the evidence that there are powerful effects over not inconsiderable lengths of time we would regard as very strong.' F.T. Blackaby,[5] after a survey of incomes policies from 1960 to 1974, concludes:

> 'In sum, if we suppose that over this period there was a variety of forces tending to produce a rising trend in the increase in money earnings, then the experience of the late 1960s and early 1970s is consonant with the view that incomes policies during that period were successful, so long as they were in force, in holding back this process.'

Sir Henry Phelps Brown[6] sums up the moral in this way: 'Instead of taking the past breakdowns of incomes policy as reasons for discarding it, we had . . . better try to learn from them how to do better in future.'

Many other democratic countries have pursued similar restraint policies for varying periods with varying degrees of success. West Germany has long operated a system by which a pay rise norm is declared annually by the central bank after discussion with industry and the unions, and price increases were kept comparatively low even in the inflationary 1970s. In Sweden in the same years an annual norm has been negotiated by central trade union and employers' organizations independent of the government; and the price rise has seldom exceeded 4 or 5 per cent. Norway and Austria have operated similar systems in recent years with at times even more successful results. France and Canada, which have attempted price control without incomes control, have been less successful. French governments have tended to trade industrial or financial concessions to various interests in return for compliance. The USA has practised various restraint policies under the Kennedy, Nixon, Carter, and later administrations, and for a time suffered heavier unemployment in 1980–2 after they had been abandoned. US governments, not unlike those in the UK, have vacillated between different policies, as one president succeeded another. In Australia compulsory last-resort pay arbitration has been in force for most of this century. Started in 1904, and continuously evolving according to changing circumstances, Australian policy is now based on a non-government Conciliation and Arbitration Commission. It is essentially a system of compulsory arbitration without compulsory compliance, but normally operates in practice as compulsory conciliation. In the full employment years it achieved in Australia a higher rise in real incomes than in the UK with a lower rise in money pay.[7] From 1975 to 1981 the Commission formulated what was in effect a six-monthly national minimum wage in the light of the consumer price index. Under the subsequent Labour government it has included in its six-monthly awards the full amount of the rise in living costs unless very good reason is shown to the contrary. This regime is an example of what can be done in a highly democratic industrial country with a strong trade union movement; but it necessarily depends on some degree of political consensus. So the verdict from practical experience in Australia and other countries such as Sweden and Switzerland is varied and indecisive, and in no sense justifies the conclusion that all incomes policies are unworkable. Assertions on the impracticability of such policies have perhaps been founded more often on ideology than on evidence.

But the difficulties, by common consent, are real and obvious. The first major difficulty is one of objectives. The purpose of the whole policy is to keep down the *average* rise in money incomes to a certain figure: say 5 per cent, so that it does not exceed the rise in *total* real output. But unfortunately the average is the result of innumerable individual settlements; and it is not desirable, or economically possible, for all these to be identical. How then do you contrive in advance to make all the individual and separate settlements end up by generating the right average? The second basic difficulty is that the umpire (assuming for the moment there is one) who has to decide in individual cases will be faced with a number of criteria which are qualitatively and not just quantitatively different. He will have to take account of rising living costs, productivity of the individual group, 'comparability', the need for more or less manpower for the job in question, differentials, recent history, and the needs of general economic policy. There will be no simple formula, mathematical or otherwise, on which he can base his verdict. He will be in the position of a judge, who has to convert general guidance into a precise individual award. But he will not be in the position of a judge in having available an Act of Parliament or book of rules to provide the answer. He will in time have precedents; but essentially his task will be to take all these various pointers and comparisons into account, and reach the general judgement that the right answer in the case in question is, say, 3½ per cent. This is what the existing, numerous 'review bodies' in the

UK do already, and have indeed long done. The trouble is that separate review bodies 'responsible' for individual groups tend after a time to become advocates for the group rather than judges; and startling pay rises tend to be granted to whichever group is politically fashionable at the moment, whether dons, police, the armed services, civil servants, lorry drivers, or solicitors. The only remedy for this particular malady is the establishment of one final appeal authority.

The third major obstacle is the familiar dilemma of sanctions. It is very easy to point out that if the whole apparatus of an incomes policy has no sanction to back it, it will become a waste of time and manpower; but that if it does involve legal sanctions, it will be widely resented as an excessive invasion of civil liberties. Which sanctions, if any, should be used, is therefore essentially an issue for public opinion to decide; but it should make its decision with a clear understanding that the employment or unemployment of several million men and women is ultimately at stake. The use of imprisonment as a backing for incomes policies is out of the question, because to imprison an employer for paying too high a salary, or an employee for striking against an award, would not be accepted as defensible. But public opinion might well accept the procedure of injunctions, followed by fines for non-compliance, which already operates over a wide field of law where the issues and evils at stake are sometimes socially trivial compared with mass unemployment. In the Australian system legal sanctions exist, but in practice are very seldom used.

At least some other conditions of a successful future incomes policy seem reasonably beyond dispute. First, it must not be used primarily for redistribution of incomes and wealth. This can only be achieved through taxation and social benefits (which are just as important as full employment, but beyond the scope of this book, though without them no incomes policy is likely to succeed for long). Certainly the pay aspect of any incomes policy must be guided by equity in the sense that similar work is rewarded with similar pay, and that appropriate differentials are maintained for special skills, responsibility, and performance. But the main purpose must be to maximize employment rather than redistribute wealth. Secondly, an incomes policy with any hope of success must be treated as something for the long term, at least for the foreseeable future. Otherwise, as in the past, every group will be waiting breathlessly for the green light, and the more aggressive will break out on the amber. Thirdly, it must be generally clear that everyone concerned is being treated fairly. This means, for instance, that in a system of conciliation backed by voluntary or compulsory arbitration, but without legal sanctions for compliance – what may be called a soft incomes policy – at least all earned incomes must be within its scope. If on the other hand effective legal sanctions for non-compliance are thought necessary, then control of prices, dividends, and rent, as in the past, would have to be brought within the range of the policy. Nothing will more quickly destroy restraint than a feeling that only one section of the public is being restrained. Fourthly, at the centre of the system there must operate an independent, impartial umpiring authority.

That authority's job cannot be performed by a minister, still less by Parliament, both of whom would soon be accused of party or sectional partiality. The umpire's attitude to the government's policy should be similar in this respect to the attitude of a judge (or the Inland Revenue) to the law. In British conditions it would probably be for the government and Parliament, after full consultation, to specify what average rise in money incomes was practicable for the year in question (the norm), and for the umpire to apply it to individual disputes (in some cases perhaps by way of appeal from existing 'review bodies'). The umpire might have some or all of three main functions, including those already performed in the UK by the existing Advisory, Conciliation and Arbitration Service (ACAS), which could without much difficulty be transformed into the wider authority. It could seek to resolve disputes by agreement rather than conflict, but taking no view on the rights and wrongs involved. It could, if asked by all parties, give a verdict on the rights and wrongs. Finally, it could give such a verdict at the request either of one or other party or of the government itself. Many variations of detail are possible, some more suited to one country and some to another.

Two serious attempts have recently been made to devise an effective incomes policy which would be acceptable in a democracy: one by Professor James Meade, and the other by Sir Henry Phelps Brown. The Meade plan[8] is based on the desire both to preserve the strike as a last-resort weapon in the employee's hands and also to get away from 'central wage-fixing' with its danger of too much bureaucratic control. By this plan, which Professor Meade calls 'not-quite-compulsory arbitration', free collective bargaining would proceed in the normal way. If voluntary agreement was reached between the parties, that would be the end of it, and nobody could interfere. But if the dispute was not settled, either party, and perhaps the government also, could take the issue to a permanent independent pay commission, whose primary job would be to give the award most likely to promote employment. In this case it is assumed that the government would be maintaining the flow of total money demand for labour at the level needed to employ the whole labour force, and also that 'a central body' would have issued a 'general guideline' for the rise in pay permissible as a national average in the year in question. If the commission's award were accepted by both sides, no difficulty would arise. Naturally, if it were rejected by either side – if the employer paid more or less than the award, or the employees struck against it and yet no sanctions were applied – the norm and the pay policy would be undermined. Under the Meade plan suggested possible sanctions are, in the case of the employer, making it unlawful for him to pay according to scales other than those awarded (with fines for non-compliance); for the employee striking against an award, the loss of certain benefit or tax concessions; and for a union backing such a strike, the loss of certain legal immunities.

The advantages of the Meade plan, then, are the avoidance of excessive centralized wage fixing, and of other than financial penalties on individuals or groups (though the plan does need a central independent pay commission and a central body to issue the 'general guideline'). The disadvantages are the plan's inability to prevent agreed but inflationary pay settlements, such as the Ford agreement in the autumn of 1978 which undermined a hitherto successful anti-inflationary policy; and secondly, the doubt whether public opinion would accept even the mild last-resort sanctions suggested. The plan certainly goes some way to escape the basic dilemma that either you have sanctions or you do not, but not the whole way. Professor Meade also somewhat weakens his case, as do others, by talking of 'wages' when he means pay.

Sir Henry Phelps Brown's alternative[9] has similarities to the Australian system and comes nearer to what Professor Meade would call 'central wage-fixing'. Under the Phelps Brown plan there would be an independent non-government Central Arbitration Commission, whose first duty would be, after due consultation, to issue from time to time a national award – a percentage or an absolute amount – which would automatically be paid under all contracts unless variations up or down were accepted by agreement. If such variations were agreed, they would come into force freely and automatically. If, however, agreement was not reached, the parties would be under obligation to take the issue – in the case of the UK – to ACAS for conciliation, and if that failed to go to arbitration before the Commission. Fines (not enforceable by imprisonment) would be the sanction against those taking industrial action before the conciliation and arbitration procedures were completed. But there would be no obligation to accept the arbitration award once it was given, and therefore no penalty on either party for resisting it.

This alternative system amounts in effect to compulsory conciliation but not compulsory arbitration; it is one degree 'softer' than the Meade scheme. It is less likely to be criticized as constituting excessive interference with basic freedoms than as being too weak a vessel to prevent a pay–price spiral when economic forces are pressing that way. But again, its ability or inability to do this is a matter of opinion which can only be finally decided by the practical test. Australian experience lends some support to the Phelps Brown plan. It is a virtue of his alternative that the whole existing UK system of individual settlements and conciliation is preserved before arbitration is invoked, and that the near-automatic basic award would normally meet the cost-of-living argument and be acceptable in very many cases. It is at the same time, however, a virtue of the Meade scheme that the arbitration body would be specifically charged to adopt as its main objective the promotion of employment, which makes explicit the real underlying issues.

Indeed it would be possible to combine some of the merits of each alternative by retaining the Phelps Brown independent but strong Central Arbitration Commission, but specifically declaring the promotion of employment to be one of its main duties, while leaving with the government the power of deciding the national guideline or norm. Both are 'soft' policies, in the sense that in each the two parties, if they agree, are free to reach any settlement however contrary to the national norm. The Meade plan is slightly less soft, in so far as after arbitration the final sanctions may be applied. A possible slightly 'harder' halfway house could be achieved if the government was given the authority to refer to the arbitrator an agreed settlement which violated the norm. Harder still would be legal powers to impose in the last resort the penalties proposed in the Meade scheme on any party defying an arbitration award.

For a future British government determined to bring down unemployment decisively the wisest course in all the circumstances would probably be to base its approach explicitly on a Stage I and Stage II incomes policy. The aim would be to move gradually, until experience proved it necessary to proceed less gradually. In Stage I, starting from say a 10–15 per cent level of unemployment similar to that prevailing in the UK in 1985, and from considerable unused productive capacity, the government could afford to begin, if possible by agreement with employers' and employees' organizations, with a soft incomes policy. This would involve at least a centrally established norm for pay increases in the relevant year, and a national arbitration body to which disputed issues could be voluntarily transferred where normal bargaining and conciliation had failed. But all settlements voluntarily agreed would freely come into force. In return for this, the government would undertake to expand demand so as gradually to achieve rising output and falling unemployment. The government itself as employer would of course also operate the policy and observe the current norm. In this stage expanding output should help to keep prices from rising too sharply. If by the time unemployment had been reduced to, say, 5 or 6 per cent, prices were still not rising too rapidly, the gradual expansion could be continued.

If, however, the rise were approaching the 10 per cent level, and appeared to be accelerating, the government would inform Parliament and representative industrial organizations that it could not extend the expansion of demand any further unless a Stage II incomes regime were agreed. This regime would have to involve the right of the government, as well as of the parties to a dispute, to refer the pay issues to arbitration, and would also involve some last-resort legal sanctions of the kind suggested by Professor Meade (excluding imprisonment) for non-compliance. In that case restraint would have to cover prices and dividends as well as pay. If the government could obtain the consent of Parliament and representative organizations of employers and labour, it could then proceed to Stage II and further expansion. It would at the same time have to explain frankly that if the pace accelerated, either the expansionist policy would have to be abandoned or the last-resort sanctions used. The Australian Labour Government of 1983–4 acted broadly on this principle and with considerable success. If on the other hand general agreement was not secured, the government should make it clear that the existing level of unemployment would have to be accepted, and demand henceforth strictly held back by budgetary and monetary means. And this in turn was the less attractive alternative accepted by the French Mitterand administration when it had to switch from active reflation to the pursuit of stability.

The practical merit of a two-stage policy such as this, whatever the variations according to different circumstances or different countries, would be that it would present the real fundamental choice to those who in reality have to make it – those who pay and receive salaries and wages throughout the economy. Either they accept the discipline necessary for full employment; or else they do not, and must accept lower employment, and incidentally lower profits. It should be their choice and not the government's. The sceptic may still retort that these paper plans and pleas for moderation are all very fine; but what happens if some maverick group inspired by the gospel of Friedman or Marx defies the law, the arbitration tribunal, and everyone else. It is perfectly true that if 100,000 men, or even 10,000, are determined to go on strike, come what may, nobody can stop them; though the employer, public or private, can still decline to give way. But on these assumptions, such a breakdown would occur in any case, and the public are no worse off than if there had been no policy at all. And it is surely common sense to believe that even the most aggrieved and aggressive of groups would be somewhat less disposed to defy the employer, the arbitration tribunal, Parliament, the courts, and the law than simply to defy their employer alone.

Fundamentally the issue at stake is the ancient one: whether you settle disputes by rational argument and the will of the majority, or by force. When the idea of law and order instead of fighting it out was first mooted by some prehistoric pioneer, it was probably mocked as preposterous and impracticable.[10] But the change came, by degrees. Fortunately the effort was not abandoned after the first failures. On the eve of the battle of Bosworth the notion that Tudor monarchs would in time bring feudal private armies to an end would have been loudly scorned by the sceptics. So probably was William Pitt's idea of the modern income tax derided in the 1790s, not to mention PAYE and National Insurance in the twentieth century. Admittedly all these devices are imperfect, laborious, and inconvenient. But the decisive question is whether they are not better than the alternative. And the alternative in the choice being examined here is mass unemployment.

Because more understanding seems at present to be what we need, this book has stuck to economics, and has nowhere mentioned the human evils of unemployment. But it is these evils which are conclusive. Deflation and unemployment in a modern society mean not merely poverty and hideous waste of human talent, but idleness, demoralization, neglect, disillusion, and the bitterness of mental as well as physical decay. An expansionist economic and social policy, on the other hand, generates activity, effort, experiment, enterprise, innovation, and pride in constructive achievement. Everyone must judge for themselves which they prefer. But in doing so they should know what they are choosing. Opinion polls, for what they are worth, have recently shown in the UK that a large and persistent majority regard unemployment as a greater evil than 'inflation'. In my judgement, to treat the tedious inconveniences of a rational economic policy as a worse evil than what Professor Meade describes[11] as an 'intolerable return to [the] wasteful folly' of mass unemployment would be grotesque and uncivilized.

Notes

[1] *The New Inflation: The Politics of Prices and Incomes*, p. 158ff.
[2] *The Reform of Pay Determination*.
[3] *Pay Board: Experience of Operating a Statutory Incomes Policy*.
[4] *Report to the House of Commons Treasury and Civil Service Select Committee*, 17 July 1980, p. 157.
[5] *British Economic Policy 1960–1974*, p. 392.
[6] *Incomes Policy: A Modest Proposal*, p. 5. See also *The Barbaric Counter-Revolution*, W.W. Rostow. p. 78-79.
[7] *Incomes Policy: A Modest Proposal*, p. 13.
[8] *Stagflation*, Vol. I, *Wage-Fixing*, Chapter VIII.
[9] *Incomes Policy: A Modest Proposal*, Unservile State Paper No. 30, pp. 8-15.
[10] Beveridge put it this way (*Full Employment in a Free Society*, p. 201):

'Wages ought to be determined by reason . . . . Ordeal by battle has for centuries been rejected as a means of settling legal disputes between citizens.'

[11] *Stagflation*, Vol. I, *Wage-Fixing*, p. 153.

28

The Future of Sterling

Management of money demand and money costs can thus ensure that existing manpower and other resources are reasonably fully used, and that consequently the gradual shift of labour from old to new industries and services is not impeded by fear of heavy unemployment. This is the biggest single contribution which *monetary* policy – the management of money demand and incomes – can make to the aim of keeping changes in money values within moderate bounds. But management of demand and costs will not be enough in itself in the special circumstances of the UK to ensure real growth or balanced international accounts, or to prevent a sharp fall in sterling in the next twenty years. Three other major strands of policy will be needed. These can only be summarized here: first, the maintenance of a higher standard of social justice in the distribution of property and income, without which income restraint will not be possible; secondly, vigorous development through the whole range of microeconomic measures, involving full government support, of the more technologically advanced industries and services; thirdly, the removal of the distortions in commercial policy and consequently in the trade balance introduced in 1972–3 and at present only concealed by large temporary oil earnings.

In particular if we mean to emulate, as we must, the successes of Japan and even France in the last twenty years, future British governments will have to shoulder some new responsibilities in economic policy with which they have so far only tentatively experimented. Those who do not realize the need for new policies are living in a bygone age. In the past thirty years Japan has created from very small beginnings massively successful steel, shipbuilding, motor car, and electronics industries France has built up aircraft, nuclear power, motor vehicle, and telecommunications industries with substantial success, if less spectacular than Japan. In each case this has been done largely because the governments of both countries committed themselves to long-term support of selected industries, and threw the whole weight of the government machine – financial, administrative, and political – behind the approved programme. It could not have been done if everything had been left to the resources of private firms competing with one another in an old-fashioned *laissez-faire* atmosphere. France could never have built up a nuclear power industry without total government support.

In addition, by whole-hearted co-operation between the government machine and their own native enterprises, private or public, Japan, France and other countries have secured a major share of the huge export contracts which are now on offer from many countries in the fields of construction, aircraft, defence, shipbuilding, nuclear power, and telecommunications. While these countries have treated industrial development as a national responsibility – almost a crusade – planned and guided by the government, too often in Britain Conservative governments have just sat back and left everything to private enterprise, and Labour governments have suffered from the hangover of regarding private industry as a somewhat awkward ally. Both these attitudes to economic policy are a hundred years out of date.

Some sporadic constructive efforts have already been made by successive British governments, and without them the prospect would be much worse than it is. But if a sustained, planned, and nationally agreed effort had been exerted comparable with those elsewhere, British industry and British exporting power would be far stronger than they are today. It follows from this that two major new responsibilities should be accepted by future UK governments. First, after thorough research and consultation, clear decisions should be taken on which industries and services have the best long-term prospect of survival and expansion; and the resources needed to back them should then be supplied over a reasonable period of time. Such policies cannot succeed if each government reverses the policies of its predecessors. Some mistakes will be made; but without these measures there will be few, if any, major successes. In contemporary conditions it is only by such methods that modern industries can be created which will absorb the labour released by the old ones.

Secondly, it should be a primary and more explicit government task to foresee and identify the large-scale export contracts available round the world (not only from OPEC countries) in the industries mentioned above, and to offer all necessary practical support by way of finance, export credits, and organizational and diplomatic assistance on a scale matching that provided by rival governments. If major new units in the government machine are needed – in the UK probably in the Department of Trade and Industry – to co-ordinate and energize both these operations, they should be created and expanded as necessary. A concerted export effort on these lines, even if it fell short of the industrial mobilization achieved in the war and early post-war years, could transform the whole outlook for the pound sterling in particular and the UK's economic future generally.

One other crucial reform is essential: the reversal of the fatal mistakes made in 1972–3 of artificially raising the price of UK food imports, which stepped up labour costs, and worsened our export competitiveness, and at the same time removed all restraint on imports of manufactured goods from the continent. The result has been the emergence of a UK trade deficit in manufactured goods with the continental EEC running in 1983–4 at £8 billion a year[1] instead of a rough balance in 1970. This in turn has brought about the disappearance in the 1980s of the export surplus in manufactured goods which the UK had till then enjoyed since the eighteenth century. The results of these policies are all the more insidious because they are temporarily masked by very large export earnings from North Sea oil; and though North Sea oil and gas reserves *may* turn out to be larger than previously thought, it would be a pure gamble to regard this as certain.

As an economic and trading nation we are, on present policies, heading for a situation in the late 1990s, when the oil supplies dwindle, which will amount to near-collapse, but which the public does not yet clearly foresee, and the government, as I write in 1984, is doing almost nothing to prevent. The UK earned surpluses on the overall current balance of payments (including oil earnings) of £4 billion in 1982 and £3.5 billion in 1985. Yet the total contribution of North Sea oil (in export earnings and imports saved) to the balance of payments has been running in these years at between £10 billion and £20 billion a year. So without the temporary oil earnings, and burdened by a £8 billion deficit in manufactured goods with the continental EEC, we should face an annual deficit on the overall current balance of payments of something like £10 billion a year.[2]

Mercifully we still have the years from 1985 to 1995 in which to steer away from this disastrous slide. But it will be a long march back after the mistakes of the last five years. And if we do not adopt the above policies in good time, and in particular reverse the errors of 1972–3, our living standards may actually fall and the pound sterling may be worth only $1 sooner than many people think.

Notes

[1] The seriousness of this was emphasized in the *Report of the House of Commons Select Committee on Trade and Industry*, 11 June 1984, which said: 'It is quite obvious that EEC membership has not provided the benefits to our manufacturing industry which were promised.'
[2] The same point was emphatically made in the *House of Lords Select Committee on Overseas Trade Report* of October 1985.

Appendix: The Purchasing Power of the Pound Sterling 1264–1983

All sorts of difficulties, both in principle and in practice, arise when measuring the real value or purchasing power of a currency – in prices at a point between the wholesale and retail stage, being based Commodities change; their quality changes; social habits and the value individuals put on different satisfactions change. But in spite of this people naturally ask: what could one have bought for £1 in 1400 or 1600 or 1800? Any attempt to answer this question is beset not merely by the above qualifications and doubts but naturally also by inadequacy of records.

The attempt below to give a rough answer is largely based on the remarkable work of Professor Sir Henry Phelps Brown and Mrs Sheila Hopkins in tracing sterling price history since the thirteenth century. Their results were originally published in *Economica* in 1955 and 1956 and later, in 1981, in *A Perspective of Wages and Prices*. In that book they provide two indices (1451–75=100): first, of the price of a 'composite unit of consumables', and secondly of the 'equivalent of wage-rate of building craftsmen', expressed in the above composite physical unit, in southern England between 1264 and 1954. The index given below reproduces the price index only, and not the 'equivalent of wage-rate'. It therefore attempts to measure only the commodity value of the pound regardless of money incomes, and not the actual real value of money incomes received.

The price index devised by Phelps Brown and Hopkins represents prices at a point between the wholesale and retail stage, being based on prices paid by major purchasers such as Oxford colleges, monasteries, hospitals and so on. The commodities selected fell into several continuous groups – food, drink, fuel, and textiles – though the individual commodities change over time. As much as 80 per cent of the weighting of the index consists of food and drink, since the proportion in actual expenditure between the groups was found hardly to differ from the fifteenth century to the 1904–13 figures adopted by the Board of Trade for the original cost-of-living index.

The Phelps Brown-Hopkins index ends in 1954. In order to offer some rough continuity in the figures up to the 1980s I have, after consultation with the Central Statistical Office and the Oxford University Institute of Economics & Statistics, made use of the CSO's 'long-term index of prices of consumer goods and services' for the eventual period 1954–84. Since for this latter index January 1974 is taken as 100, the figures have been converted from 1954 onwards on to the same base years as the Phelps Brown-Hopkins index, and the last few figures rounded off.

The extension to a still longer period, together with the changed basis of the figures, naturally makes the post-1954 estimates an even rougher comparison with earlier years. They are no more than a long shot at comparing the level of sterling consumer prices in this and earlier centuries. But it is doubtful if any better shot could be made. For what it is worth, this series shows sterling prices of consumable goods as having risen over thirty-fold between 1451–75 and 1954, and nearer 300-fold between 1451–75 and 1984. This emphatically does not mean that living standards, or real incomes, have fallen – in order to measure that, figures of money incomes would have to be included in the calculation. Though I have not included here the Phelps Brown-Hopkins index of the 'wage-equivalent' (in ordinary language, the real wage), that index in fact shows for 1954 a level some 94 per cent *above* 1451–75, most of the rise having occurred since 1880.

Index (1451–75 = 100) of price of composite unit of consumables in southern England, 1264–1983

Year	Index	Year	Index	Year	Index	Year	Index
1264	83	1302	93	1340	96	1379	94
1265	80	1303	89	1341	86		
1266	83	1304	94	1342	85	1380	106
1267	—	1305	97	1343	84	1381	119
1268	70	1306	100	1344	97	1382	111
1269	83	1307	94	1345	98	1383	108
		1308	105	1346	88	1384	116
1270	—	1309	119	1347	109	1385	112
1271	98			1348	116	1386	104
1272	130	1310	135	1349	97	1387	100
1273	98	1311	123			1388	102
1274	95	1312	108	1350	102	1389	100
1275	100	1313	101	1351	134		
1276	96	1314	112	1352	160	1390	106
1277	97	1315	132	1353	138	1391	133
1278	103	1316	216	1354	117	1392	104
1279	94	1317	215	1355	115	1393	100
		1318	154	1356	121	1394	101
1280	94	1319	119	1357	133	1395	93
1281	93			1358	139	1396	99
1282	104	1320	106	1359	126	1397	116
1283	111	1321	121			1398	121
1284	120	1322	141	1360	135	1399	113
1285	83	1323	165	1361	131		
1286	91	1324	137	1362	153	1400	104
1287	91	1325	127	1363	155	1401	130
1288	72	1326	124	1364	151	1402	127
1289	69	1327	96	1365	143	1403	119
		1328	96	1366	121	1404	99
1290	80	1329	119	1367	137	1405	99
1291	106			1368	139	1406	100
1292	96	1330	120	1369	150	1407	99
1293	93	1331	134			1408	107
1294	110	1332	131	1370	184	1409	120
1295	131	1333	111	1371	164		
1296	104	1334	99	1372	132	1410	130
1297	93	1335	96	1373	131	1411	106
1298	106	1336	101	1374	125	1412	103
1299	96	1337	111	1375	125	1413	108
		1338	85	1376	146	1414	108
1300	113	1339	79	1377	112	1415	115
1301	89			1378	95	1416	124

1417	129	1459	95	1500	94	1542	172
1418	114			1501	107	1543	171
1419	95	1460	97	1502	122	1544	178
		1461	117	1503	114	1545	191
1420	102	1462	115	1504	107	1546	248
1421	93	1463	88	1505	103	1547	231
1422	97	1464	86	1506	106	1548	193
1423	108	1465	108	1507	98	1549	214
1424	103	1466	109	1508	100		
1425	109	1467	108	1509	92	1550	262
1426	103	1468	106			1551	285
1427	96	1469	107	1510	103	1552	276
1428	99			1511	97	1553	259
1429	127	1470	102	1512	101	1554	276
		1471	103	1513	120	1555	270
1430	138	1472	104	1514	118	1556	370
1431	115	1473	97	1515	107	1557	409
1432	102	1474	95	1516	110	1558	230
1433	112	1475	90	1517	111	1559	255
1434	109	1476	85	1518	116		
1435	105	1477	81	1519	129	1560	265
1436	95	1478	89			1561	283
1437	93	1479	97	1520	137	1562	266
1438	128			1521	167	1563	—
1439	154	1480	103	1522	160	1564	—
		1481	115	1523	136	1565	290
1440	140	1482	145	1524	133	1566	287
1441	93	1483	162	1525	129	1567	282
1442	85	1484	128	1526	133	1568	281
1443	97	1485	99	1527	147	1569	276
1444	102	1486	86	1528	179		
1445	87	1487	103	1529	159	1570	300
1446	95	1488	110			1571	265
1447	100	1489	109	1530	169	1572	270
1448	102			1531	154	1573	274
1449	106	1490	106	1532	179	1574	374
		1491	112	1533	169	1575	—
1450	102	1492	103	1534	145	1576	309
1451	109	1493	117	1535	131	1577	363
1452	97	1494	96	1536	164	1578	351
1453	97	1495	89	1537	155	1579	326
1454	105	1496	94	1538	138		
1455	94	1497	101	1539	147	1580	342
1456	101	1498	96			1581	347
1457	93	1499	99	1540	158	1582	343
1458	99			1541	165	1583	324

Year	Value	Year	Value	Year	Value	Year	Value
1584	333	1626	552	1668	602	1710	798
1585	338	1627	496	1669	572	1711	889
1586	352	1628	466			1712	638
1587	491	1629	510	1670	577	1713	594
1588	346			1671	595	1714	635
1589	354	1630	595	1672	557	1715	646
		1631	682	1673	585	1716	645
1590	396	1632	580	1674	650	1717	602
1591	459	1633	565	1675	691	1718	575
1592	370	1634	611	1676	652	1719	609
1593	356	1635	597	1677	592		
1594	381	1636	593	1678	633	1720	635
1595	515	1637	621	1679	614	1721	604
1596	505	1638	707			1722	554
1597	685	1639	607	1680	568	1723	525
1598	579			1681	567	1724	589
1599	474	1640	546	1682	600	1725	610
		1641	586	1683	587	1726	637
1600	459	1642	557	1684	570	1727	596
1601	536	1643	553	1685	651	1728	649
1602	471	1644	531	1686	559	1729	681
1603	448	1645	574	1687	580		
1604	404	1646	569	1688	551	1730	599
1605	448	1647	667	1689	535	1731	553
1606	468	1648	770			1732	557
1607	449	1649	821	1690	513	1733	544
1608	507			1691	493	1734	518
1609	559	1650	839	1692	542	1735	529
		1651	704	1693	652	1736	539
1610	503	1652	648	1694	693	1737	581
1611	463	1653	579	1695	645	1738	563
1612	524	1654	543	1696	697	1739	547
1613	549	1655	531	1697	693		
1614	567	1656	559	1698	767	1740	644
1615	561	1657	612	1699	773	1741	712
1616	562	1658	646			1742	631
1617	537	1659	700	1700	671	1743	579
1618	524			1701	586	1744	518
1619	494	1660	684	1702	582	1745	528
		1661	648	1703	551	1746	594
1620	485	1662	769	1704	587	1747	574
1621	461	1663	675	1705	548	1748	599
1622	523	1664	657	1706	583	1749	609
1623	588	1665	616	1707	531		
1624	543	1666	664	1708	571	1750	590
1625	534	1667	577	1709	697	1751	574

1752	601	1794	978	1836	1141	1878	1281
1753	585	1795	1091	1837	1169	1879	1210
1754	615	1796	1161	1838	1177		
1755	578	1797	1045	1839	1263	1880	1174
1756	602	1798	1022			1881	1213
1757	733	1799	1148	1840	1286	1882	1140
1758	731			1841	1256	1883	1182
1759	673	1800	1567	1842	1161	1884	1071
		1801	1751	1843	1030	1885	1026
1760	643	1802	1348	1844	1029	1886	931
1761	614	1803	1268	1845	1079	1887	955
1762	638	1804	1309	1846	1122	1888	950
1763	655	1805	1521	1847	1257	1889	948
1764	713	1806	1454	1848	1105		
1765	738	1807	1427	1849	1035	1890	947
1766	747	1808	1476			1891	998
1767	790	1809	1619	1850	969	1892	996
1768	781			1851	961	1893	914
1769	717	1810	1670	1852	978	1894	982
		1811	1622	1853	1135	1895	968
1770	714	1812	1836	1854	1265	1896	947
1771	775	1813	1881	1855	1274	1897	963
1772	858	1814	1642	1856	1264	1898	982
1773	855	1815	1467	1857	1287	1899	950
1774	863	1816	1344	1858	1190		
1775	815	1817	1526	1859	1214	1900	994
1776	797	1818	1530			1901	986
1777	794	1819	1492	1860	1314	1902	963
1778	826			1861	1302	1903	1004
1779	756	1820	1353	1862	1290	1904	985
		1821	1190	1863	1144	1905	989
1780	730	1822	1029	1864	1200	1906	1016
1781	760	1823	1099	1865	1238	1907	1031
1782	776	1824	1193	1866	1296	1908	1043
1783	869	1825	1400	1867	1346	1909	1058
1784	874	1826	1323	1868	1291		
1785	839	1827	1237	1869	1244	1910	994
1786	839	1828	1201			1911	984
1787	834	1829	1189	1870	1241	1912	999
1788	867			1871	1320	1913	1021
1789	856	1830	1146	1872	1378	1914	1147
		1831	1260	1873	1437	1915	1317
1790	871	1832	1167	1874	1423	1916	1652
1791	870	1833	1096	1875	1310	1917	1965
1792	883	1834	1011	1876	1370	1918	2497
1793	908	1835	1028	1877	1330	1919	2254

1920	2591	1937	1275	1953	3735	1970	6564
1921	2048	1938	1274	1954	3825	1971	7183
1922	1672	1939	1209	1955	3960	1972	7695
1923	1726			1956	4130	1973	8395
1924	1740	1940	1574	1957	4265	1974	9742
1925	1708	1941	1784	1958	4382	1975	12104
1926	1577	1942	2130	1959	4409	1976	14106
1927	1496	1943	2145			1977	16342
1928	1485	1944	2216	1960	4454	1978	17697
1929	1511	1945	2282	1961	4579	1979	20068
		1946	2364	1962	4759		
1930	1275	1947	2580	1963	4849	1980	23677
1931	1146	1948	2781	1964	5010	1981	26488
1932	1065	1949	3145	1965	5244	1982	29010
1933	1107			1966	5450	1983	29260
1934	1097	1950	3155	1967	5594	1984	30873
1935	1149	1951	3656	1968	5854		
1936	1211	1952	3987	1969	6169		

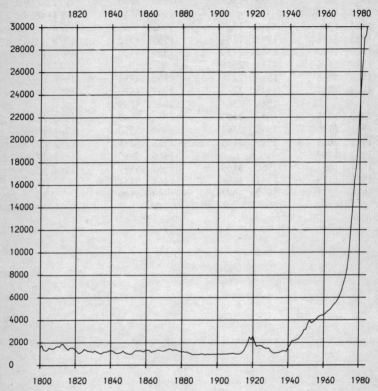

280

CHART A
Consumer Price Index in Sterling (1451–75=100)

Chart A. The Phelps Brown–Hopkins figures are the sources for the figures in this chart.

CHART B
UK* Index of Industrial Production per capita (1980=100)

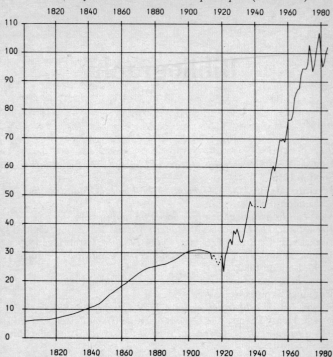

* Including Ireland until 1922, and N. Ireland thereafter.

Sources for Chart B are as follows:
(1) Mitchell, B.R. and Deane, P., Abstract of British Historical Statistics, Cambridge University Press, 1962. pp. 271–72.
   Population 1801–1939.
   Total Industrial Production (including building) 1801–1938.
(2) Lomax, K.S., Journal of the Royal Statistical Society, Vol. 122, Series A, 1959.
   Total Industrial production (all industries) 1900–1957.
(3) Mitchell, B.R. and Jones, H.G., Second Abstract of British Historical Statistics, CUP, 1971.
   Population figures 1938–1965.
   Total Industrial Production (all industries) 1938–1965.
(4) CSO.
   Population and Total Industrial Production 1965–1984 (1984 figure estimated).

Bibliography

Ashton, T.S., *An Economic History of England. The Eighteenth Century.* London 1955.

Beveridge W.H., *Unemployment: A Problem for Industry.* 2nd edition, London 1930.

———*Full Employment in a Free Society.* London 1944.

Black, John, *The Economics of Modern Britain.* 3rd edition, Oxford 1982.

Blackaby, F.T., *British Economic Policy 1960–74.* Cambridge 1979.

Brittan, Samuel, *How to End the Monetarist Controversy.* Hobart Paper 90, London 1982.

———*The Role and Limits of Government,* London 1983.

Brookings Reports: see Caves.

Brown, A.J., *World Inflation Since 1950.* Cambridge 1985.

Brown, Henry Phelps, *The Origins of Trade Union Power.* Oxford 1983.

———*Incomes Policy: A Modest Proposal.* Unservile State Papers No. 30, Oxford.

———and Margaret H. Browne, *A Century of Pay.* London 1962.

———and Sheila V. Hopkins, *A Perspective of Wages and Prices.* London 1981.

Buitter, Willem H., and Marcus H. Miller, *The Macroeconomic Consequences of a Change in Regime: The UK under Mrs Thatcher.* London 1983.

Cairncross, Alec, and Barry Eichengreen, *Sterling in Decline.* Oxford 1983.

———*Britain's Economic Prospects Reconsidered.* London 1971.

———*Years of Recovery 1945–51.* London, New York 1985.

Caves, Richard E., and Lawrence B. Krause, *Britain's Economic Prospects.* Brookings Institution, Washington DC 1968.

———*Britain's Economic Performance.* Brookings Institution, Washington DC 1980.

———*Charter for Jobs. We Can Cut Unemployment.* London 1985.

Clapham, John, *The Bank of England: A History.* Cambridge 1944.

Cooper, John, *The Management and Regulation of Banks.* London 1984.

Crafts, N.C.R. *The Industrial Revolution.* Oxford 1985.

Dalton, Hugh, *High Tide and After*. London 1962.

Dornbush, R., *Sound Currency and Full Employment*. Employment Institute. London 1985.

Dow, J.C.R., *The Management of the British Economy 1945–60*. Students' edition, Cambridge 1970.

Feavearyear, Sir Albert, *The Pound Sterling*. 2nd edition, revised by E. Victor Morgan, London–Oxford 1963.

Feinstein, C.H. *National Income, Expenditure and Output*. Cambridge 1972.

Friedman, Milton, *Unemployment versus Inflation?* Occasional Paper 44, London 1975.

——and Anna Schwartz, *Monetary Trends in the US and UK: their Relation to Income, Prices, and Interest Rates 1867–1975*. Chicago 1982.

Gilbert, Martin, *Winston S. Churchill*. Vol V. London 1976.

Gilmour, Ian, *Britain Can Work*. Oxford 1983.

Hahn, Frank, *Money and Inflation*, Oxford 1982.

Harrod, R.F., *The Trade Cycle*, Oxford 1936.

——*The British Economy*. 1963.

Figgures, F., *Pay Board: Experience of Operating a Statutory Incomes Policy*, July 1974.

Hayek, F.A., *Prices and Production*. London 1931.

——*Monetary Theory and the Trade Cycle*. London 1933.

Hendry, David, and Neil Ericsson, *Assertion without Empirical Basis: An Econometric Appraisal of 'Monetary Trends in the UK' by Milton Friedman and Anna Schwartz*. Oxford 1983.

Hicks, J.R., *Trade Cycle*. Oxford 1956.

——*Are There Economic Cycles?* Stirling 1981.

Howson, Susan, and Donald Winch, *The Economic Advisory Council 1930–39*.

Jay, Douglas, *Change and Fortune*. London 1980.

——*After the Common Market*. London 1968.

Jones, Aubrey, *The New Inflation: The Politics of Prices and Incomes*. London 1973.

——*The Reform of Pay Determination*. Unservile State Papers No. 27.

Kaldor, Nicholas, *Essays on Economic Stability and Growth*. 2nd edition, London 1980.

——*The Scourge of Monetarism*. Oxford 1982.

——*The Economic Consequences of Mrs Thatcher*. Fabian Tract 486, 1983.

Keegan, William, *Mrs Thatcher's Economic Experiment*. London 1984.

Keynes, J.M., *A Tract on Monetary Reform*, London 1923.

——'The Economic Consequences of Mr Churchill'. London 1925.

——*A Treatise on Money*. London 1930.

——*The General Theory of Employment, Interest and Money*. London 1936.

Layton and Crowther, *The Study of Prices*. 3rd edition, London 1938.

Macmillan Committee, *Report on Finance and Industry*, 1931.

Malthus, A., *Principles of Political Economy*. 1st edition, London 1820.

Meade, James E., *Stagflation*. Vol. I, *Wage-Fixing*. London 1982. Vol. II, *Demand Management*. London 1983.

Minford, A.P., 'A Return to Sound Money'. *The Banker*, July 1962.

Mitchell and Deane, *Abstract of British Historical Statistics*. Cambridge 1962.

Mitchell and Jones, *Second Abstract of Historical Statistics*. Cambridge 1971.

Moggridge, D.E., *Keynes*. London 1980.

Morgan, E. Victor, *A History of Money*. London 1965.

Outhwaite, Brian, *Inflation in Tudor and Early Stuart England*. London 1982.

Radcliffe Committee, *Report on the Working of the Monetary System*. Cmnd. 827, 1959.

Ramsey, Peter, *The Price Revolution in Sixteenth-Century England*, London 1971.

Rees, Goronwy, *The Great Slump*, London 1970.

Reid, Margaret, *The Secondary Banking Crisis 1973–75*. London 1982.

Robbins, Lionel, *The Great Depression*. London 1934.

Roll, Eric, *About Money*. London 1934.

Rostow W.W., *The World Economy: History and Prospect*. London 1978.

——*The Barbaric Counter-Revolution*. London 1949; Austin, USA 1983.

Salter, Arthur, *Recovery*. London 1932.

Sayers, R.S., *Modern Banking*. 4th edition, Oxford 1958.

Smith, Adam, *Wealth of Nations*, 2nd edition, 1837.

Strange, Susan, *Sterling and British Policy*. Oxford 1971.

Treasury and Civil Service Committee of the House of Commons on Monetary Policy: *Memoranda on Monetary Policy*. 17 July 1980.

——*Report*. 24 February 1981.

Truman, H., *Year of Decisions*. New York 1955.

Worswick, G.D.N. and P.H. Ady (eds), *The British Economy in the Nineteen-Fifties*. Oxford 1962.

Index

OXFORD

MORE OXFORD PAPERBACKS

Details of a selection of other books follow. A complete list of Oxford Paperbacks, including The World's Classics, Twentieth-Century Classics, OPUS, Past Masters, Oxford Authors, Oxford Shakespeare, and Oxford Paperback Reference, is available from the General Publicity Department, Oxford University Press (JH), Walton Street, Oxford, OX2 6DP.

In the USA, complete lists are available from the Paperbacks Marketing Manager, Oxford University Press, 200 Madison Avenue, New York, NY 10016.

Oxford Paperbacks are available from all good bookshops. In case of difficulty, please order direct from Oxford University Press Bookshop, 116 High Street, Oxford, Freepost, OX1 4BR, enclosing full payment. Please add 10% of published price for postage and packing.

LAW, LIBERTY, AND MORALITY

H. L. A. Hart

Professor Hart deals in this book with the use of the criminal law to enforce morality, in particular sexual morality. He first considers John Stuart Mill's famous declaration: 'The only purpose for which power can be rightfully exercised over any member of a civilized community is to prevent harm to others.'

The author then examines the arguments of Sir James Fitzjames Stephen, the great Victorian judge, and Lord Devlin, that the use of the criminal law to enforce morality is justified. He sets out to demonstrate that these challenges fail to recognize distinctions of vital importance for legal and political theory.

'All who lay claim to an educated conscience should make themselves familiar with the issues presented in these incisively argued lectures.' *Twentieth Century*

INTRODUCTION TO ENGLISH LAW

New Edition

William Geldart

Edited by D. C. M. Yardley

Geldart's *Elements of English Law* has established itself over the years as a classic account of the English legal system. Now reaching its ninth edition, it has a new title, and has been substantially rewritten to take account of recent legislation.

An OPUS book

LAW AND MODERN SOCIETY

P. S. Atiyah

'The Oxford University Press has done well to publish this brief, lucid and stimulating appraisal by P. S. Atiyah of English law as it operates in our society today. And it is refreshing to find that Professor Atiyah describes the law in action before he asks his questions. His study is critical, but not damning. Though Atiyah is careful not to state his own position and sensibly emphasizes that without judges educated by training and experience to handle and develop constitutional safeguards a Bill of Rights is unlikely to achieve its purpose, I find the conclusion to be drawn from his reasoning inescapable. It points to the need for constitutional reform. Atiyah leaves it to his readers to decide what they want. It is good, therefore, that the book is designed to be read by all who are interested; that it is written in a style which all can appreciate; that it is brief; and that it is modestly priced.' Leslie Scarman, *Times Literary Supplement*

'The author surveys the legal system rather than substantive law and has views on judges, the legal profession generally, the way lawyers themselves regard law, law and the state and "Bad law". Throughout the text he tries to be fair where there are two political viewpoints . . . the book is a stimulating introduction to the legal system for the intelligent layman.' *Solicitors Journal*

An OPUS book

MARXISM AND LAW

Hugh Collins

In this introduction to Marxism and the law, Hugh Collins presents a unified and coherent view of Marxism, which he uses to examine the specific characteristics of legal institutions, rules, and ideals. He pays particular attention to the place of ideology in law, the distinction between base and superstructure, and the destiny of law in a Communist society, and frequently subjects the Marxist approach to criticism, suggesting that many of the Marxist claims about law are unproven or misconceived.

'enthusiastically and warmly recommended' *New Law Journal*

THE MORAL STATUS OF ANIMALS

Stephen R. L. Clark

Most of us exploit animals for our own purposes. The Moral status of animals has long been a subject of heated debate. According to the great philosophers, morality has nothing to say about our relations with non-humans. Modern liberals, though, have allowed that animals should at least be spared unnecessary pain Stephen Clark discussed the arguments and rationalizations offered in defence of our behaviour in farms, laboratories, and at home, and reveals their roots in neurotic fantasy.

'an erudite, intriguing, provocative, disturbing book which deserves close attention' *Month*

'An impassioned, detailed and wide-ranging polemic . . .' *Sean French, Sunday Times*

THE LANGUAGE OF MORALS

R. M. Hare

'It is indeed the accuracy, the thoroughness of this analysis that makes *The Language of Morals* by far the best introduction to moral philosophy to appear for many years.' *New Statesman*

'This then is a book upon which all serious students of moral philosophy—dons as well as undergraduates—will have to ponder.' *Mind*

'It is a perceptive contribution toward the solution of many fundamental problems of ethics.' *Philosophical Review*

MORAL PHILOSOPHY

D. D. Raphael

Do moral philosophers have anything to say which is useful, let alone comprehensible, to people with more down-to-earth concerns? Professor Raphael would answer 'Yes' on both counts. Unlike most 'introductions' to moral philosophy, this book is written expressly for the beginner. Also, it is not confined to the theory of ethics in any narrow sense, but makes a point of showing the connections between abstract ethics and practical problems.

'It would be difficult to find a clearer introduction to modern moral philosophy.' *Tablet*

An OPUS book

A THEORY OF JUSTICE

John Rawls

When this book was first published in 1972, the *New York Review of Books* hailed it as 'the most substantial and interesting contribution to moral philosophy since the war', and the *Times Literary Supplement* claimed it would 'exercise a significant and perhaps lasting influence on the central questions of political philosophy with which it deals'. In this important and major work. Professor Rawls sets out the principles of justice that free and rational persons would accept in an initial position of equality.

'compulsory reading for every student of the subject' *Times Higher Education Supplement*

THE PROBLEMS OF PHILOSOPHY

Bertrand Russell

First published in 1912, this classic introduction to the subjects of philosophical inquiry has proved invaluable to the formal student and general reader alike. It has Russell's views succinctly stated on material reality and idealism, knowledge by acquaintance and by description, induction, knowledge of general principles and of universals, intuitive knowledge, truth and falsehood, the distinctions between knowledge, error, and probable opinion, and the limits and the value of philosophical knowledge.

A foreword Russell wrote in 1924 for a German translation has been added as an appendix. Here Russell gave details of how some of his views had changed since *The Problems of Philosophy* was written.

An OPUS book

EXISTENTIALISM

Mary Warnock

Existentialism is the name of a kind of philosophical activity which had a wave of popularity in the 1940s and 1950s, and which has had a far wider influence upon literature than most systems of philosophy. Itself the product mainly of German thought, it has flowered in both Germany and France. The strength of Existentialism lies in its sources, which are both epistemological and ethical. It is a philosophy which concerns itself with all aspects of man in his world, not only with his perception or his moral behaviour, but with his feelings, his freedom, and his possibilities. The aim of this book is to trace the common interests and ancestry of Existentialism in the work of Heidegger, Merleau-Ponty, and Sartre.

An OPUS book

THE CHARACTER OF MIND

Colin McGinn

Colin McGinn's book provides a general introduction to the philosophy of mind, and covers all the main topics currently at the forefront of philosophical debate. McGinn writes in non-technical language, but does not shirk the considerable difficulties of the subject, and what he writes will certainly be useful to advanced students as well as to beginners.

'Brilliant . . . Colin McGinn's admirable book manages to give a comprehensive picture of the state of play in the subject at the present time. In a compressed and well-written work, and without any loss of subtlety, he contrives to lead the reader on a guided tour of the problems . . . This format is entirely successful. The result is a lucid and impressive discussion of the issues in their own right. And it should be added that at all times McGinn's own contributions to the problem under discussion are noteworthy.' *London Review of Books*

An OPUS book

CONSCIOUSNESS REGAINED

Chapters in the Development of Mind

Nicholas Humphrey

'This is a bold book. Nicholas Humphrey, in a series of separate but well-stitched essays, attacks the human mind with a gigantic "Why?", eschewing all "Hows". His answer is so elegant in argument and language as to leave one thinking "I wish I had thought of that."

'The author is a rare beast: a scientist who writes beautifully. Dr Humphrey conveys the excitement of a scientific approach. Too often scientists flounder in detail and qualification, sapping the mystery of their subject. Or they degrade mystery into problem. Nicholas Humphrey's vision is as captivating and rich as any work of fiction.' *Economist*